LOST CHATHAM

PHILIP MACDOUGALL

AMBERLEY

First published 2024

Amberley Publishing
The Hill, Stroud
Gloucestershire, GL5 4EP

www.amberley-books.com

British Library Cataloguing in Publication Data.

A catalogue record for this book is available from the British Library.

ISBN 978 1 3981 1554 5 (print)
ISBN 978 1 3981 1555 2 (ebook)

Typesetting by SJmagic DESIGN SERVICES, India.
Printed in the UK.

Contents

Introduction

Lost Chatham looks at the Chatham that is no more, the way things were and the buildings and traditions that have simply slipped away. As a town, Chatham has undergone great change. In the Middle Ages it was a place with absolutely no pretensions, an outlier of Rochester. Sufficiently isolated from the rest of society, it had bestowed upon it during the thirteenth century a hospital for lepers, the site marked to this day by St Bartholomew's Chapel in the modern-day High Street. Farming and fishing was the source of livelihood for those living in the parish in those years, although some must also have taken advantage of the main road from London to Dover that passed through Chatham, establishing no doubt a hostelry to quench the thirst of a passing traveller and a blacksmith or two for the re-shoeing of a horse or fixing a broken carriage wheel.

All was to change during the latter years of the sixteenth century when the King's navy began using the Medway as an anchorage, although to begin with most ships were provisioned and fitted out at 'Jillyngham' where storehouses were built. But it was Chatham where the dockyard was constructed, this during the reign of Elizabeth I (1558–1603). Nobody could then have guessed the consequences of building that yard; Chatham transforming out of that small fishing and farming village into a massive military-industrial complex that would become the envy of the world. Before long, as the number of labourers and artisans employed in the dockyard continued to multiply, all available land close to the dockyard was quickly developed for housing – some of high quality for the officers of the yard but most rapidly constructed of timber and not really built to last.

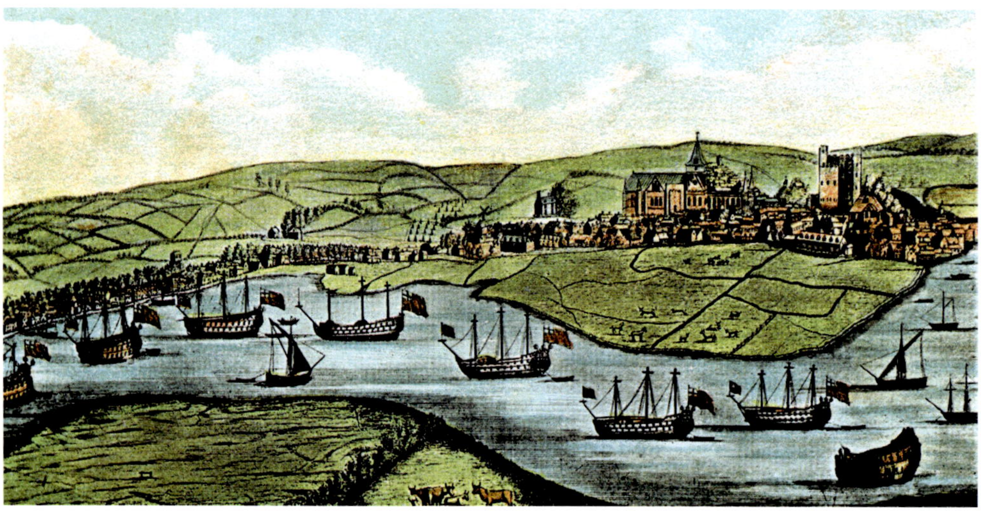

An early representation of the emerging industrial-military complex. Chatham and the dockyard are to be seen on the left, housing in Chatham already seamlessly linking the City of Rochester with the, by then, town of Chatham.

Following the arrival of the navy, came the army, essentially to defend the dockyard from an enemy attack. Initially few in number, but the Dutch Raid of 1667 changing all this. Although a Dutch squadron under Willem Joseph van Ghent failed in its objective of destroying the dockyard, the intent had been there, and it was realised that others might succeed where van Ghent had failed. To this end, a small number of forts and forlets were constructed, but the biggest project was the Chatham Lines, built to defend the dockyard from a land attack. To man these defences more and more soldiers were required, with newly constructed barracks adding to the overcrowding of a town that was already bulging at the seams.

With space at a premium, those employed in the dockyard were soon living further and further away, with those who could afford it turning to the City of Rochester, viewed as more select and refined. Only in the nineteenth and early twentieth centuries was the problem of housing such vast numbers finally resolved – this through the spiralling of the yard into Gillingham and so allowing for the opening of a major new entrance into the yard through Gillingham Gate. It was in Gillingham where many of the newly employed workers would take up residence, housing slowly pushing out from this new gateway onto farmland rapidly acquired by profit-seeking developers. But even this did not solve the problem, after all the new extension, through requiring an increased labour force, also increased the demand for housing. Ultimately though, it was the arrival of the tram and the opening of routes designed to swiftly move large numbers of passengers into the more far-flung areas of the Medway Towns, but especially Luton on the edge of Chatham and the further reaches of Gillingham.

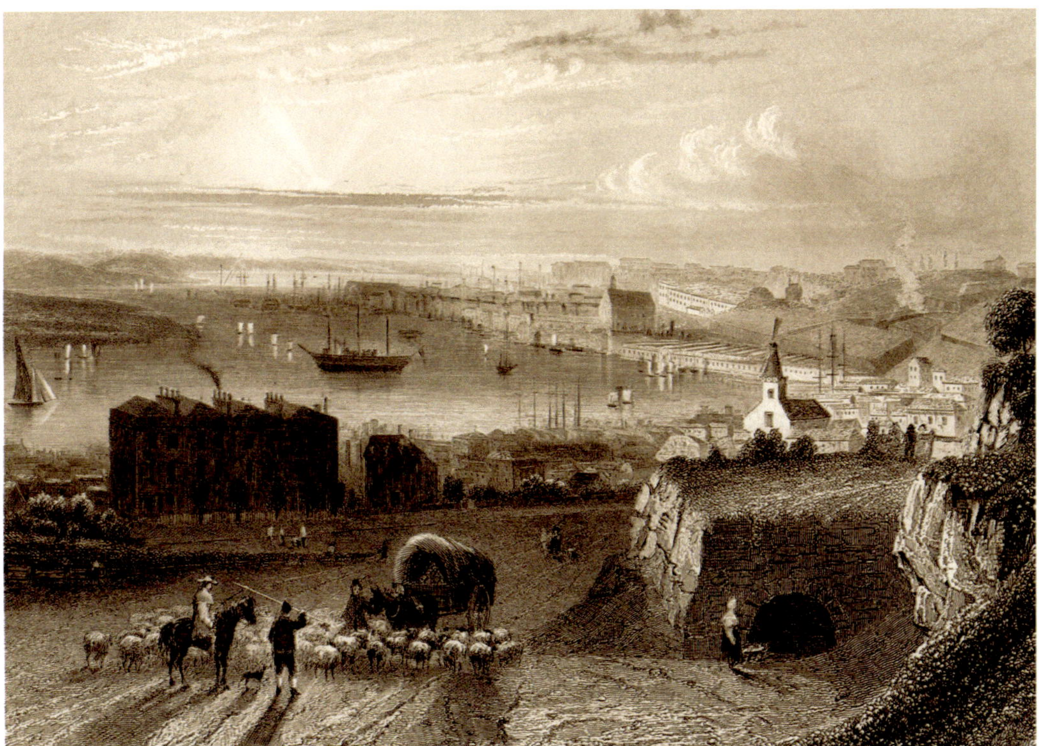

An early nineteenth-century view of the dockyard and town of Chatham.

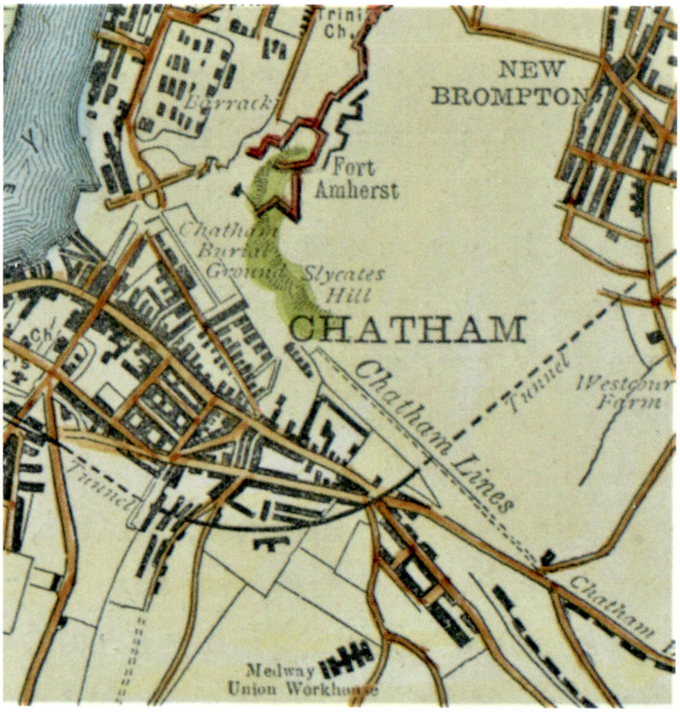

Chatham during the late nineteenth century. That an extensive gap existed between modern-day Gillingham and the town of Chatham was because this was a military zone, required to give an uninterrupted field of fire should an enemy attack the dockyard from this direction.

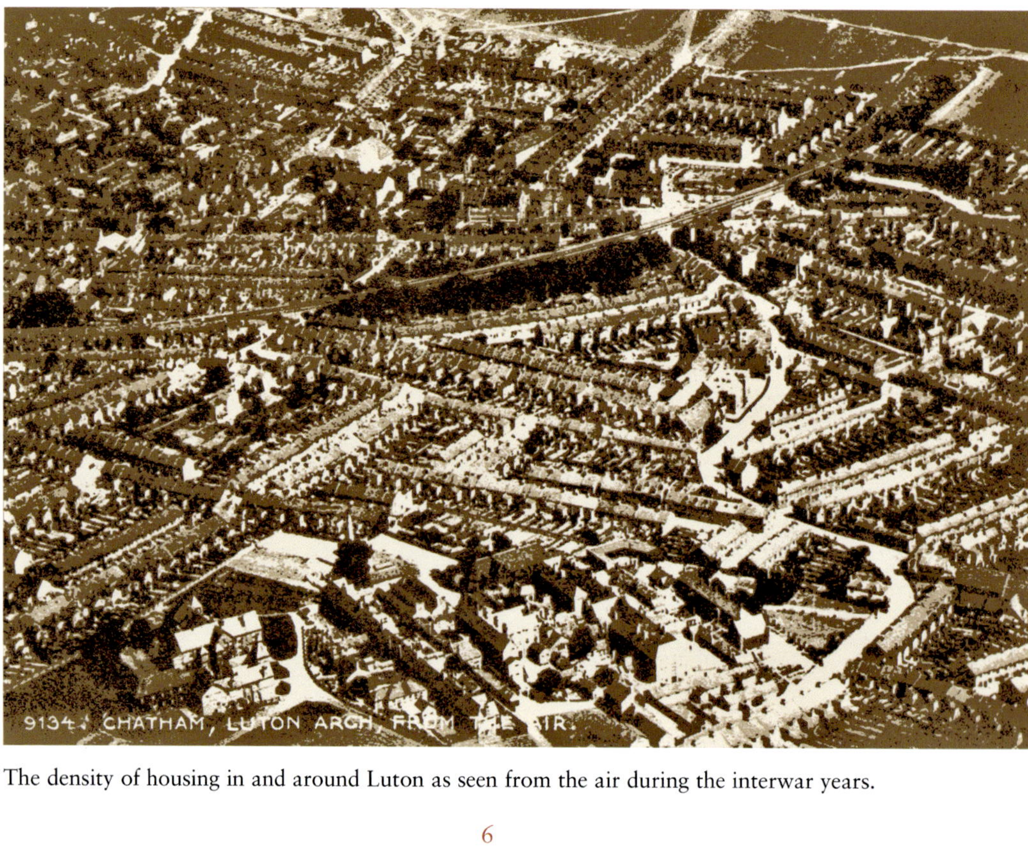

The density of housing in and around Luton as seen from the air during the interwar years.

Throughout the dockyard, the Royal Navy and the Amy combined to make Chatham what it had become. If you were not employed in the dockyard or a member of the Armed Services, you were still heavily dependent upon the Admiralty or War Office for an income. After all, there was more to life than dockyard work or life within the barracks. Families of dockyard workers needed to spend their hard-earned money locally on food and entertainment, as did off-duty servicemen. This in itself created a local economy equally dependent upon the continuance of the dockyard and military barracks.

All of this was to eventually fall apart during the 1980s, the decade in which both the dockyard and Royal Naval Barracks closed, while the number of soldiers in the town had long been in steady decline. Unemployment rocketed, both Chatham and Gillingham losing direction with the heart of both communities having been ripped asunder. It was a massive forced change of direction, one that differed markedly from those earlier changes. While it had taken more than a hundred years for Chatham to transform into an industrial community and another 300 years for that industry to entrench and advance, it took no more than a decade for all this to be destroyed. While, just over thirty-five years later, Chatham has come far in the process of regenerating itself, it is no longer the community it once was. Employment opportunities clearly exist, but the ease of commuting into London is a magnet that takes many out of the town on a daily basis while there is more poverty in one area of Chatham than any other area in Kent. Much still needs to be done to repair the damage inflicted upon it by the closure of the dockyard and restoration of the pride that the community of Chatham once possessed.

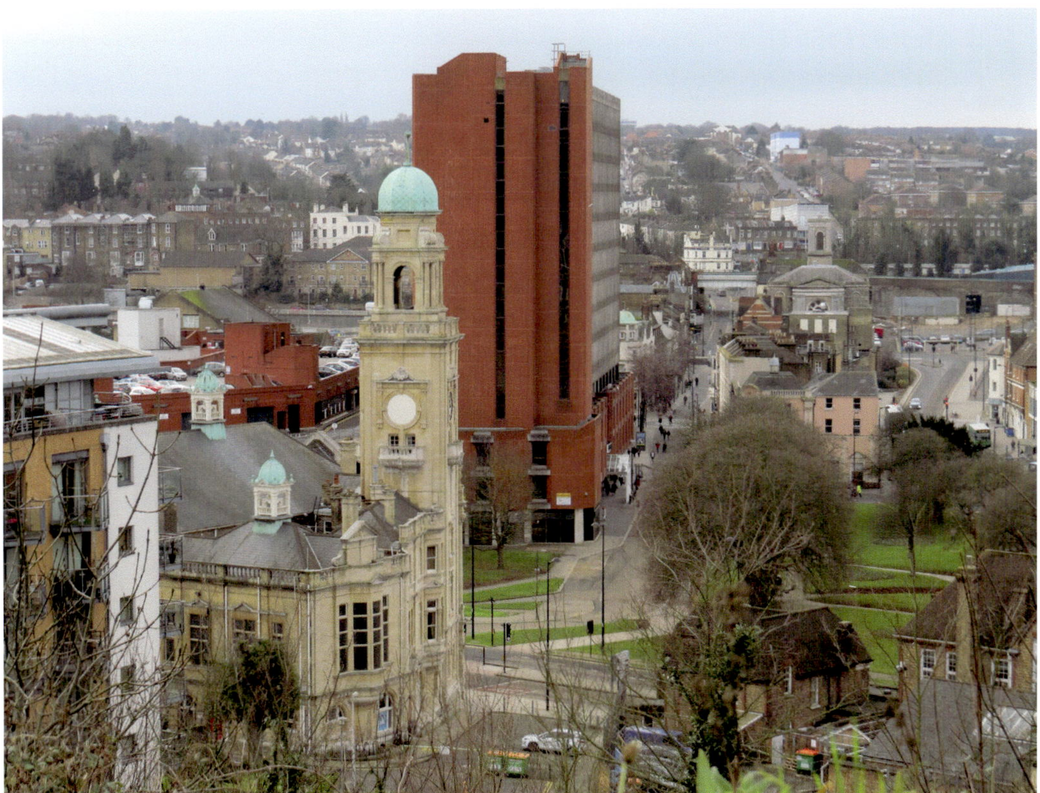

Chatham as viewed in 2018 from Fort Amherst.

I

Theatres, Music Halls and Cinemas

Along the length of Chatham High Street were once to be found a mixed range of entertainment venues, of which the largest and most impressive were theatres, music halls and cinemas. These catered not only for the resident population but also for thousands of soldiers and naval seamen billeted in the various barracks in and around the town. In the age before the arrival of television, Chatham High Street was a magnet for those seeking a break from the monotonous chores of a daytime job or life in a regimental institution.

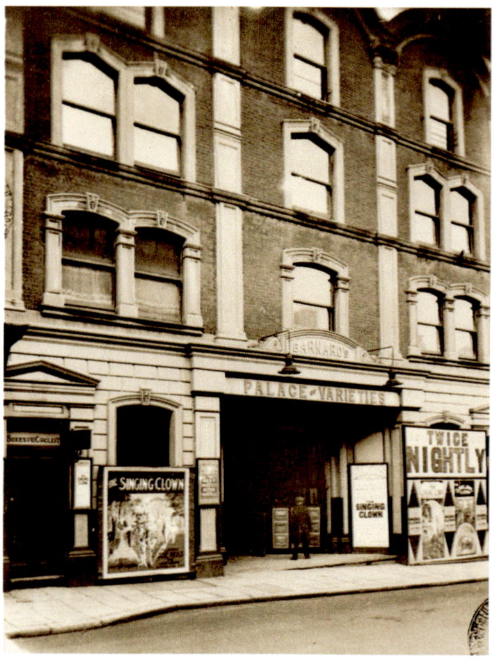

Chatham once possessed one of the earliest music halls in the country. Situated in the High Street, just by Holborn Lane, this was Barnard's Palace of Varieties. The building seen here, the New Palace of Varieties, first opened in July 1886, replacing an earlier variety theatre that had first seen performances sometime around 1850. In those very early days artists performing had to compete with the disturbing accompaniment of orange sellers bawling out their selection of 'Oranges, sweet oranges!' alongside noisy talk and the clattering of pots at the bar. Barnard's, though, gave hours of good entertainment just for one penny! Besides such famous names as Charlie Chaplin and Marie Lloyd, there was the lesser-known Madame Buck who appeared in bloomer costume and delivered a lecture on 'bloomerism', and W. D. Holmes who specialised in unusual cat imitations as well as other grotesques. A twice-nightly system was long adopted, this for the convenience of sailors and soldiers billeted in the port and garrison and which had to return by a set early evening time.

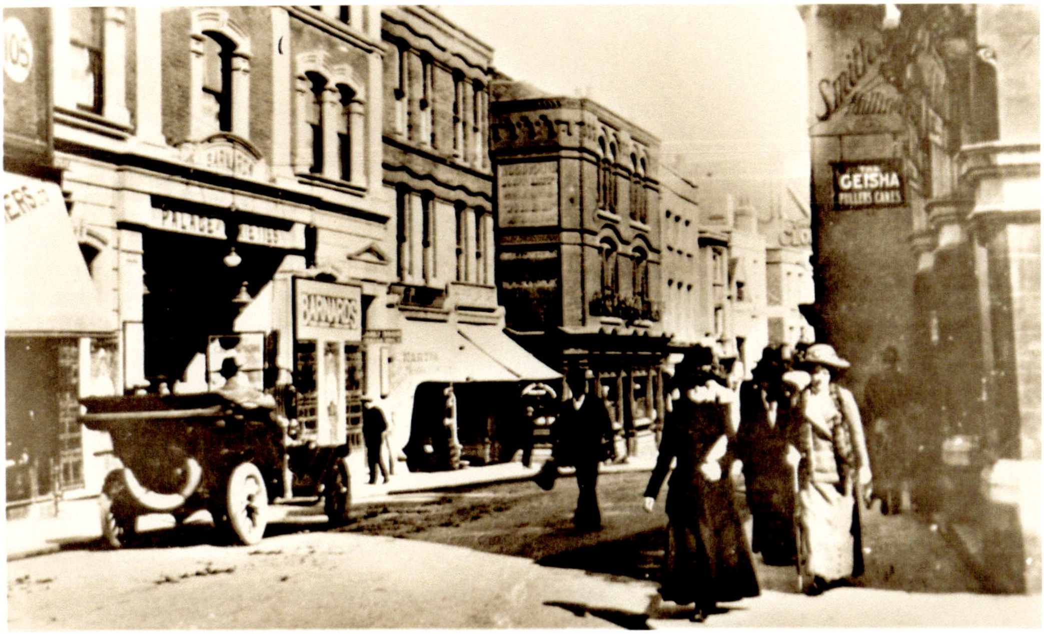

Above: While the previous view of the Palace of Varieties dates to 1930 with the outside billboard advertising a stage musical entitled *The Singing Clown*, this view shows the theatre and surrounding buildings as they appeared shortly before the First World War.

Right: The Palace of Varieties building itself came to a sensational end, destroyed by fire in March 1934 and seen here under final demolition.

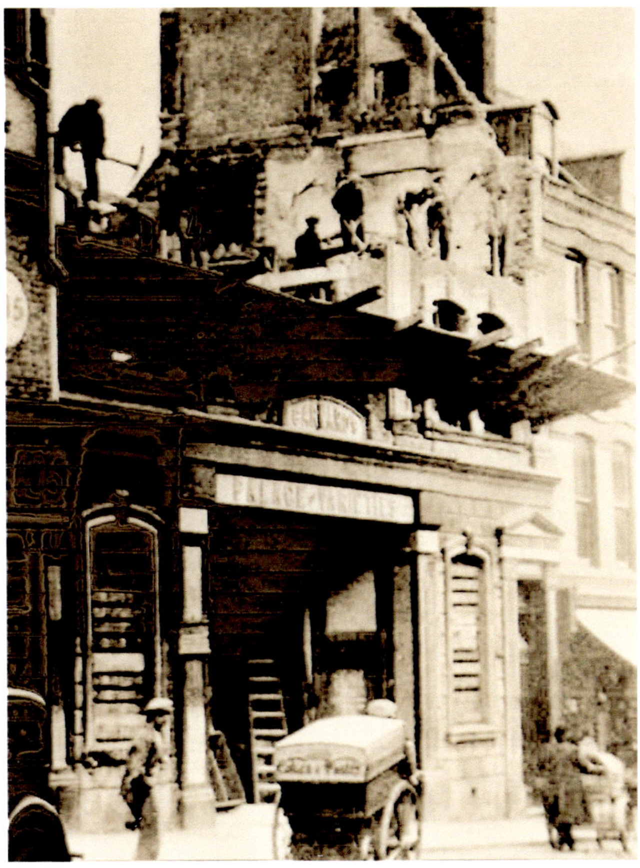

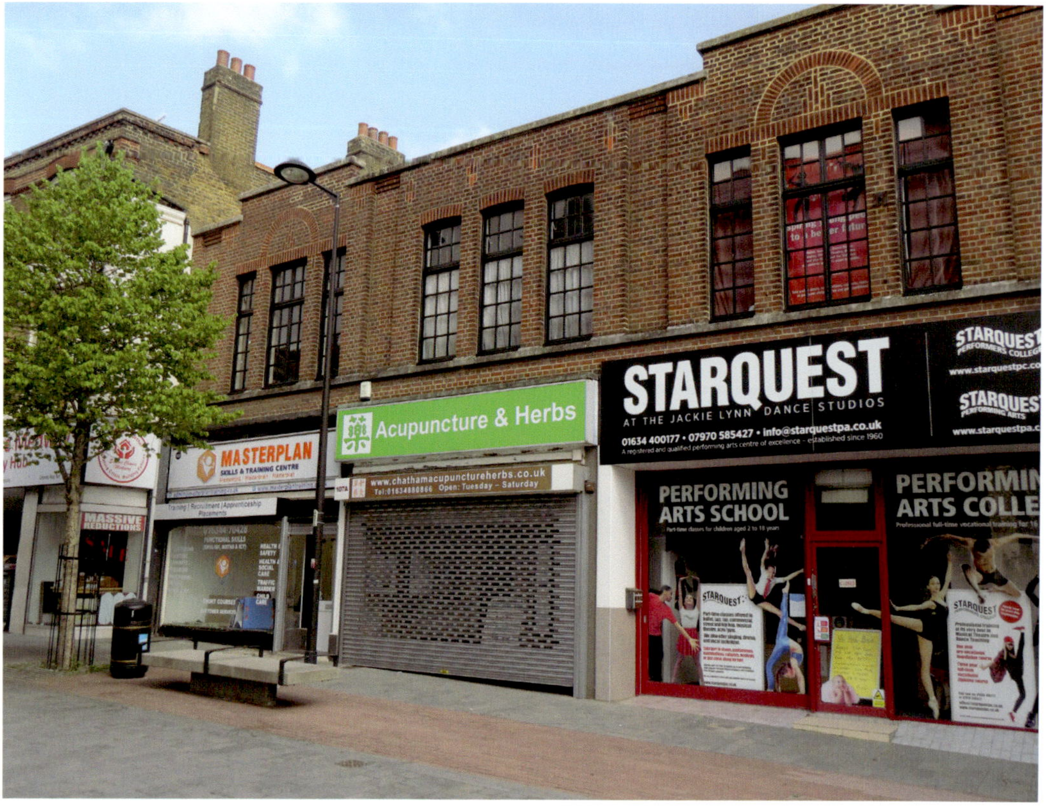

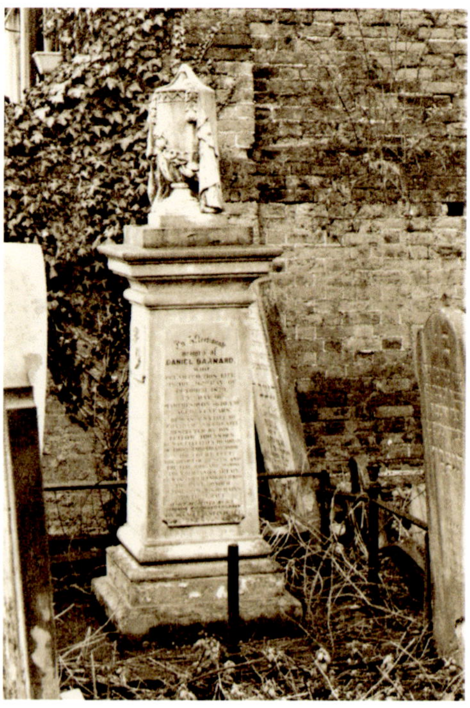

Above: The exact site of where Barnard's Palace of Varieties once stood can easily be determined, as it is these buildings, set further back from the now pedestrianised stretch of road that replaced the theatre following the devastating fire that brought about its destruction.

Left: Daniel Barnard was the man who first brought variety to Chatham, that first music hall of the 1850s created out of the Granby Coffee Tavern, and in which name the theatre licence was held to the very end. A Chatham man through and through, becoming High Constable in 1862, 'Old Dan', as he was known, was buried in the cemetery of the town's synagogue and is marked by the memorial stone seen here.

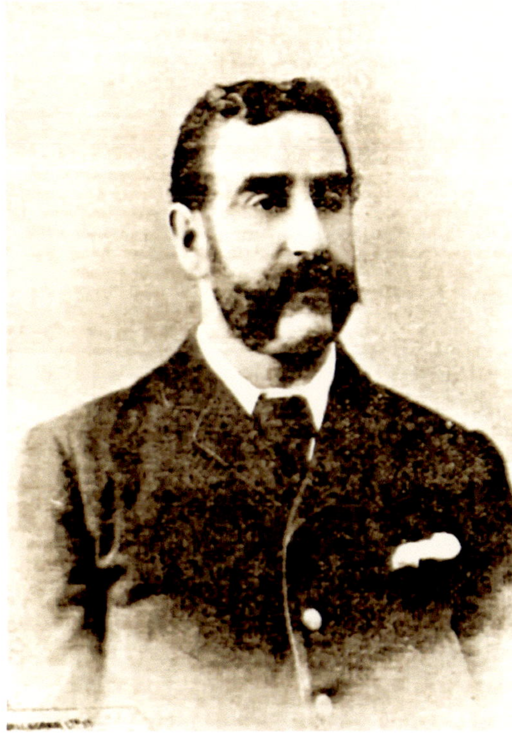

Lou Barnard, Daniel's son, seen here in this portrait picture, succeeded his father in 1871 as the proprietor of Barnard's, overseeing construction of the new theatre which was described as a comfortable and compact building admirably adapted to the purpose for which it was built.

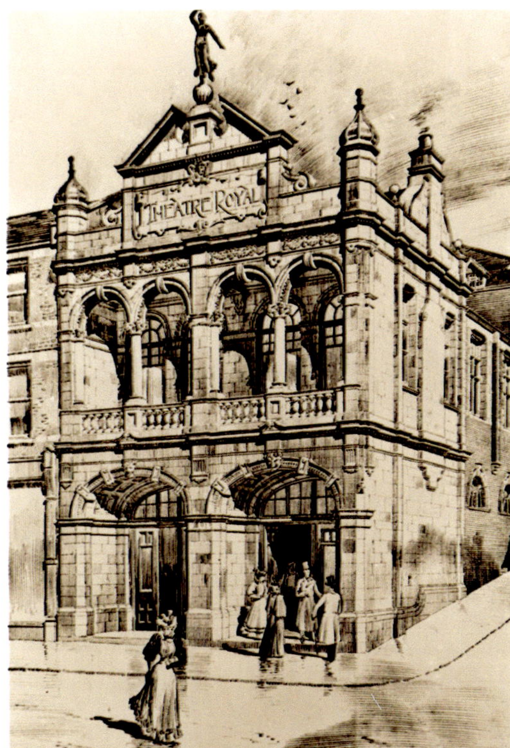

A second Barnard venture in Chatham was the Theatre Royal, a purpose-built theatre depicted here at the time of its opening in July 1899. It was designed by George E. Bond, Medway's leading architect of the time. Bond also designed the Town Hall and the Chatham Masonic Hall in Manor Road. In the building of the New Palace of Varieties he had served as Clerk of Works.

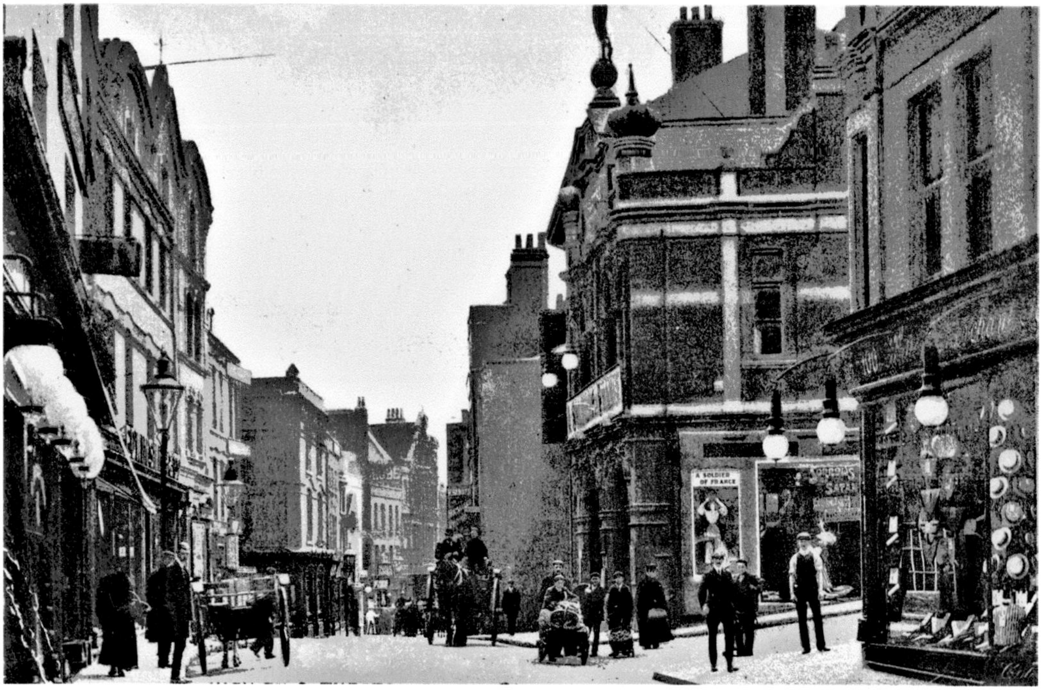

The Theatre Royal sometime around 1907. Unlike the Palace of Varieties, the Theatre Royal aimed itself at a less raucous audience with a fare of popular theatrical productions staged by weekly visiting companies. On this occasion, the billboard outside is advertising *A Soldier of France*, a possible indication that this picture was produced during the time of the First World War.

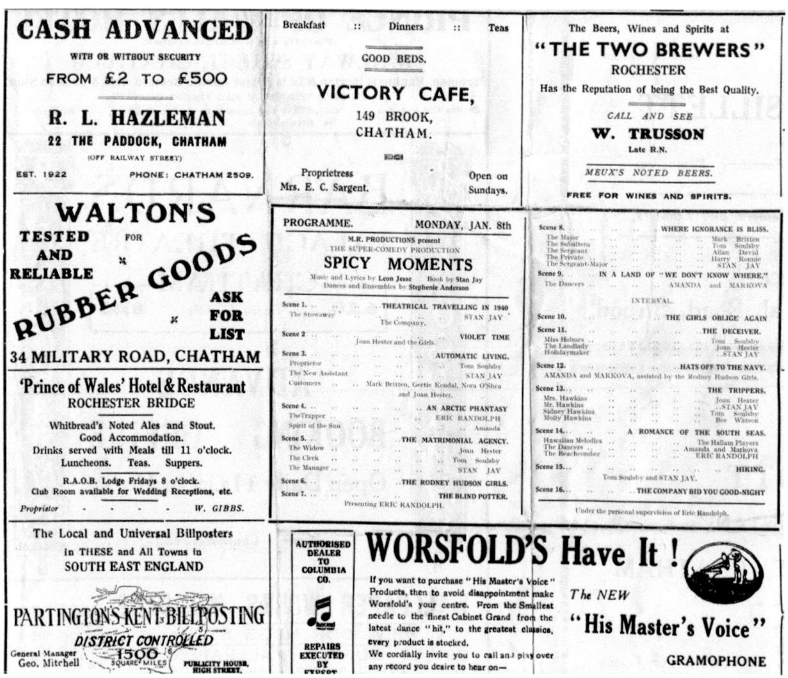

CASH ADVANCED
WITH OR WITHOUT SECURITY
FROM £2 TO £500
R. L. HAZLEMAN
22 THE PADDOCK, CHATHAM
(OFF RAILWAY STREET)
EST. 1922 PHONE: CHATHAM 2509.

WALTON'S
TESTED AND RELIABLE
FOR
RUBBER GOODS
ASK FOR LIST
34 MILITARY ROAD, CHATHAM

'Prince of Wales' Hotel & Restaurant
ROCHESTER BRIDGE
Whitbread's Noted Ales and Stout.
Good Accommodation.
Drinks served with Meals till 11 o'clock.
Luncheons. Teas. Suppers.
R.A.O.B. Lodge Fridays 8 o'clock.
Club Room available for Wedding Receptions, etc.
Proprietor - - - - *W. GIBBS.*

The Local and Universal Billposters
in THESE and All Towns in
SOUTH EAST ENGLAND
PARTINGTON'S KENT BILLPOSTING
DISTRICT CONTROLLED
1500 SQUARE MILES
General Manager Geo. Mitchell
PUBLICITY HOUSE, HIGH STREET.

Breakfast :: Dinners :: Teas
GOOD BEDS.
VICTORY CAFE,
149 BROOK,
CHATHAM.
Proprietress Mrs. E. C. Sargent.
Open on Sundays.

The Beers, Wines and Spirits at
"THE TWO BREWERS"
ROCHESTER
Has the Reputation of being the Best Quality.
CALL AND SEE
W. TRUSSON
Late R.N.
MEUX'S NOTED BEERS.
FREE FOR WINES AND SPIRITS.

PROGRAMME. MONDAY, JAN. 8th
M.R. PRODUCTIONS present
THE SUPER-COMEDY PRODUCTION
SPICY MOMENTS
Music and Lyrics by Leon Jesse Book by Stan Jay
Dances and Ensembles by Stephenie Anderson

Scene 1. .. THEATRICAL TRAVELLING IN 1940
The Stowaway .. STAN JAY
The Company.
Scene 2 .. VIOLET TIME
Joan Hester and the Girls.
Scene 3. .. AUTOMATIC LIVING.
Proprietor .. Tom Soulsby
The New Assistant .. STAN JAY
Customers .. Mark Britten, Gertie Kendal, Nora O'Shea and Joan Hester.
Scene 4. .. AN ARCTIC PHANTASY
The Trapper .. ERIC RANDOLPH
Spirit of the Sun .. Amanda
Scene 5. .. THE MATRIMONIAL AGENCY.
The Widow .. Joan Hester
The Clerk .. Tom Soulsby
The Manager .. STAN JAY
Scene 6. .. THE RODNEY HUDSON GIRLS.
Scene 7. .. THE BLIND POTTER.
Presenting ERIC RANDOLPH.
Scene 8. .. WHERE IGNORANCE IS BLISS.
The Major .. Mark Britten
The Subaltern .. Tom Soulsby
The Sergeant .. Allan David
The Private .. Harry Rennie
The Sergeant-Major .. STAN JAY
Scene 9. .. IN A LAND OF "WE DON'T KNOW WHERE."
The Dancers .. AMANDA and MARKOVA
INTERVAL.
Scene 10. .. THE GIRLS OBLIGE AGAIN
Scene 11. .. THE DECEIVER.
Miss Holmes .. Tom Soulsby
The Landlady .. Joan Hester
Holidaymaker .. STAN JAY
Scene 12. .. HATS OFF TO THE NAVY.
AMANDA and MARKOVA, assisted by the Rodney Hudson Girls.
Scene 13. .. THE TRIPPERS.
Mrs. Hawkins .. Joan Hester
Mr. Hawkins .. STAN JAY
Sidney Hawkins .. Tom Soulsby
Molly Hawkins .. Bee Watson
Scene 14. .. A ROMANCE OF THE SOUTH SEAS.
Hawaiian Melodies .. The Hallam Players
The Dancers .. Amanda and Markova
The Beachcomber .. ERIC RANDOLPH
Scene 15. .. HIKING.
Tom Soulsby and STAN JAY.
Scene 16. .. THE COMPANY BID YOU GOOD-NIGHT
Under the personal supervision of Eric Randolph.

AUTHORISED DEALER TO COLUMBIA CO.
REPAIRS EXECUTED BY
WORSFOLD'S Have It !
If you want to purchase "His Master's Voice" Products, then to avoid disappointment make Worsfold's your centre. From the Smallest needle to the finest Cabinet Grand from the latest dance "hit," to the greatest classics, every product is stocked.
We cordially invite you to call and play over any record you desire to hear on—
The NEW
"His Master's Voice"
GRAMOPHONE

In 1935, the Theatre Royal underwent a change of ownership and, in an attempt to overcome a decline in audiences, a move was made away from serious drama to revues and, as can be seen in this playbill for 1940, slightly more risqué productions such as *Spicy Moments*.

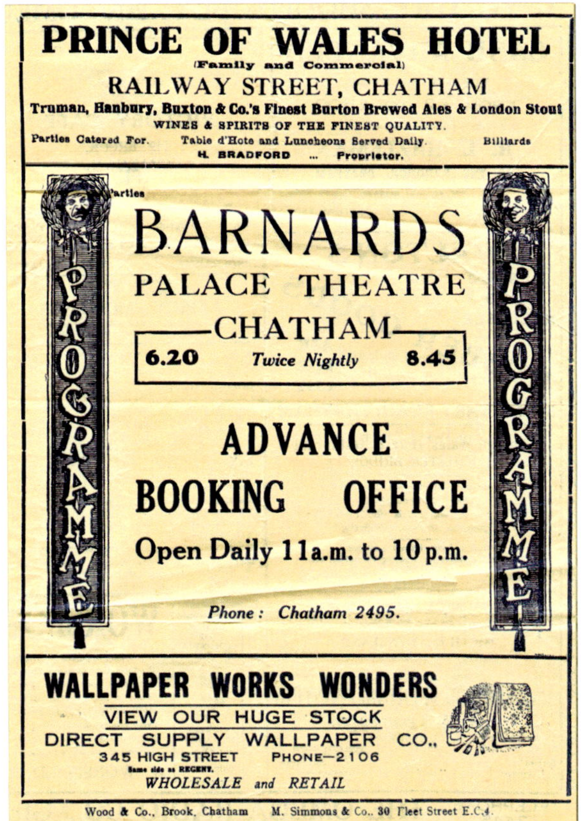
PRINCE OF WALES HOTEL
(Family and Commercial)
RAILWAY STREET, CHATHAM
Truman, Hanbury, Buxton & Co.'s Finest Burton Brewed Ales & London Stout
WINES & SPIRITS OF THE FINEST QUALITY.
Parties Catered For. Table d'Hote and Luncheons Served Daily. Billiards
H. BRADFORD ... Proprietor.

PROGRAMME

BARNARDS
PALACE THEATRE
CHATHAM
6.20 Twice Nightly 8.45

ADVANCE
BOOKING OFFICE
Open Daily 11 a.m. to 10 p.m.

Phone: Chatham 2495.

PROGRAMME

WALLPAPER WORKS WONDERS
VIEW OUR HUGE STOCK
DIRECT SUPPLY WALLPAPER CO.,
345 HIGH STREET PHONE—2106
Same side as REGENT.
WHOLESALE and RETAIL

Wood & Co., Brook, Chatham M. Simmons & Co., 30 Fleet Street E.C.4.

At that time, in 1940, the theatre had also taken on a new name, making a clear connection with the earlier Barnard Palace of Varieties.

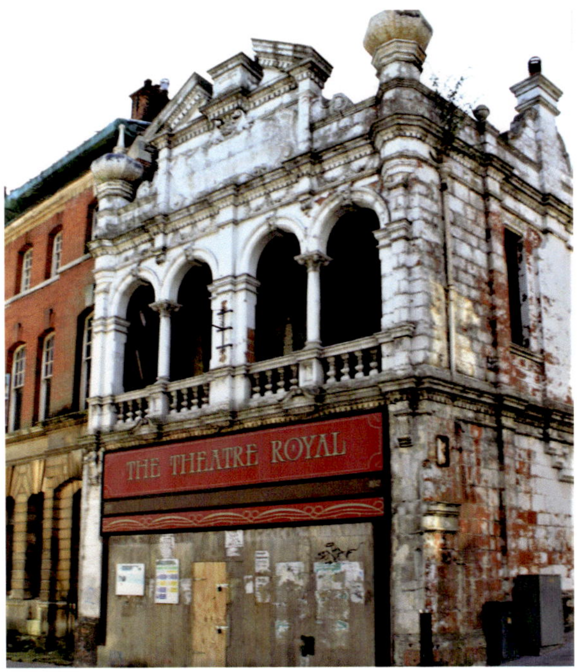

Closed as a theatre in 1955, the Theatre Royal became much neglected, and for many years was threatened with demolition. However, the result of a determined local campaign, the building, or at least the former front of house, was saved and provides this part of the High Street with an impressive piece of Victorian architecture. The auditorium and stage house were, however, demolished in 2009, and replaced by apartments given the appropriate name 'The Auditorium'.

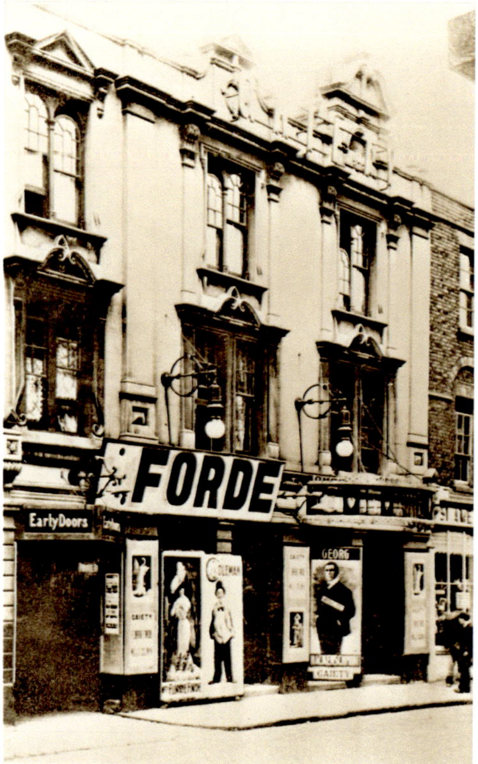

In 1890, the music hall as established by Barnham met with a rival in the form of the Gaiety (49 High Street), a new theatre also at the east end of the High Street that was more or less opposite Hammond Street. A slightly more upmarket venue, the Gaiety, as well as having three bars, also possessed a tearoom. It remained a popular venue for the next twenty-one years, with a new owner deciding upon a partial rebuilding that gave it a much grander entrance.

Gaiety Theatre of Varieties

High Street, CHATHAM.

Licensee and General Manager - - - A. E. HEGLEY.

OPEN ALL THE YEAR ROUND

. . WITH . .

First-Class London Talent only.

The Theatre is delightfully cool in Summer, and heated in the Winter by Hot Water Pipes.

COPY OF UNSOLICITED TESTIMONIAL.

DEAR SIR,

I trust you will excuse this, but I feel that I must thank you for providing a Variety Entertainment in Chatham which decent people can attend. During all the years I have resided in Chatham I have but on two occasions visited a Music Hall—the second was on Wednesday evening, when my wife and I attended the Second House at the Gaiety; and I was so struck with the clean nature of the entertainment that I have given permission to my daughters to attend this (Friday) evening.

MR. A. E. HEGLEY.

Two Performances Nightly, at 6.15 & 8.55.

DOORS OPEN AT 5.40 & 8.30.

The Gaiety was particularly careful about the acts booked, attempting always to attract a more discerning audience, a point underlined in its advertising.

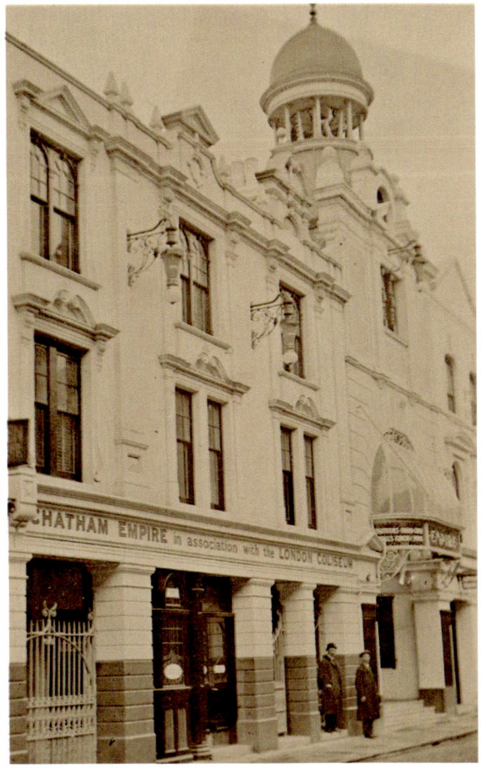

Opened in March 1912, the former Gaiety had now become the Empire, its grand entrance designed by Frank Matcham for Oswald Stoll of the London Coliseum.

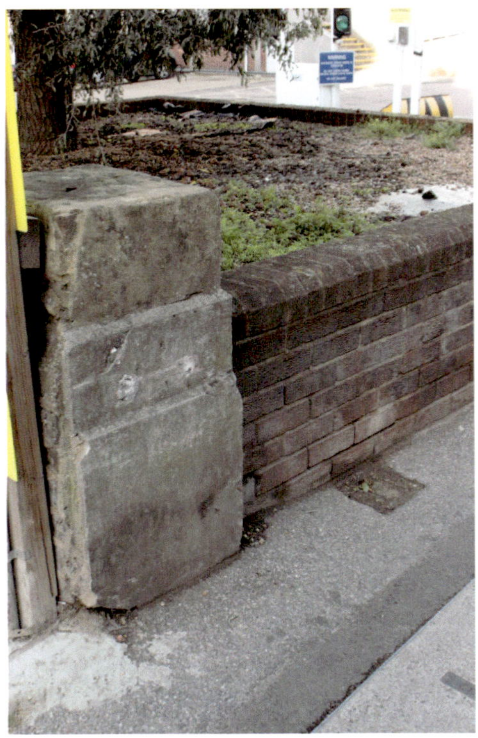

All that remains of the Empire (former Gaiety theatre) is this pillar and the adjoining wall. The Empire itself was closed in 1960, unable to effectively compete with cinemas built in the town and the home attraction of television.

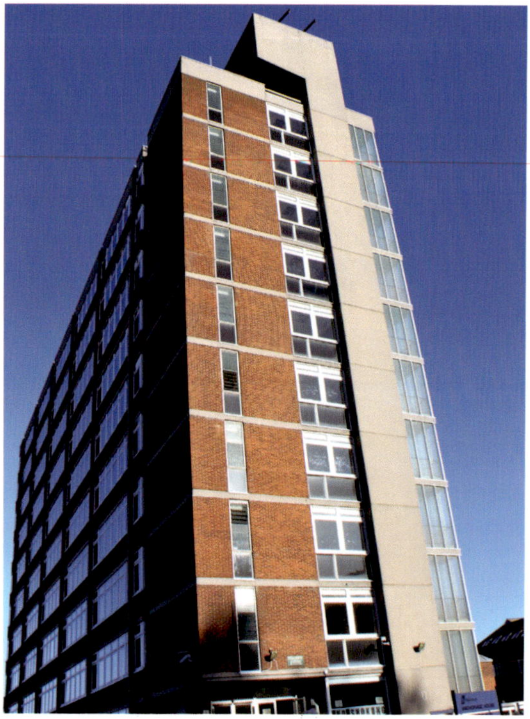

It was the demolition of the Empire Theatre and a small attached cinema, the latter more of a fleapit, that created space for a car park and the building of Anchorage House for HM Revenue and Customs. As for this building, seen here while still serving as an office block, it is currently being converted into eighty-one flats, despite Medway Council stating in its Building Heights Policy as adopted in 2000 that the outright removal of Anchorage House 'would be desirable'. Anchorage House also once housed Medway County and Family Court, this now transferred to Medway Council's Gun Wharf building.

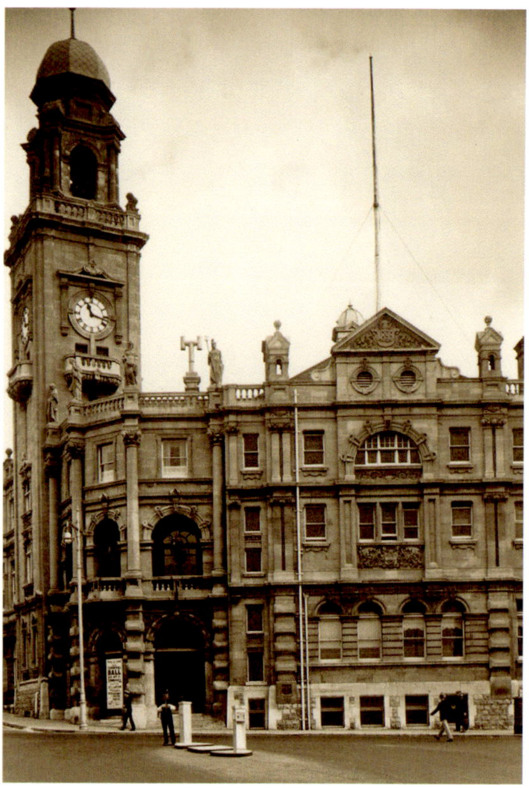

The Town Hall, while once the seat of local government for the town of Chatham, also contributed to the town's entertainment, through possessing both a ballroom and stage. Designed by George E. Bond who had also designed the Theatre Royal, the poster to be seen outside is advertising the annual carnival ball, a once annual event held within the Town Hall during the month of August. The theme of entertainment is maintained within the building to this day, for upon the City Council relocating its main offices to Strood (and subsequently to the former Lloyds riverside building), the former Town Hall was reopened as the Medway Arts Centre, becoming in 1997 the Brook Theatre.

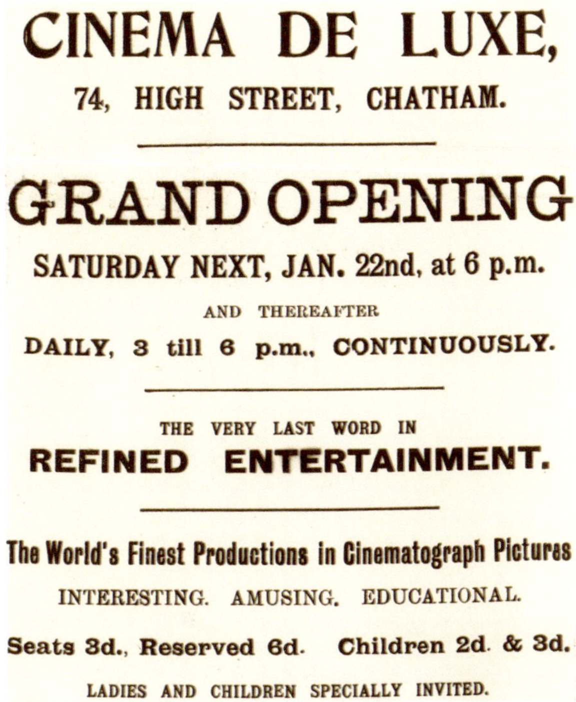

The beginning of the twentieth century saw the arrival of cinemas in the town, the earliest being the Cinema de Luxe (74 High Street) which opened in 1910. At the time it prided itself in offering 'the very last word in refined entertainment' but was soon overshadowed by other more comfortable larger theatres with improved picture reproduction.

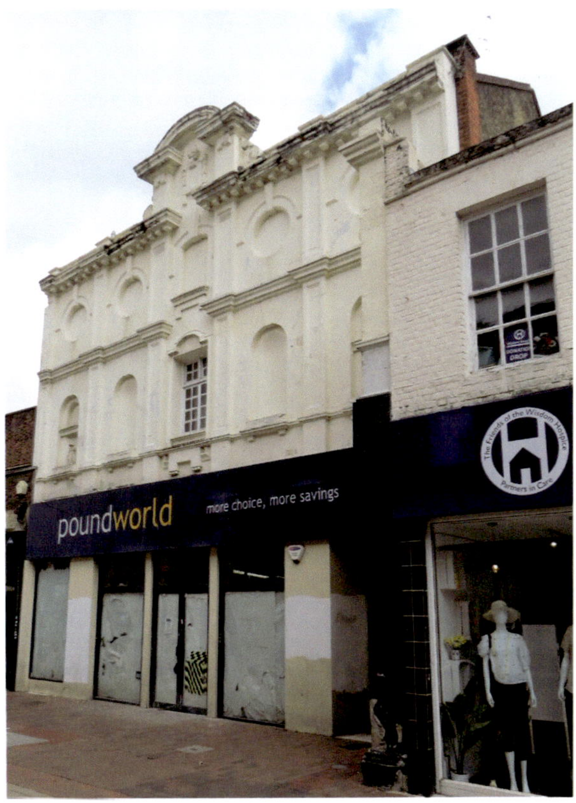

Chatham's first purpose-built cinema was the National Electric Theatre (205 High Street). It was opened in April 1911 and by the 1930s was managed by Denman Picture Houses, part of the Gaumont British Theatres chain. Eventually closing as a cinema in 1950, the building was converted into a shop and has seen a number of different businesses using the building, mostly those of the fashion industry. It was empty at the time of writing. On the upper floor of the building, once housing the circle seats, a few reminders of the building's earlier use, such as usherette seating, were certainly extant up until a few years ago. On first opening, the National Electric had one particular unique selling point: it was the first major point of entertainment built away from the west end of the High Street and where all of the preceding music halls, theatres and also the Cinema de Luxe were located. This placed it much closer to Luton, where so much of the newer housing in Chatham had been built.

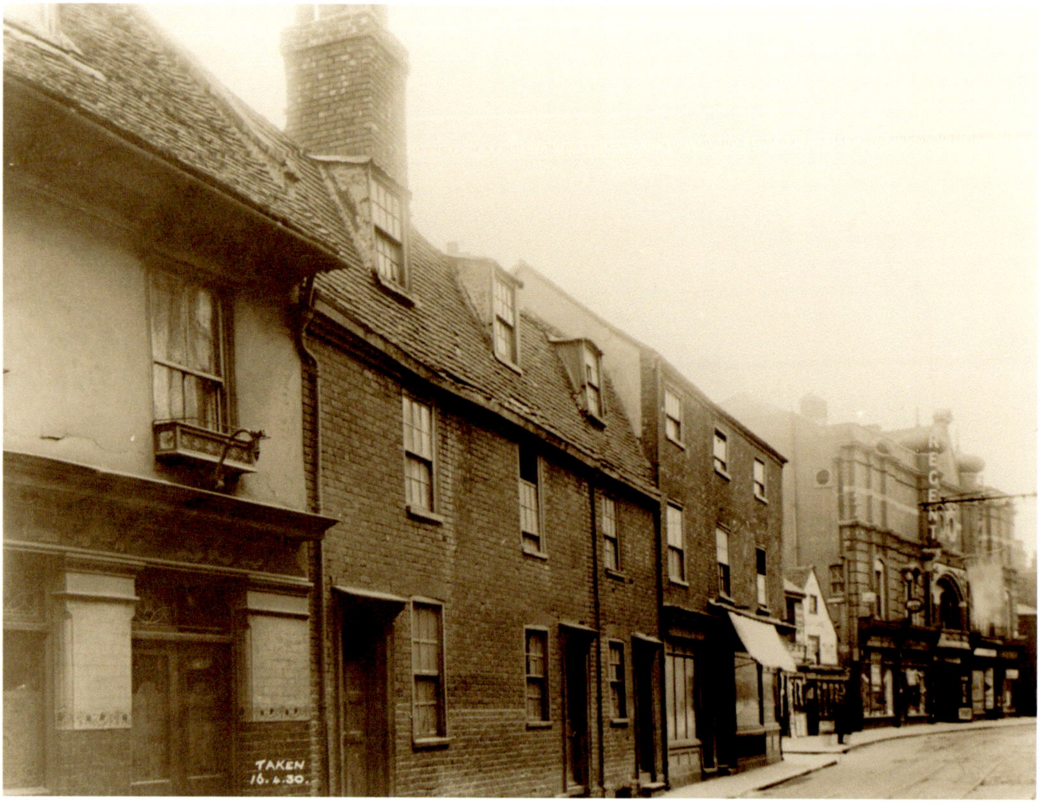

Close on the heels of Chatham's first two cinemas was a decision by the Barnards to show moving pictures at the Theatre Royal while the Empire opened its own cinema. Much more significant was the opening in 1914 of the Imperial Picture Palace, known as the IPP, at the extreme east end of the High Street on a site later rebuilt as a Tesco store, and later occupied by 'Go Outdoors'. It was one of the buildings designed by Medway architect George E. Bond, with the IPP, later becoming the Regent, remaining here until 1937. Construction of such a large cinema at the east end of the High Street took much of the audience from the now seemingly diminutive National Electric Theatre.

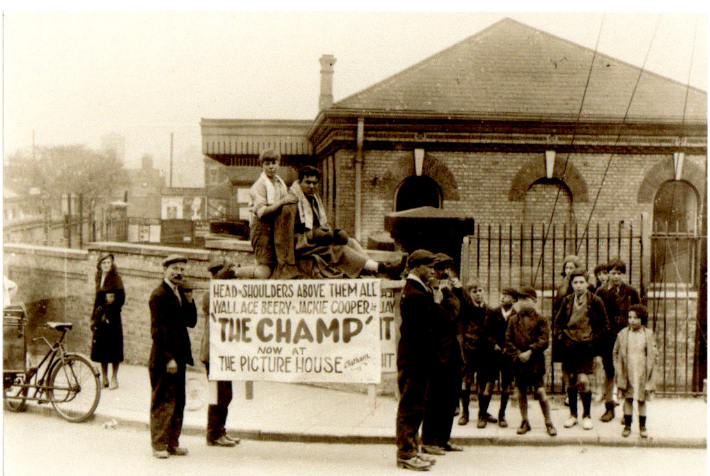

How to advertise films – this was The Regent way in 1931. *The Champ*, a highly acclaimed film, won two Academy awards (Oscars). It told the story of a washed-up alcoholic boxer.

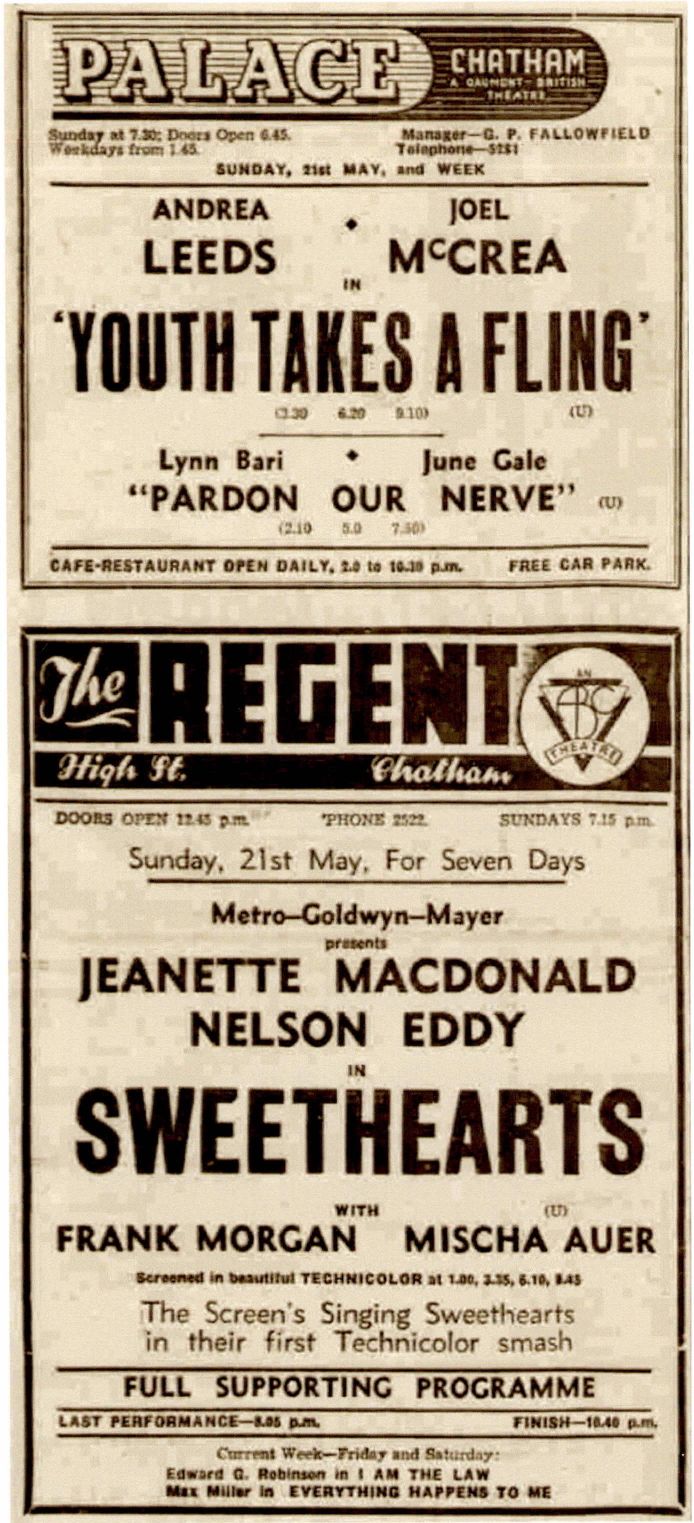

A more traditional form of advertising from 1938.

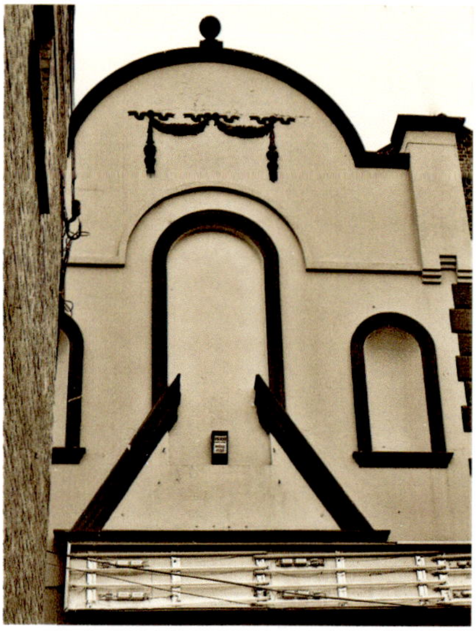

The Invicta, opened in February 1916, was a cinema located in Fullager's Yard, just off the High Street. Locally owned by the Croneen family of Gillingham, it had a rather dull and unexciting entrance, approached only by way of the narrow alleyway that was Fullager's Yard. Admittedly, some attempt was made to provide a little bit of élan, this by way of its period-style facade that overlooked the main point of entry but was probably missed by most cinemagoers.

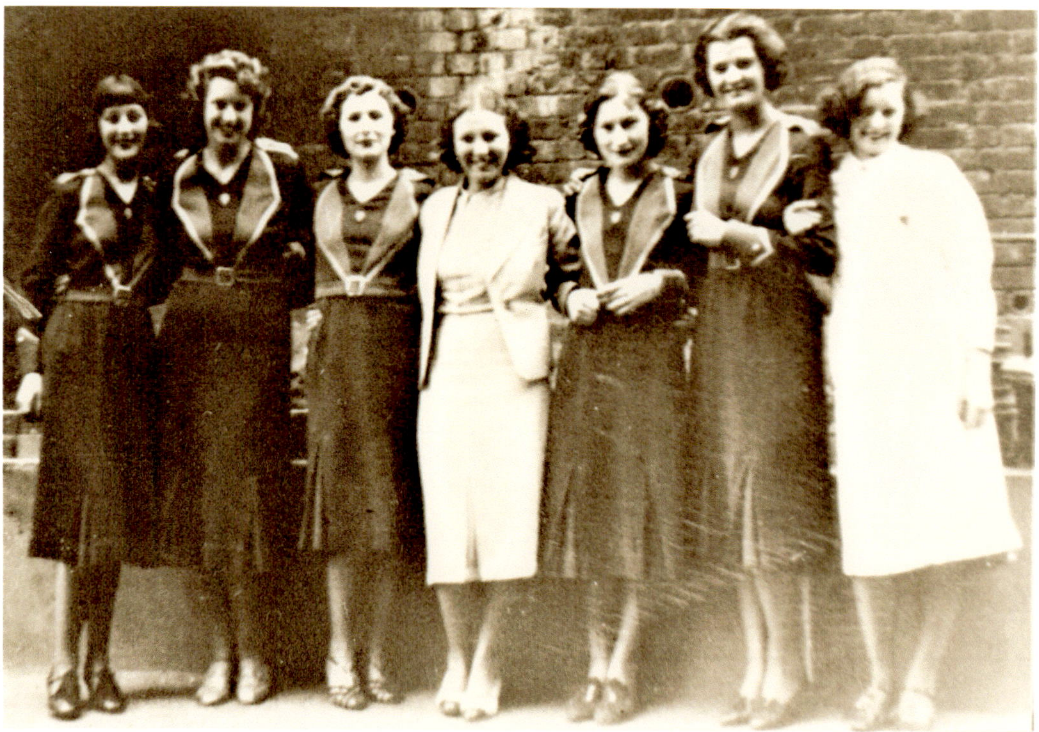

Having closed in 1937, the by then Regent was demolished, with Associated British Corporation (ABC) financing a brand-new cinema that was in a class of its own as regards, sound, picture projection, seating and overall ambience. Starting out life as the Super Regent, it was officially opened by the Mayor of Chatham, H. J. Stearne, at midday on 11 July 1938, and boasted seating for 1,115 in the stalls and 755 in the circle. Built by the William S. Blay company, the building was designed by William Riddell Glen, the appointed architect to Associated British Cinemas. Here can be seen a line-up of the Regent cinema staff of 1938.

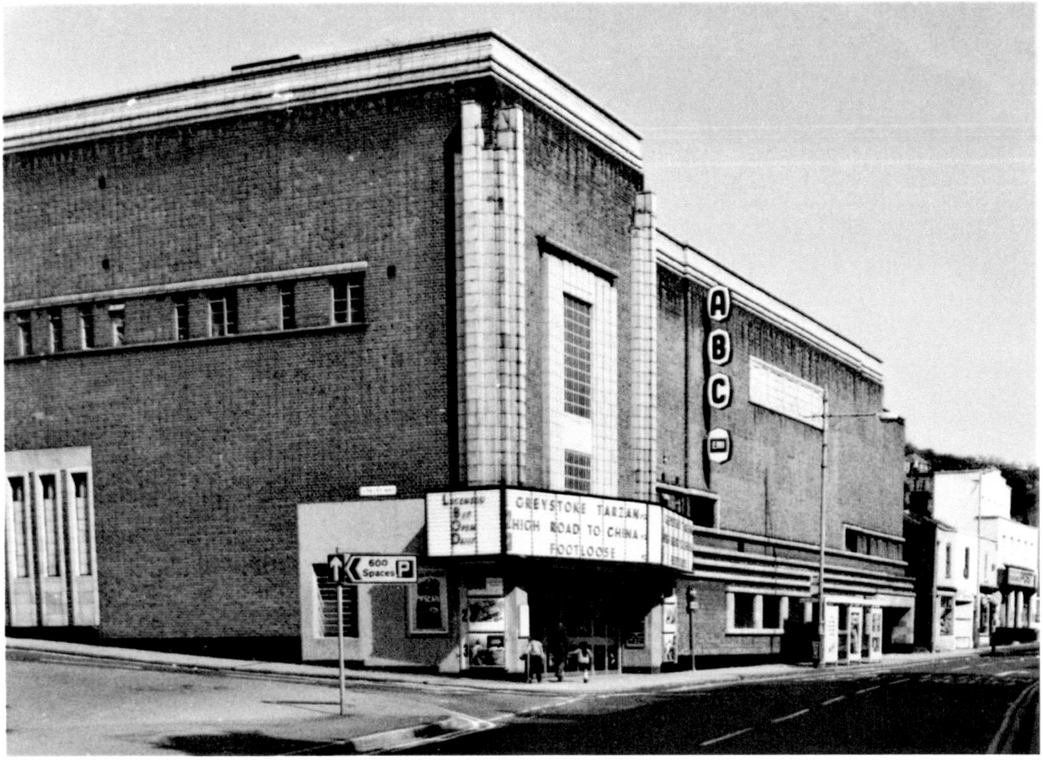

The name Regent was retained until October 1961 when it became the ABC.

The same building, but now Cannon, but formerly the Regent/ Super Regent/ABC, had seen further conversion in 1972, an internal refit creating three separate screens, each showing different films. Its acquisition and renaming by the Cannon Group took place 1986.

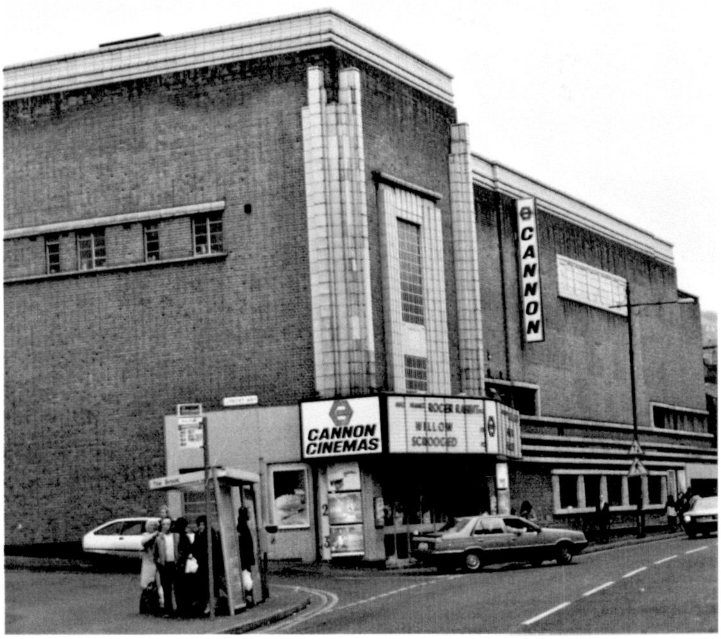

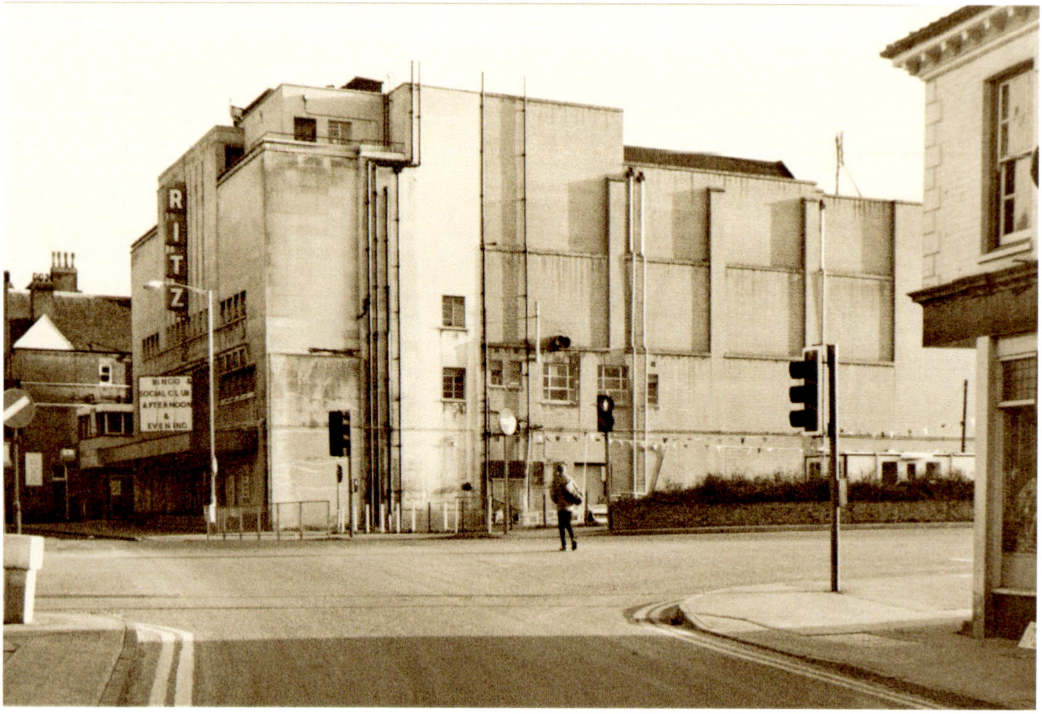

Owned by Union Cinemas, the Ritz, which once stood more or less opposite the Regent, was opened in March 1937 and was the grandest of all the Chatham cinemas. On that occasion it had seen the star of stage and screen Jack Buchanan, who had opened the cinema, with the Mayor of Chatham, H. J. Stearne, again in attendance. The opening was slightly unusual, as Buchanan opened The Ritz in Barnsley at the same time, his speech from the stage at Chatham relayed, through a special arrangement with the General Post Office (GPO), to the stage at Barnsley. In later days the Ritz at Chatham came to offer bingo rather than films. Following a devastating fire that broke out during the early morning of 30 September 1998, much of the Ritz was substantially destroyed leading to its demolition and replacement by a new structure, the Gala Bingo Club.

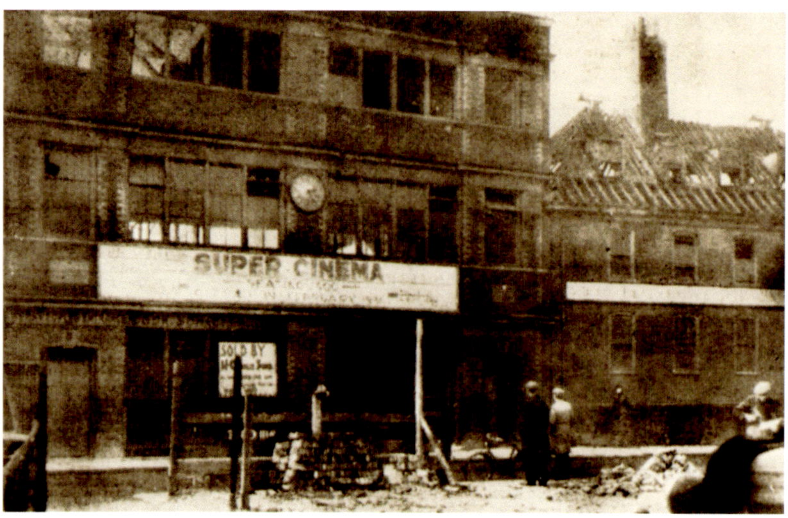

The Ritz was, itself, built on the site of the former Axe Brand clothing works factory that had, for many years, occupied this site and which was purchased by the Union Cinema Company. In preparation for the new cinema, work is in hand on demolishing the factory.

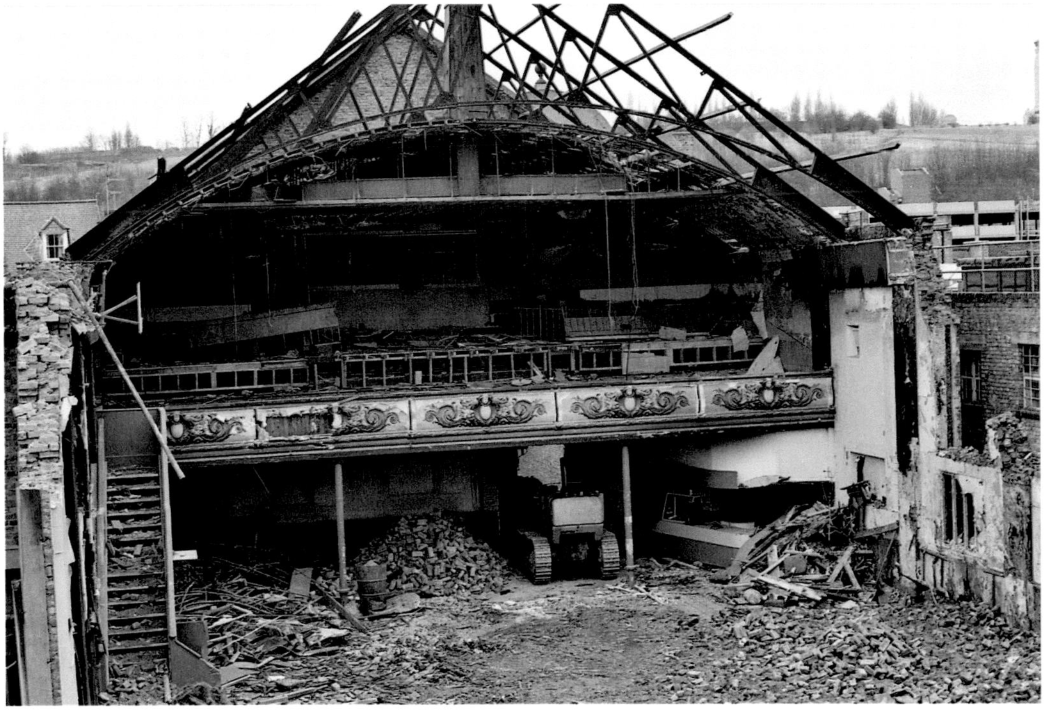

Above and below: In 1987 the Invicta cinema was demolished. These images show the auditorium during its final few days.

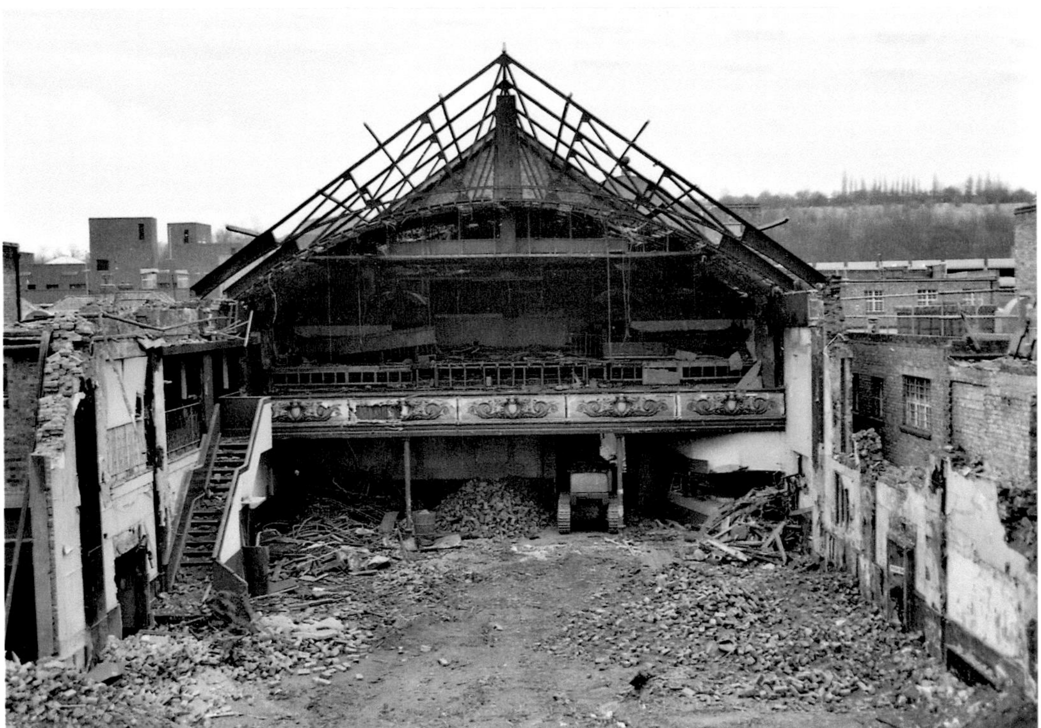

2

The Shopping Experience

Within the Medway area, Chatham High Street as a shopping centre once went unrivalled, possessing by the end of the nineteenth century not just numerous butchers, bakers, fishmongers and grocery stores, but at its more fashionable west end, department stores alongside more exclusive clothing outlets and jewellers. In other words, the High Street shopping experience was one that met not just the daily needs of everyday life but the unfulfilled dreams of every customer. The importance of the High Street is now much diminished, despite the building of the Pentagon shopping centre during the 1970s. Instead, the internet and out-of-town retail centres have taken their toll, forcing many shops to either close or relocate.

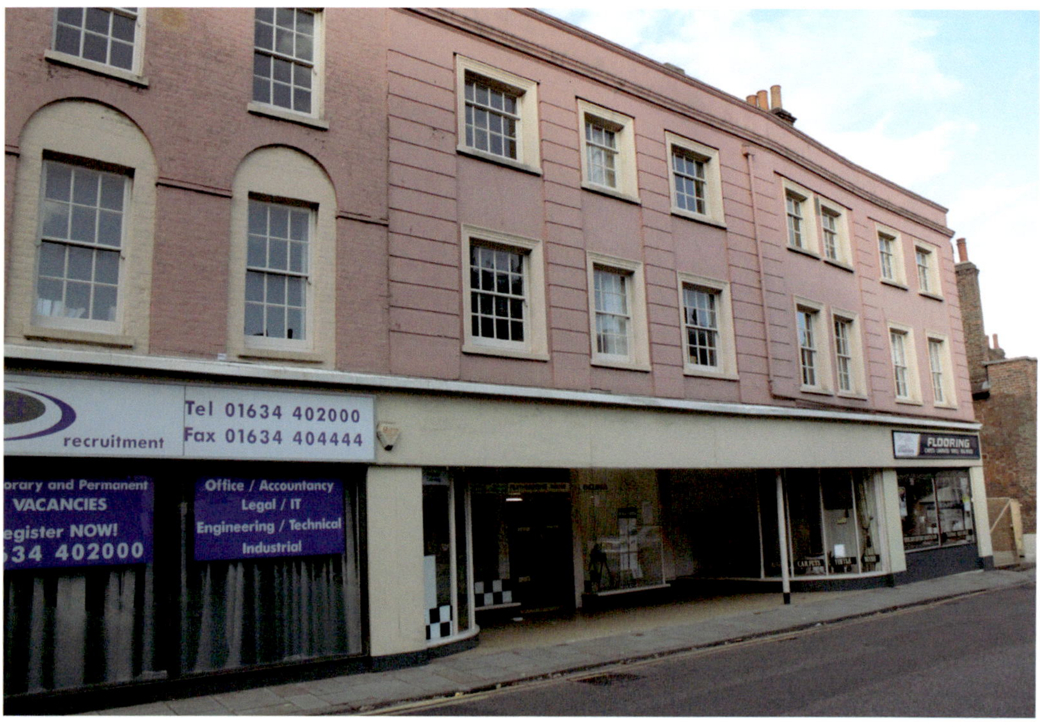

Seen here in 2010, the building was once occupied by a department store first established in 1901 by Thomas Featherstone. In its day, the Featherstone store sold a remarkable range of goods, from bespoke tailored garments to coal. Although just within the boundary of Chatham, located next to the Sir John Hawkins Almshouse, the store always declared itself as having a Rochester address. The Featherstone family continued to run the store, together with others subsequently opened, until 1981, when it changed its business focus to that of property management.

A Featherstones' advert dating to 1936.

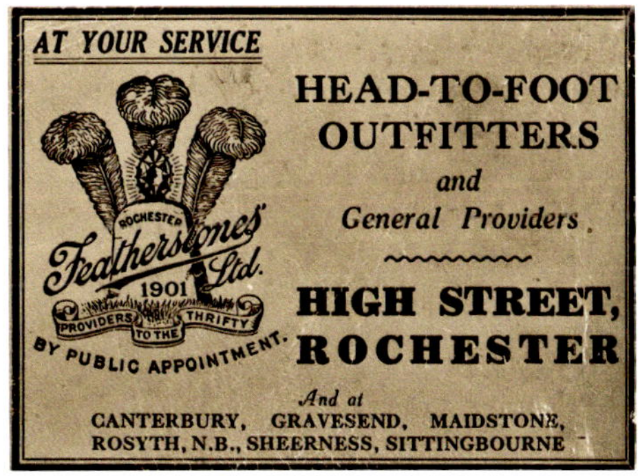

Right: Further along the High Street from Featherstones' was another department store, originally the business premises of Edward Bates (125–7 High Street) which opened in 1963. As with Featherstones', the Bates family had a long-time connection with Chatham, first opening a High Street store in 1869 and moving to a further location (94–6 High Street) in 1900. The store, as seen here in 1981, had by that time been acquired by Bentalls, this company retaining the store until 1984. One of their advertising slogans was 'Bentalls – at the better end of Chatham High Street'.

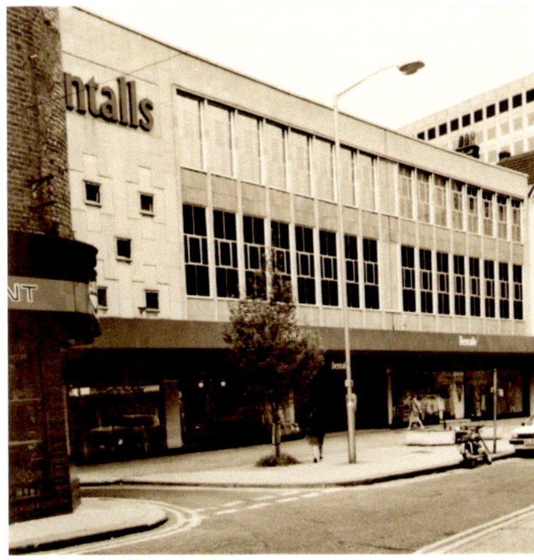

Below: More recently Argos traded from this same store as once occupied by Bentalls. Argos ceased trading here at the beginning of 2022.

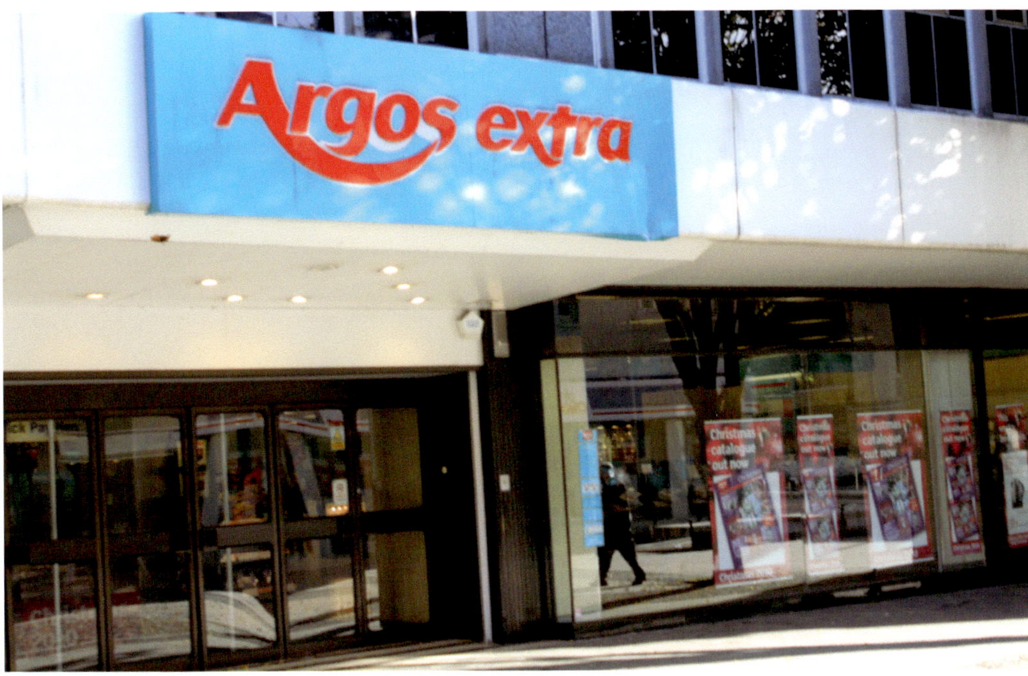

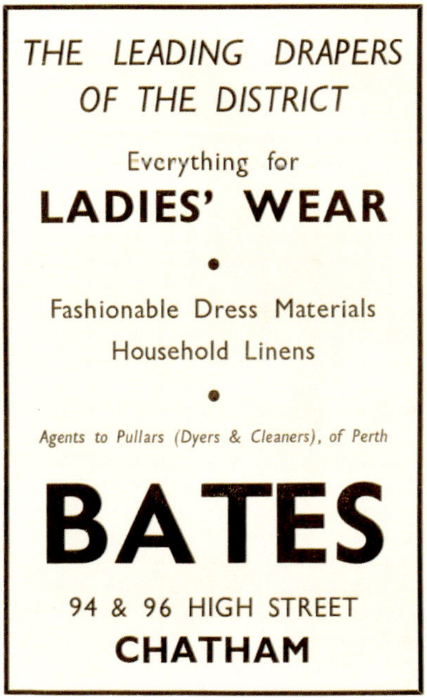

Left: An advertisement for the Edward Bates store prior to its later relocation.

Below: Here, in this photo, which was taken during the 1920s, shops viewed (and moving away from the camera) are Murdoch & Co., piano and music merchants (86–88 High Street), the Carlton Oriental Café (84 High Street), David Grieg's (82 High Street) and the Chatham Furnishing Company (80 High Street).

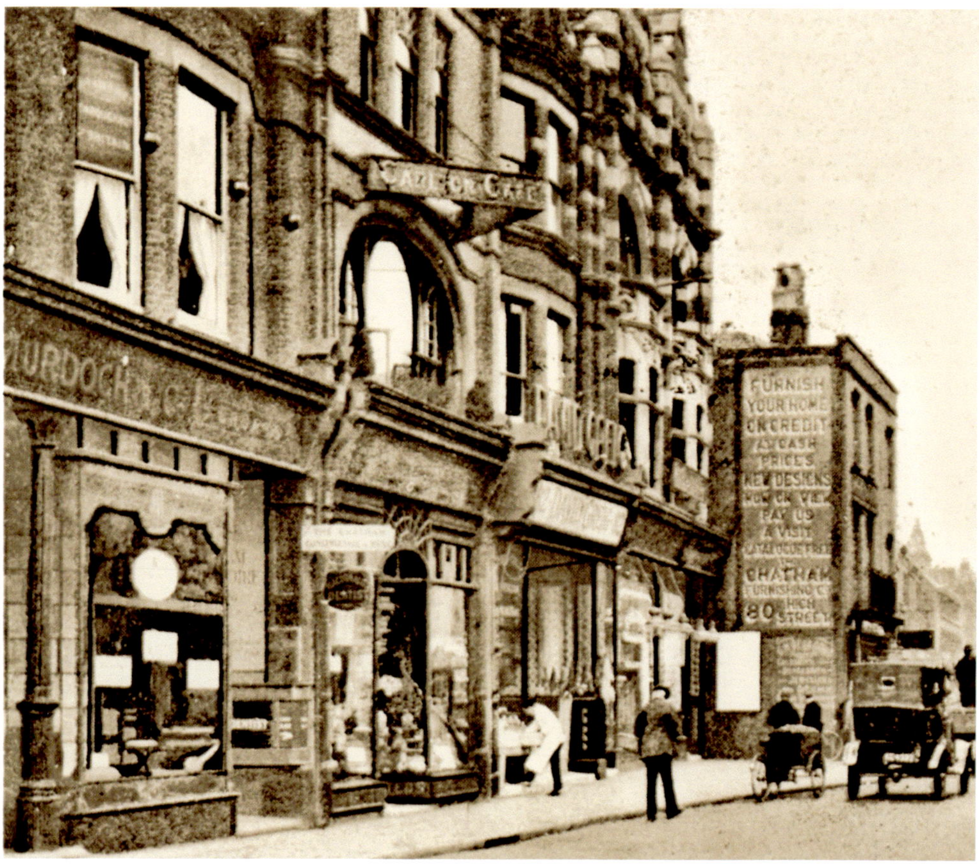

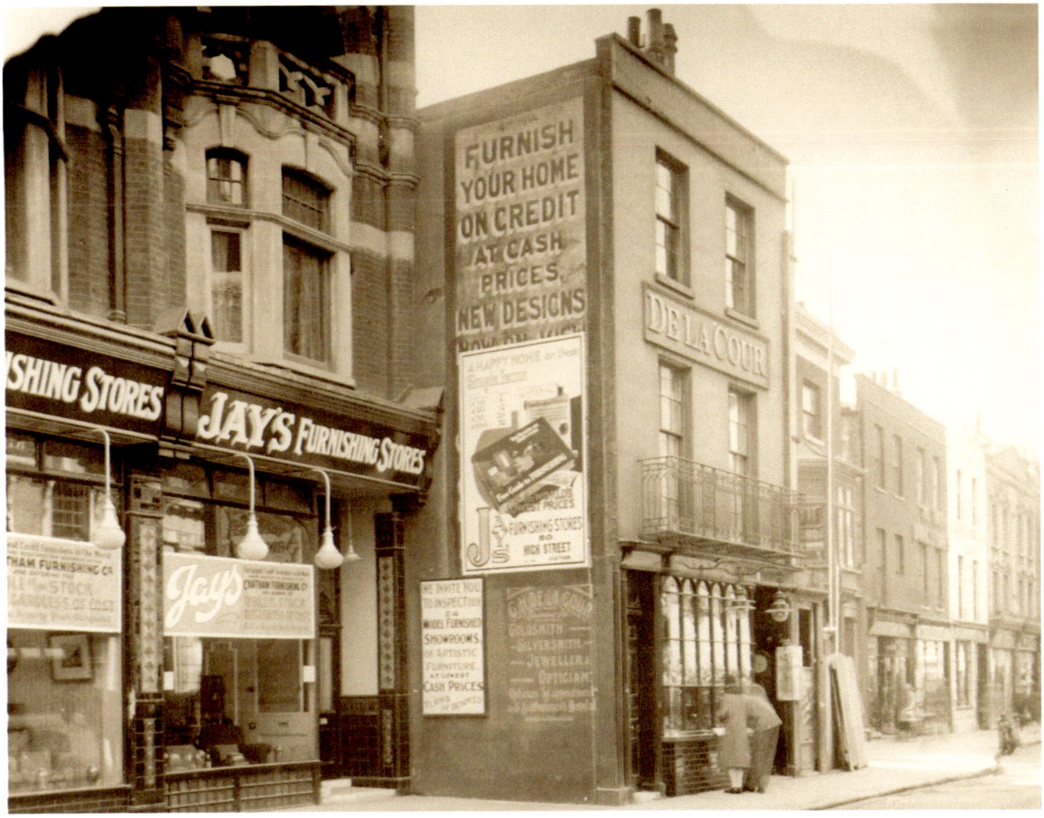

Jay's Furnishing Store (80 High Street) opened its Chatham shop during the 1930s following its acquisition from the Chatham Furnishing Company. In having taken over the premises, the earlier shop advert for the Chatham Furnishing Company has been reused, but with the name of the earlier company covered over by a large pasted poster declaring Jay's to possess within the store some twenty-four showrooms. Jay's was a national company with workshops in Brighton. It could redesign and furnish an entire home, promising householders a no-obligation visit by a 'Home Service Expert'.

This time the photographer taking this photograph during the 1920s has the Chatham Furnishing Company behind the camera. The group of shops are the retail outlet of Edward Bates Ltd (94–6 High Street), the Domestic Bazaar Company (92 High Street), Home Supply Footwear Co., bootmakers (90 High Street) and, once again, Murdoch & Co., piano and music merchants (88 High Street).

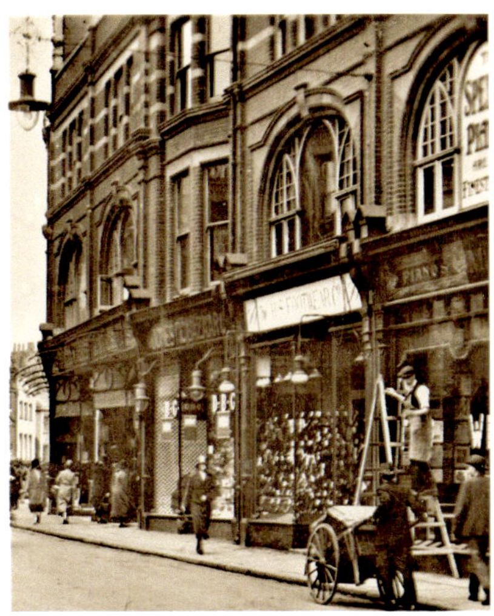

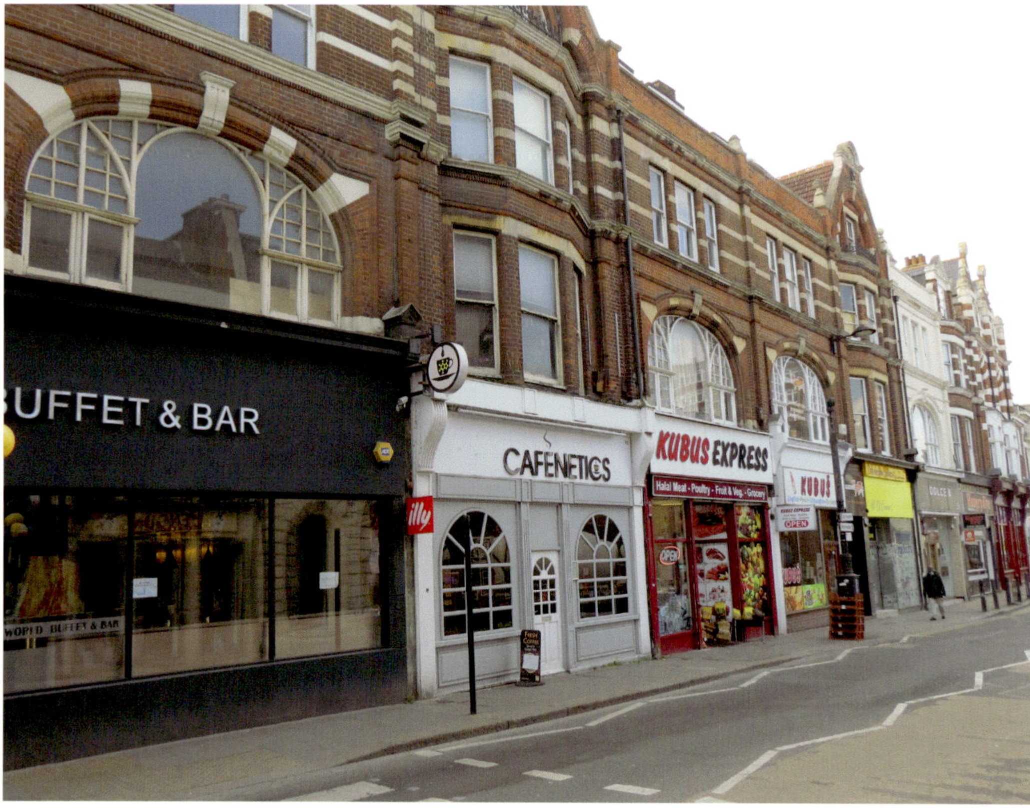

The same group of shops as they appear today.

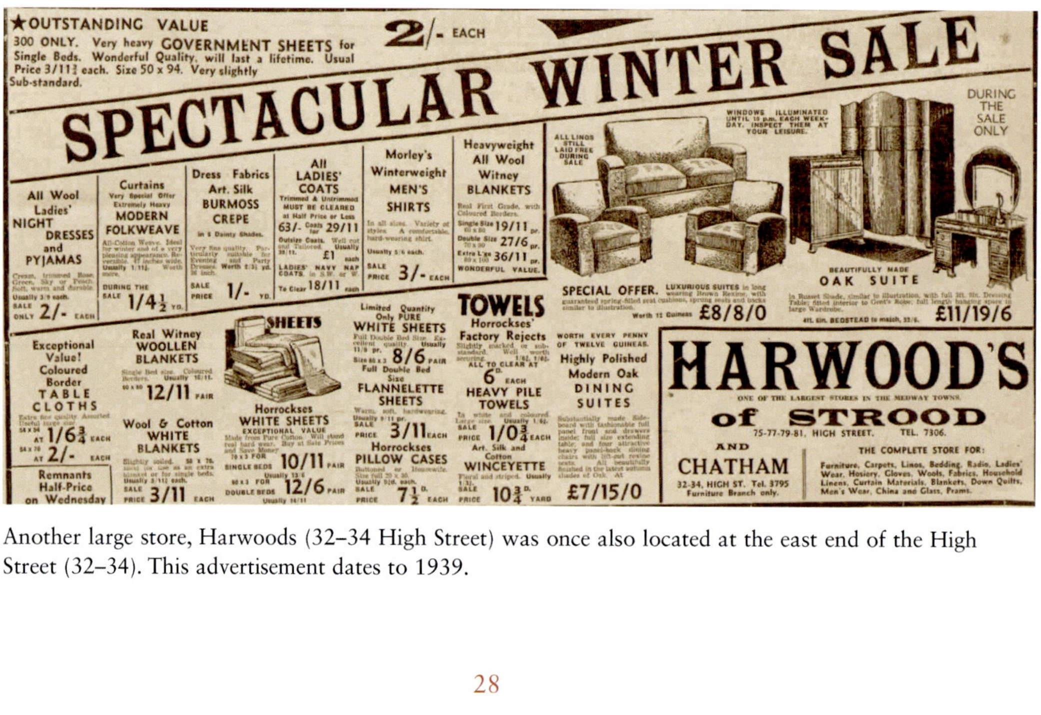

Another large store, Harwoods (32–34 High Street) was once also located at the east end of the High Street (32–34). This advertisement dates to 1939.

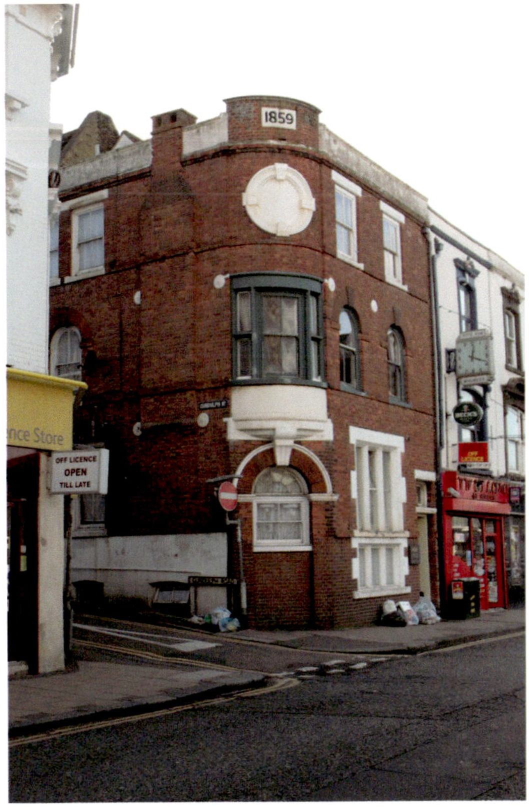

Right: Media House on the corner of the High Street and Gundulf Road was, when this picture was taken in 1981, the home of BBC Radio Medway, a station that has now been subsumed into BBC Radio Kent and which is now located at Sun Pier. That the building, which dates to 1859, is known as Media Hose is because, prior to BBC Radio Medway, it was the offices of Parrett & Neves, the owners of the *Chatham News* and the *Chatham Standard*.

Below: Formerly H. C. Lawrence & Sons Ltd (2 High Street), this distinctly different building seen in 2010 had just been taken over as a Chinese restaurant, the 'New Hong Kong' but now 'The Orchid Garden'. Lawrence & Sons, with a long association with the High Street, marketed themselves in the 1930s as 'nurserymen, seedsmen & florist'.

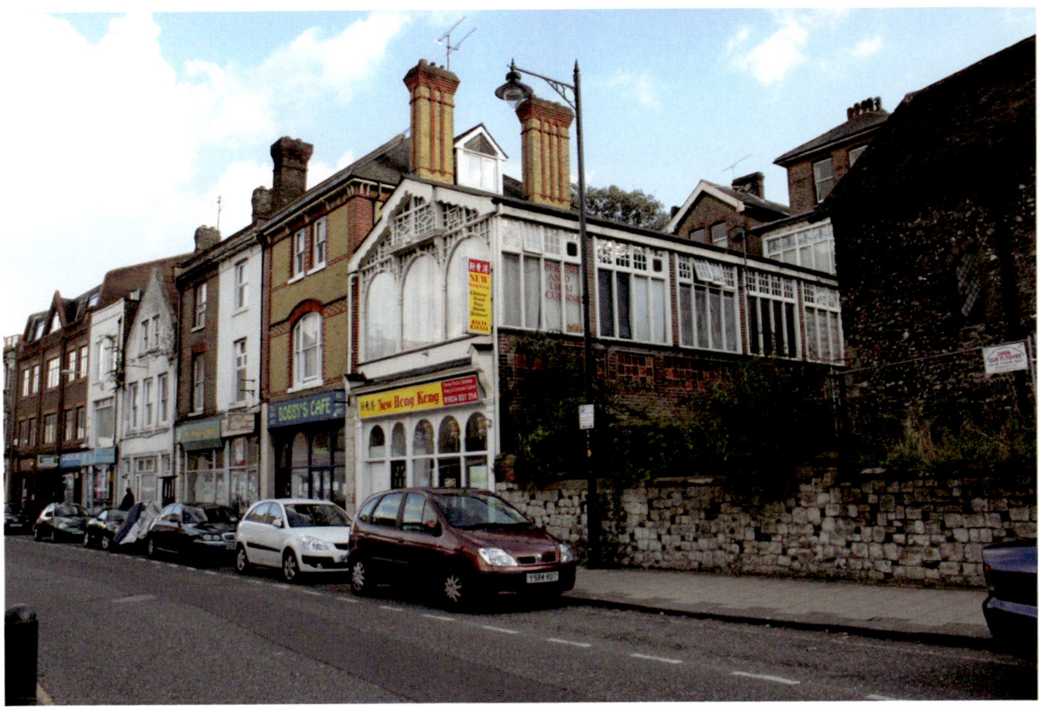

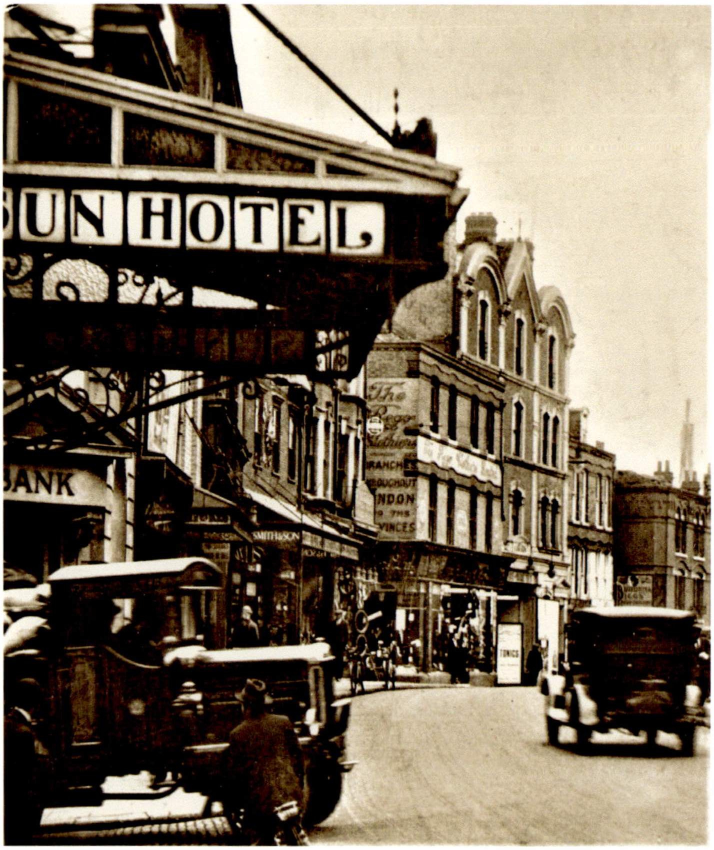

A long-time stalwart of the High Street until its move into the Pentagon during the 1970s was W.H.Smith and Son (95–7 High Street). Their premises is seen here in the 1920s, viewed through the panoply of the Sun Hotel (85 High Street). The Sun Hotel once stood on the corner of the High Street and Medway Street.

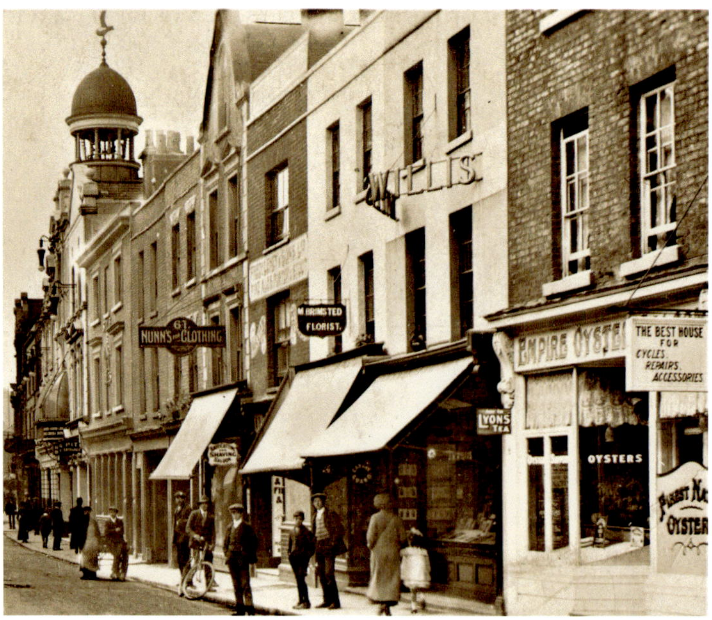

To be seen in this photograph is the long-demolished Empire Theatre of Varieties (47 High Street) with its clearly recognisable roof dome designed to provide both light and ventilation to the hall below. Closest to the camera is the Empire Oyster Bar (69 High Street) and moving away from the camera S. E. Wills, Photographer (67 High Street) and Miss D. Wolf, Milliner (65 High Street).

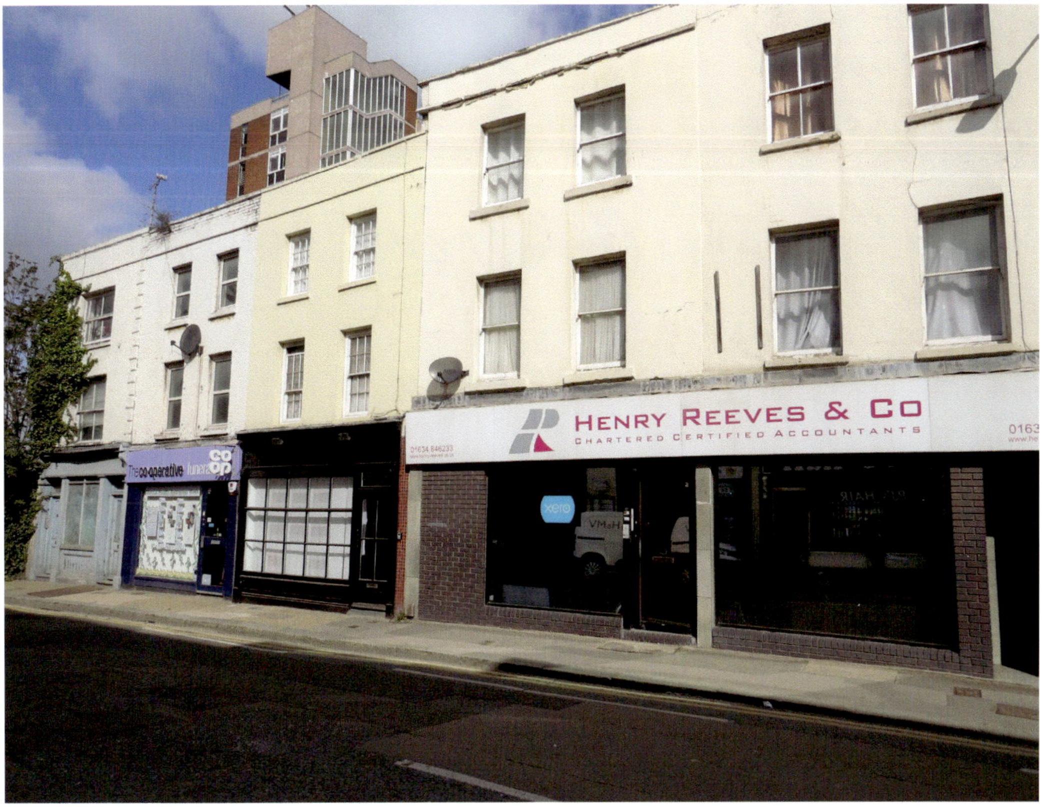

Above: This same group of shops as they appear today. The Empire Oyster Store is now Henry Reeves (69 High Street); Wills the Photographer is now a recruiting agency (67 High Street); and the milliners is now part of the Co-Op (63 High Street); while to the far left, a former beer retailer (61 High Street) has long been in need of some loving care and attention.

Right: Moving closer to Railway Street, a view of Timothy White's (126 High Street), a national pharmacy chain that was once Boots' greatest rival before the latter bought out Timothy White's in 1968 but with the name not disappearing until 1985.

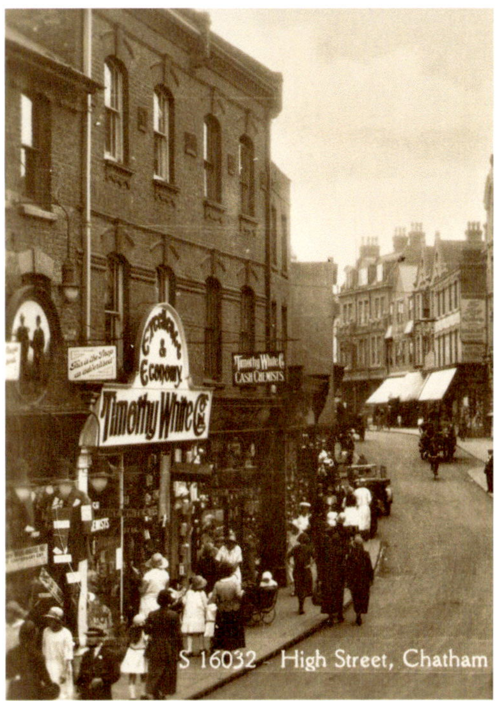

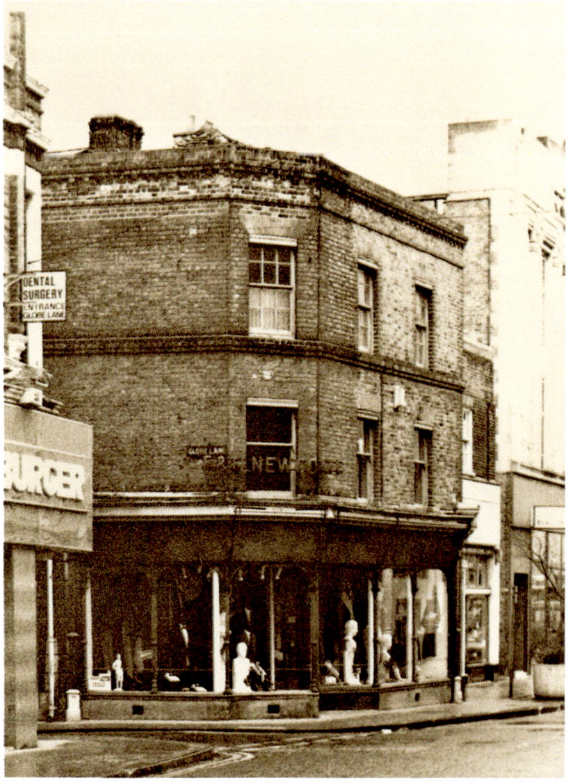

This is the High Street where, in former times, Globe Lane was situated. F & H Newcomb (133 High Street), a firm once describing itself as a clothier and hatters, was situated here for just over 150 years. To make way for a flyover named after the slave trader Sir John Hawkins, and which thankfully no longer exists, Newcomb's was forced to relocate (now 87–9 High Street) and their former premises, together with shops adjoining, were demolished.

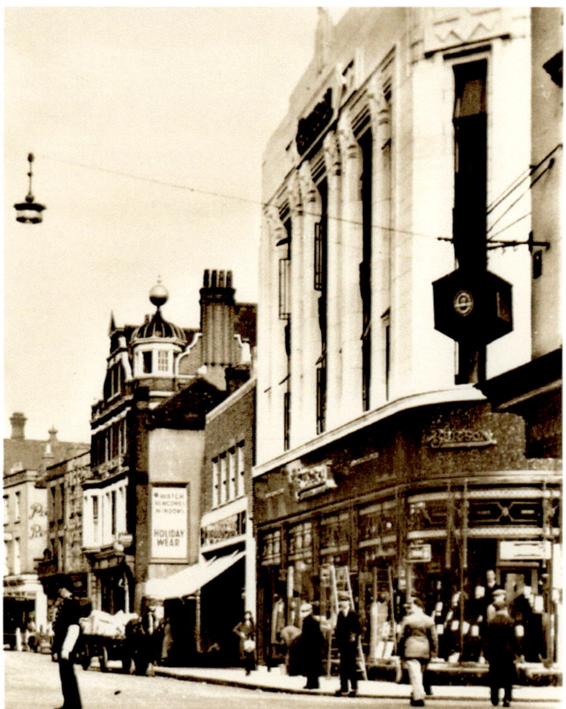

Another view of this demolished section of the High Street, seen here in 1938. Burton's Ltd (139–43 High Street), the men's fashion shop, is the large building in the foreground and was not part of the later demolition programme, remaining there for many more years, but with the premises now occupied by Halifax. A keen eye will note the placard, an advertisement for Newcomb's summer wear.

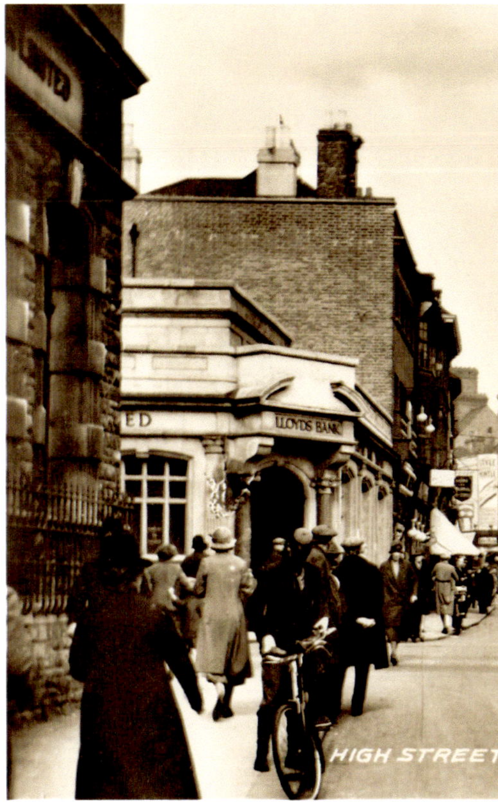

Right: Lloyds Bank (144–6 High Street) in 1938 and still located on the same site adjoining Railway Street but a building that has seen considerable alteration. For while the structure seen here still remains. It has been enshrouded with both an extension to the rear and much heightened.

Below: Possibly the oldest building in the High Street at the time of its demolition in 1984, then occupied by Platform 9 (250 High Street). Since the early nineteenth century this same shop had served as the premises of Thomas Fowle, funeral directors. The building in the foreground (248 High Street) was the former Fountain Inn.

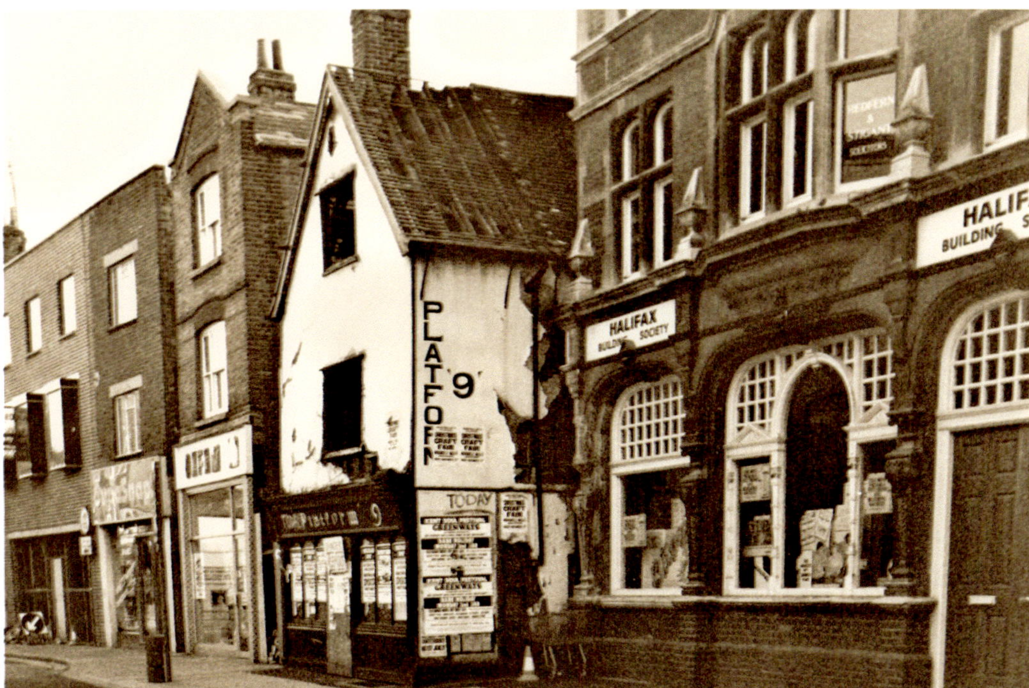

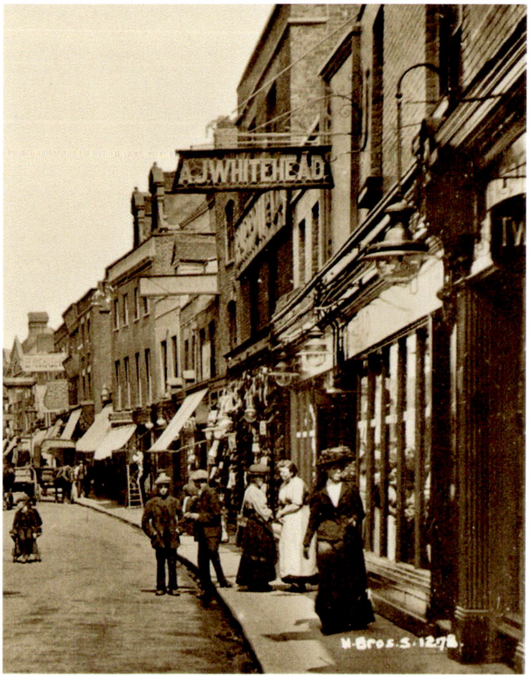

Left: The middle section of the High Street looking west sometime around 1905. A. J. Whitehead (195–9 High Street) is the most prominent shop in this photograph. A. J. Whitehead, in its advertising, proclaimed itself to be an upholsterer, cabinetmaker, carpet factory and complete house furnisher.

Below: Another High Street stalwart, Marks & Spencer (167–9 High Street), as seen in the years before the First World War. (Marks & Spencer plc)

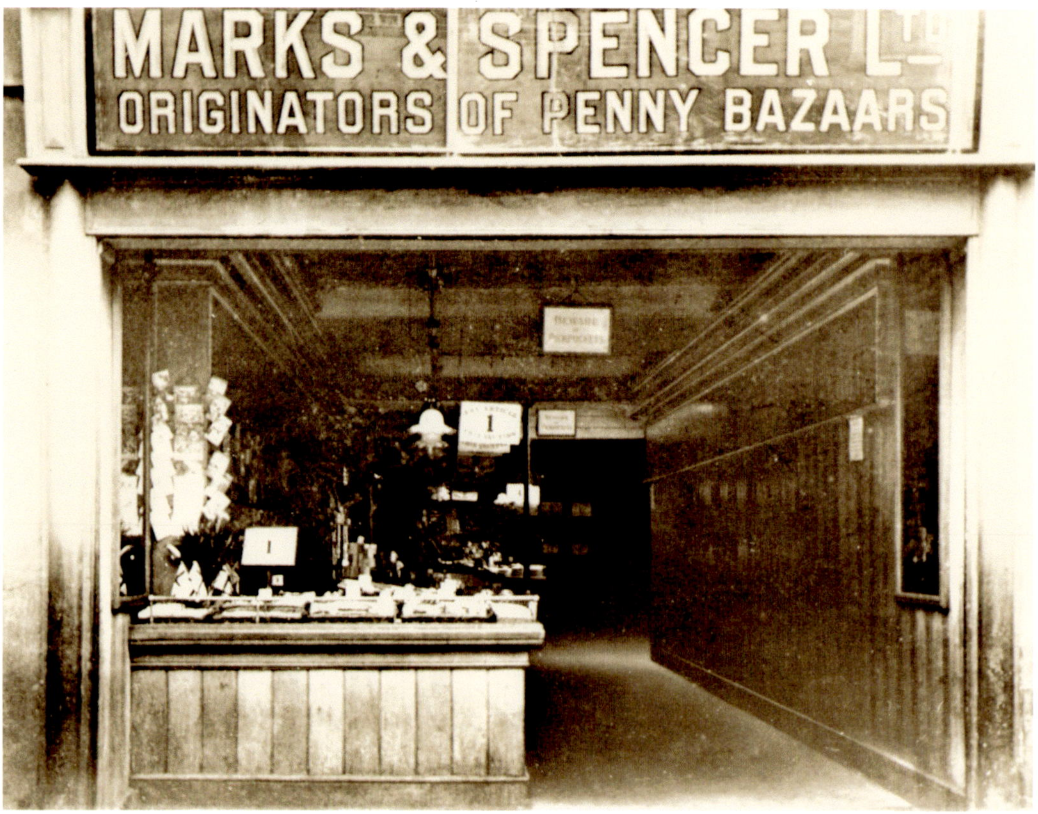

By the time of this photo, which possibly dates to the late 1920s, the Marks & Spencer's store (167–9 High Street), which is jut visible on the left-hand side of this photograph, had been completely refurbished. Above were the district offices of the London & North Eastern Railway and next door (169 High Street), the Chatham Billiard Hall.

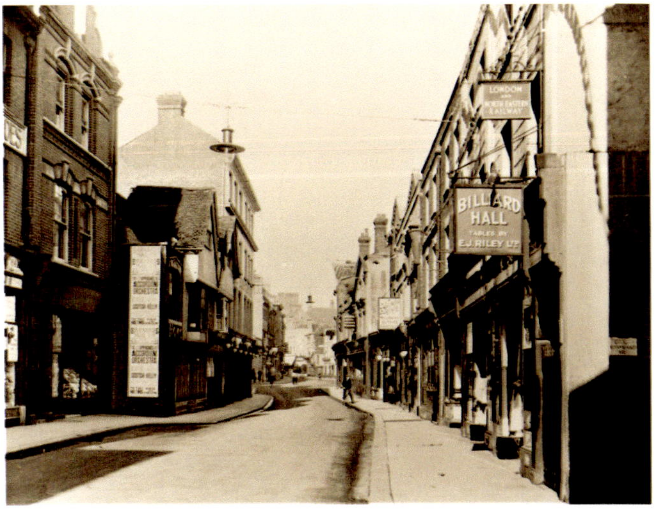

Among shops to be seen in this early 1950s shot of the High Street are F. W. Woolworth's (186–90 High Street). First established in Chatham in 1913 (198 High Street), the first Woolworth's was destroyed by bombing during the Second World War. Work commenced on a new building in 1948, this on the site of a once notorious pub, the United Services. Woolworth's closed in 2008 and the shop is now Primark.

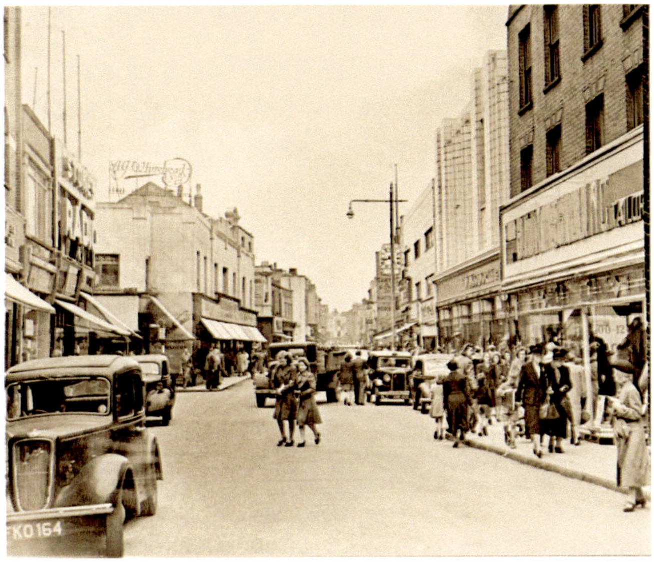

A further picture of the 1948 Woolworth's store (186–90 High Street) that stood close by Fullager's Yard, the alleyway which served as the entry passageway into the Invicta Cinema, a fact highlighted by the overhead sign.

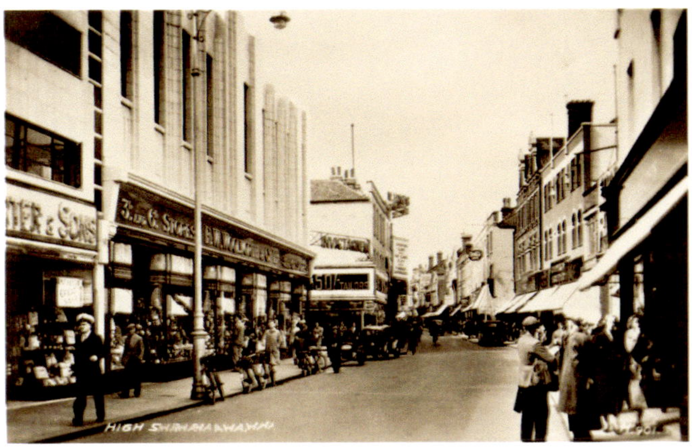

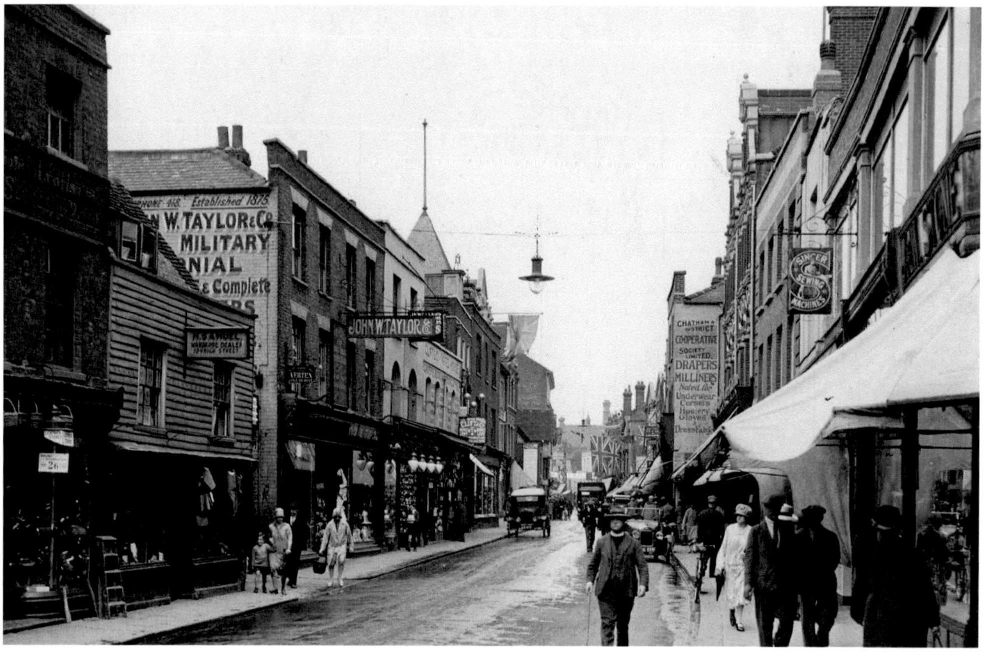

The narrowness of Fullager's Yard that once gave entry to the Invicta can be readily appreciated from this late 1920s High Street photograph. The entrance into Fullager's Yard is just visible, being the narrow gap separating John W. Taylor, a tailor (182 High Street), and Mark Samuel, wardrobe dealer (184 High Street). Easily missed, it led in later days to the erection of that overhead sign seen in the preceding photograph and the one following.

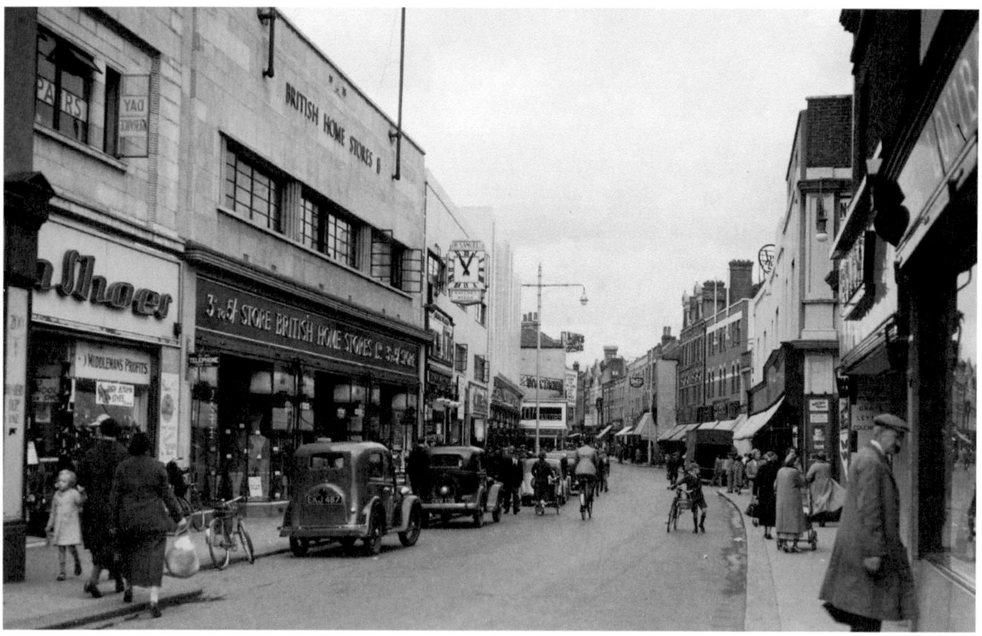

Seen here during the early 1950s is British Home Stores (194–8 High Street), with F. W. Woolworth's and the entryway leading to the Invicta Cinema also visible.

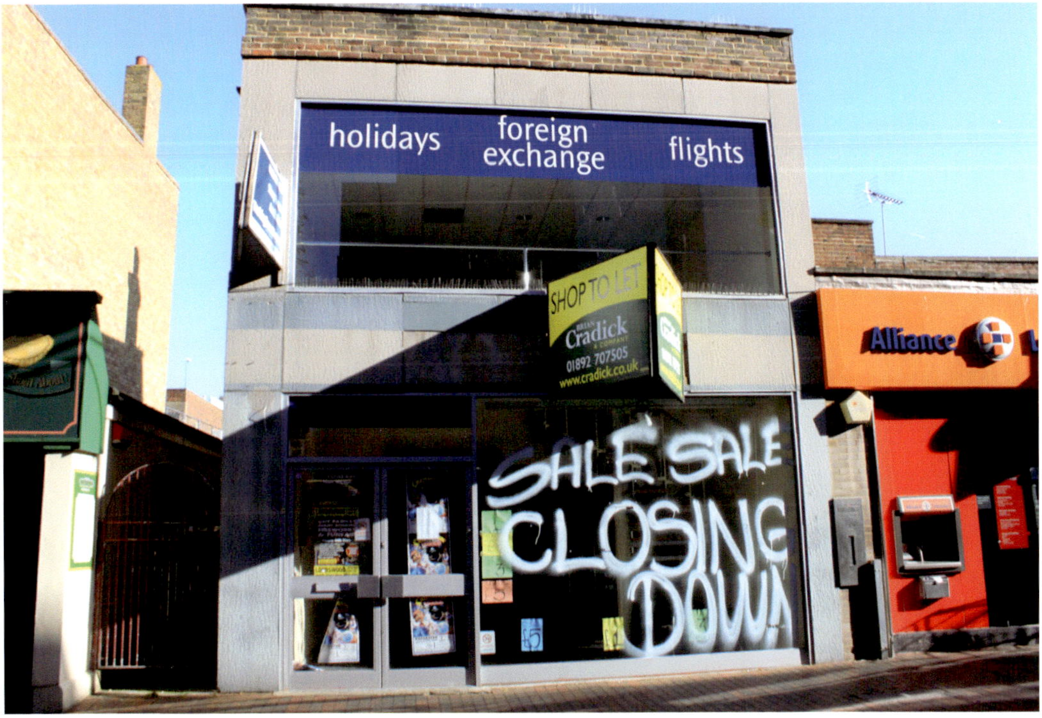

Above: Unfortunately the fate of many shops in the High Street, especially in more recent years as a result of the popularity of the internet and the effects of Covid-19, has been closure. This travel shop (233 High Street) closed in 2010.

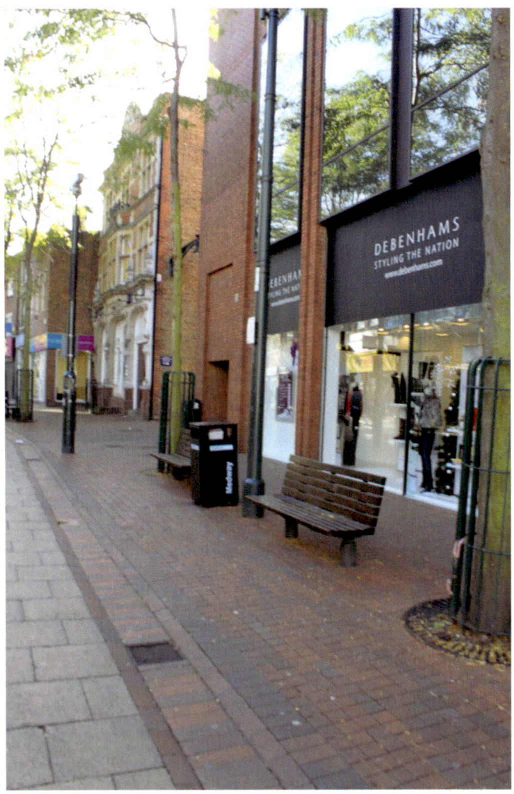

Right: For a long while before 2020, Chatham had been battling against a downturn in trade, and the pandemic has been bookended by major shop closures, with Debenhams closing in 2020 and Argos in 2022. But there are reasons to be optimistic. The Waterfront development is planned to form the hub of a grand new city centre for Medway. In addition, Medway Council plans to invest millions into Chatham town centre, buying up property for more residential and commercial space, transforming the first floor of the Pentagon, creating a new 'city square, civic hub and recreational space' to connect the Pentagon and Brook to the High Street, and converting the former Debenham's shop site, as seen in this photograph (240–6 High Street), for commercial and residential use.

3

An Industrial Past

Although Chatham from the seventeenth century onwards can be viewed as a major industrial town, the industry it possessed was very much centred on the needs of one particular consumer – the British Royal Navy. The Royal Dockyard was responsible for not just building and repairing naval warships but manufacturing all that was required to get warships to sea, whether it be masts, rigging, anchors, flags or a myriad of other items. Adjacent to the dockyard was the gunwharf which was responsible for the repair and maintenance of ships' armament, again for ships of the Royal Navy. This does not mean that other manufacturing enterprises did not exist. The Axe Brand factory, demolished in 1930 to make way for the new Ritz cinema, was an example of one alternative employer. Such enterprises when they existed were minor by comparison, with the workforce demanded by the navy so immense that any other employer faced the inevitable problem of recruitment. Another reason for the failure of alternative industries to emerge was that of the dockyard and gunwharf occupying the most suitable sites for industrial development, so preventing an alternative employer putting down roots with a view to later expansion. Outside of clothing manufacture and providing the needs of the navy, a number of breweries certainly existed in Chatham, but again these were relatively small in size.

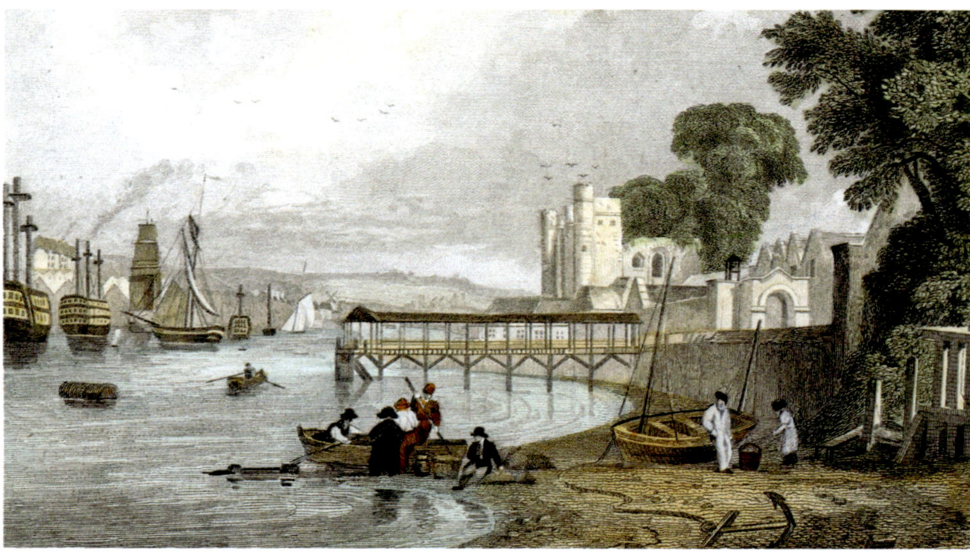

An early nineteenth-century view along Chatham Reach looking towards the dockyard with Upnor Castle on the right. During times of war, this would be an incredibly busy area, with naval warships constantly in the process of being readied for sea. The position of the artist when sketching this picture was roughly the same position reached by the Dutch in 1667 when, under Willem van Gent, they attempted to destroy the yard at Chatham. It was the guns of Upnor Castle that defeated the Dutch and forced them to return downriver.

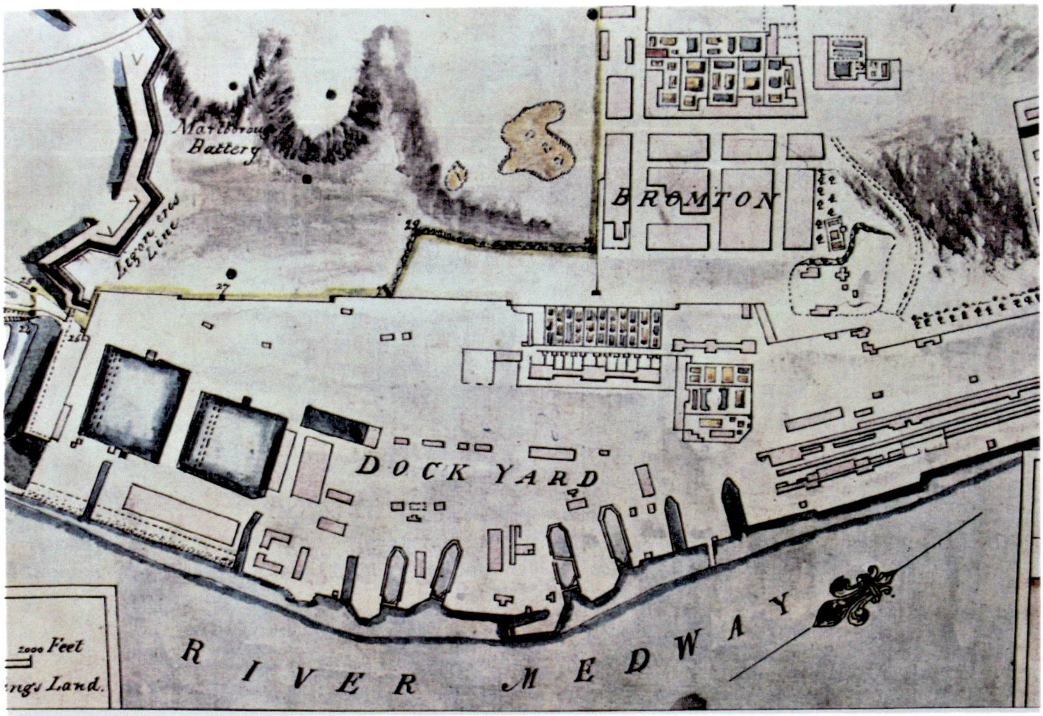

A plan of the dockyard as it appeared at the beginning of the eighteenth century, showing also Lines built to provide a land defence against possible enemy attack. The Lines were to be much strengthened later in the century and were to be frequently used for the training of troops barracked at Chatham. Fort Amherst was part of this later strengthening of the Lines, this starting life as a redoubt dating to the last quarter of the eighteenth century.

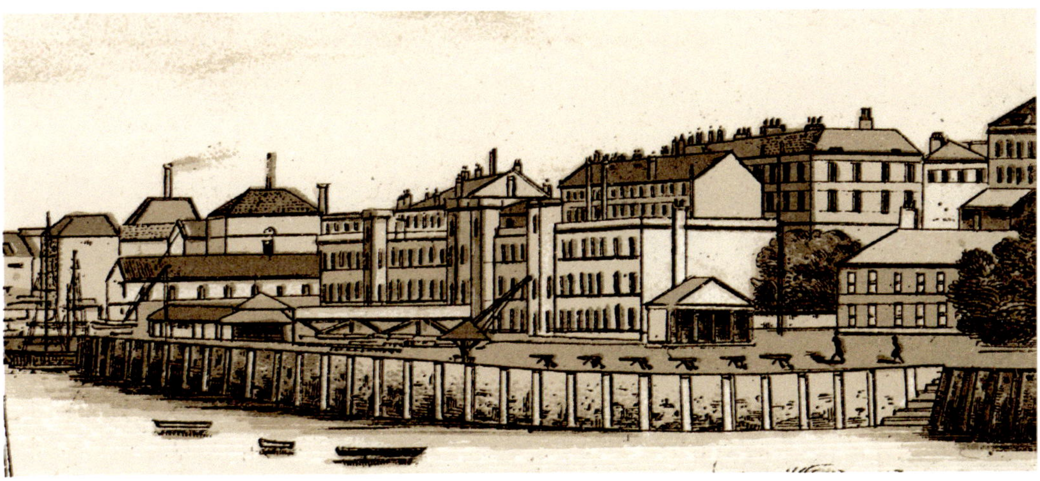

Immediately adjacent to the dockyard, and below the former parish church of St Mary's, was the ordnance wharf, seen here at the end of the nineteenth century. Responsible for the maintenance and storage of ships' ordnance, the ordnance wharf actually stood on the site of the original Tudor dockyard that had first been established during the reign of Elizabeth I (1558–1603) but was later displaced by a second and larger yard built during the early seventeenth century on the site of the present Historic Dockyard.

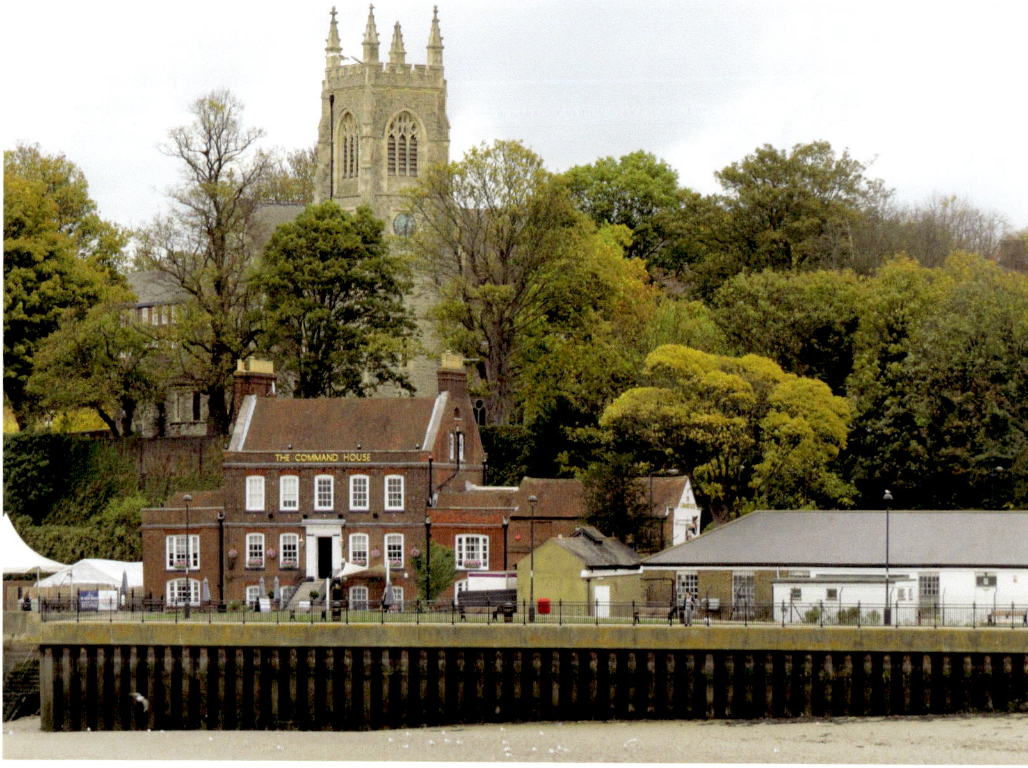

Just a few of the buildings belonging to the Ordnance Wharf, such as the Command House, as seen here, still survive. Most other structures associated with the Ordnance Wharf were demolished during the twentieth century.

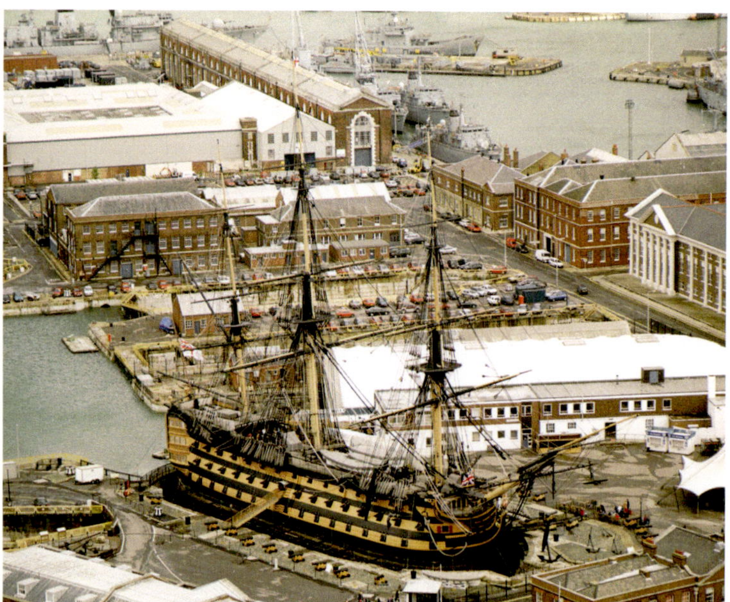

The primary role of the dockyard at Chatham for much of its life was for the construction of the navy's largest ships, of which *Victory*, seen here in its permanent home in the Victory Dock at Portsmouth, is Chatham's most famous. Launched at Chatham in 1765, *Victory* was, in her day, among the largest warships afloat, a first-rate three-decker of 100 guns. She was, of course, Lord Nelson's flagship at the Battle of Trafalgar. (MOD/Crown copyright, 2004)

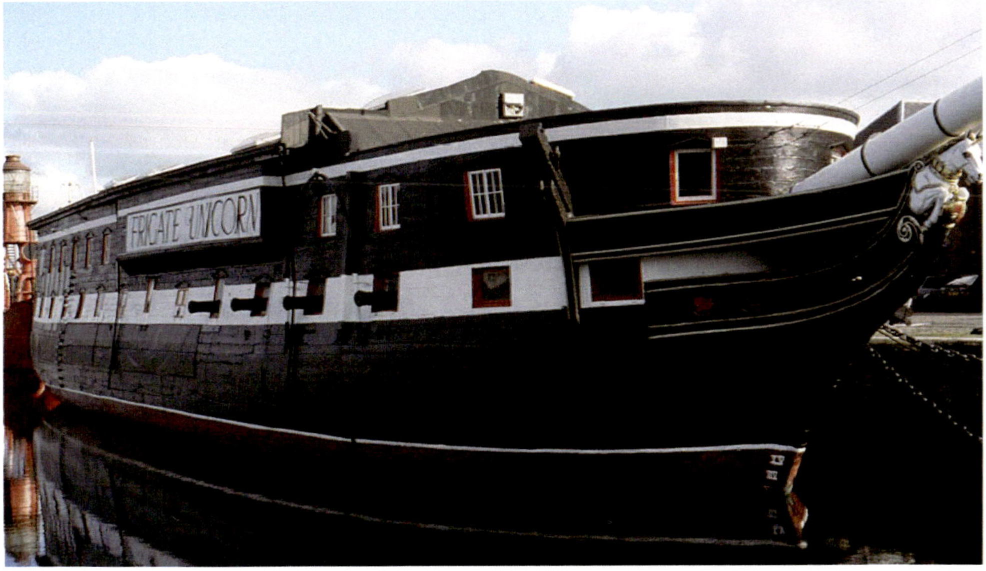

Another surviving Chatham warship is the frigate *Unicorn*, launched at Chatham in 1824 and now a tourist attraction in the Scottish city of Dundee. Unlike *Victory*, the frigate *Unicorn* represents a slightly later stage in warship construction through making greater use of iron, this in the form of iron bracing to provide internal support. Known as knees, these braces are 'L' shaped and in *Victory* were formed from oak tree branches that had grown into the required shape.

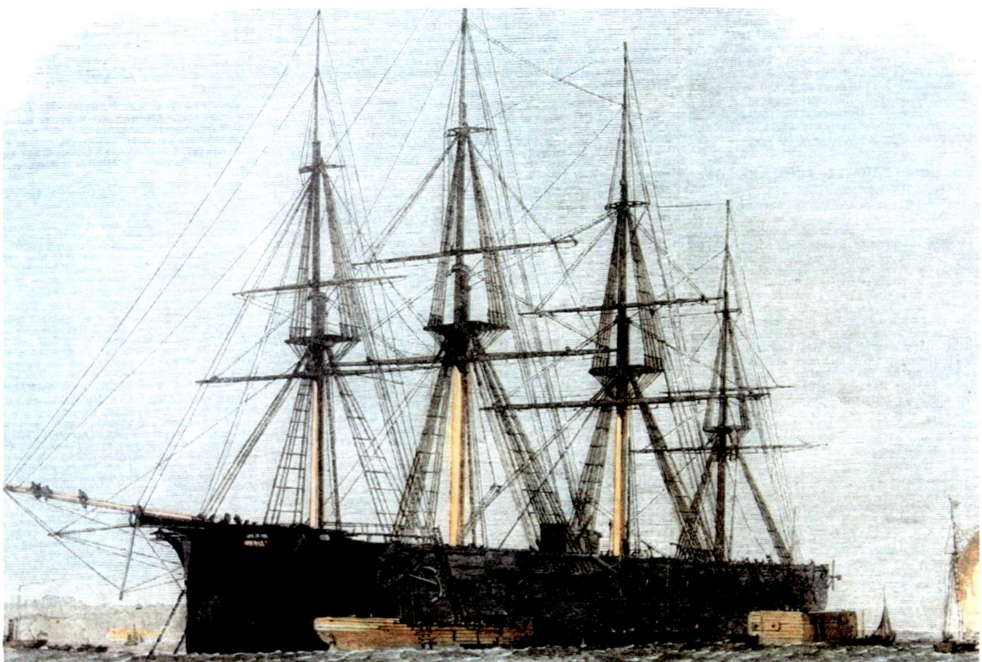

For the dockyard at Chatham, a real game changer was *Achilles*, the first iron battleship built in a British naval dockyard and launched in 1863. Seen here in the River Medway during 1864, she is being fitted out prior to her commissioning for the Channel Squadron.

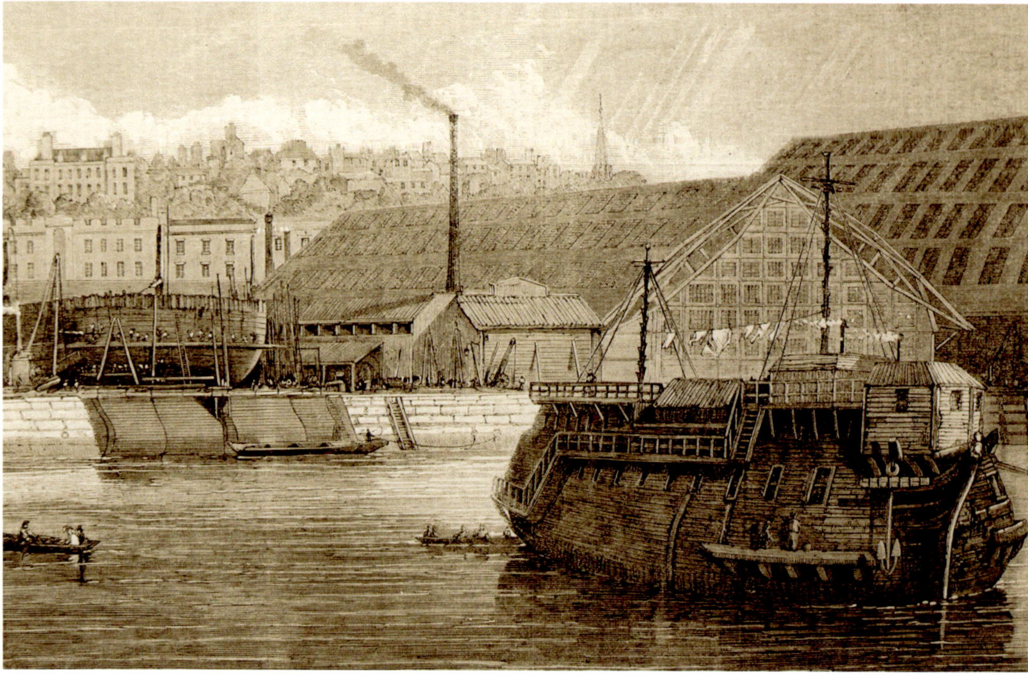

Achilles under construction in the No. 2 Dock prior to being floated out on 23 December 1863. Her particular importance for Chatham was proving that iron battleships could be built here, with a massive expansion to the yard at Chatham, for the purpose of building and maintaining such ships, following soon after. In referring to ships built at Chatham, some were constructed in a dry dock and others on a slipway. If built in a dry dock, once water entered the dock, a newly built ship was floated out. If built on a slipway, a sloping area of ground that led down to the edge of the water, and designed only for the building of ships, the newly constructed hull of a ship could slide along the ways upon which she rested. This launched her into the River Medway – a much more exciting event than a gentle floating out from a dry dock. Nevertheless, whether a floating out or a launching, huge crowds always gathered to witness the event.

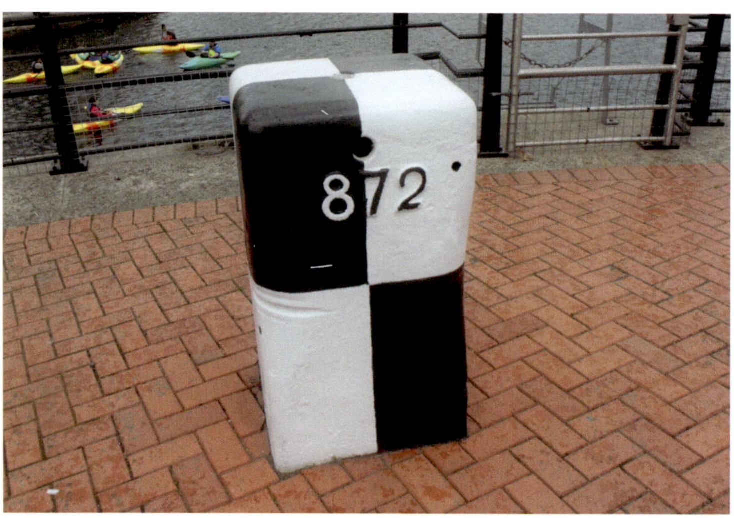

The extension to Chatham dockyard was carried out during the middle years of Queen Victoria's reign, a point highlighted by some of the bollards still to be found in this area of the yard which, technically, it must be admitted, falls within the old borough of Gillingham.

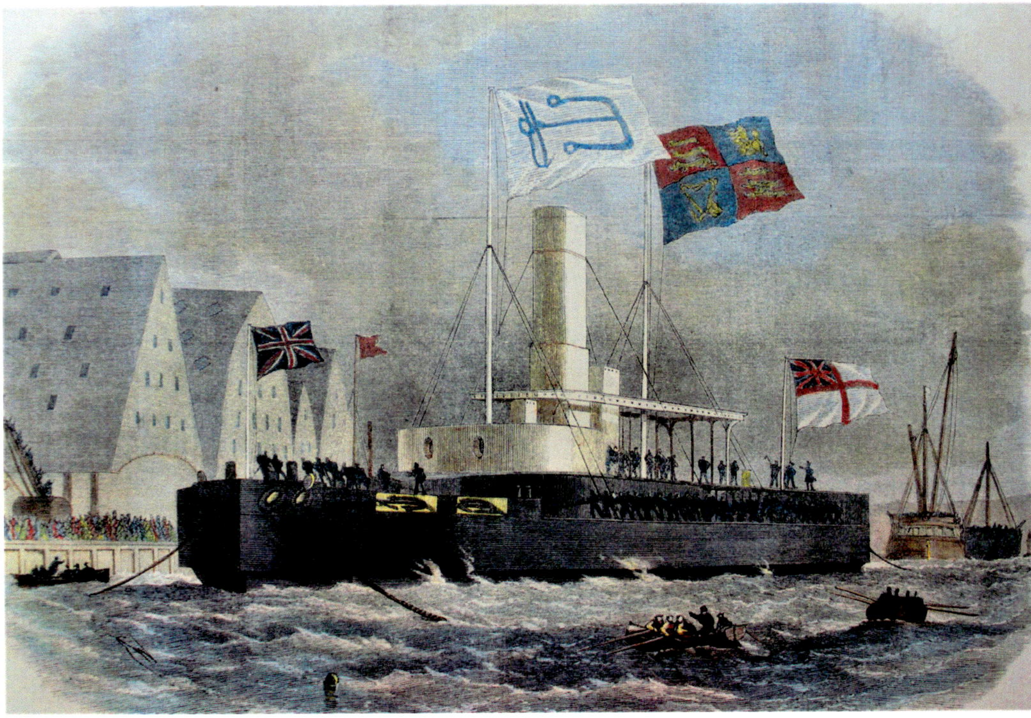

Throughout the later years of the nineteenth century, Chatham continued to build massive iron ships such as *Glatton*, her hull built in the No. 3 Dock. She is seen here passing along the dockyard's river frontage on the day of her floating out, 8 March 1871.

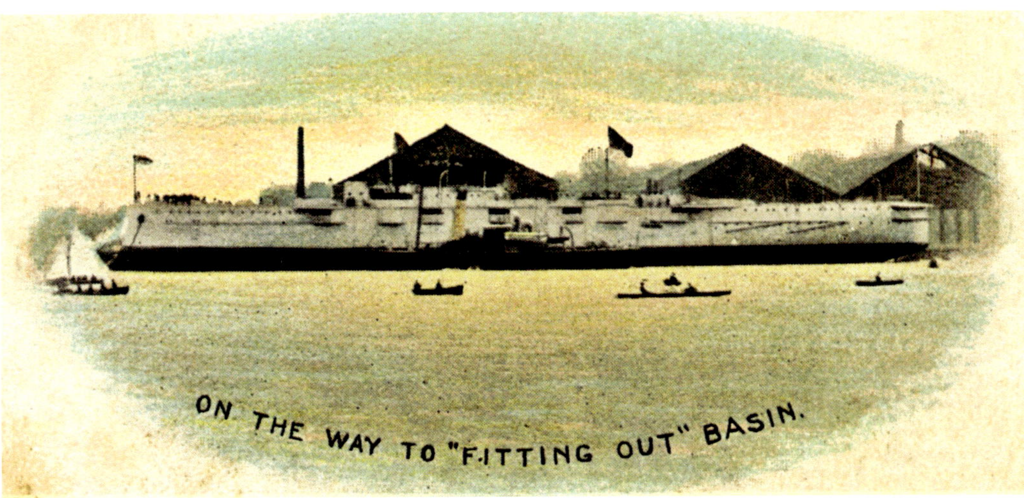

The final battleship built at Chatham was *Africa*, seen here on the day of her launch, 20 May 1905. Built on the No. 8 slip, which no longer exists, she is on her way to the No. 1 Basin where work was to continue on her completion and full readiness for sea. This was a task that would take another eighteen months.

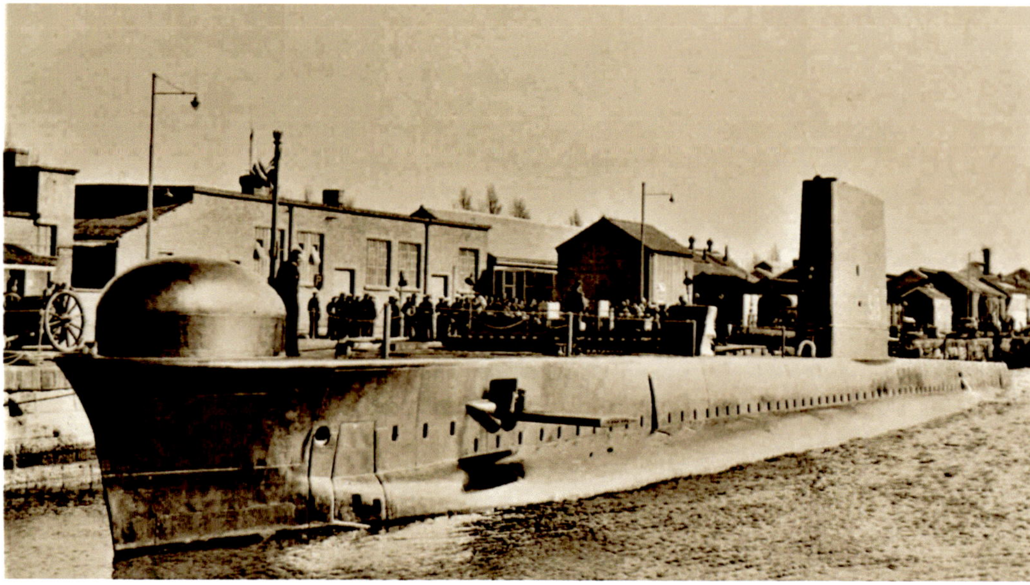

During the twentieth century, Chatham came to specialise in the construction of submarines – a total of fifty-seven launched at the yard between 1908 and 1966. This is *Oberon*, the name class of a final batch of six submarines built at the yard during the 1960s. *Oberon* is seen here at the time of her commissioning in February 1961.

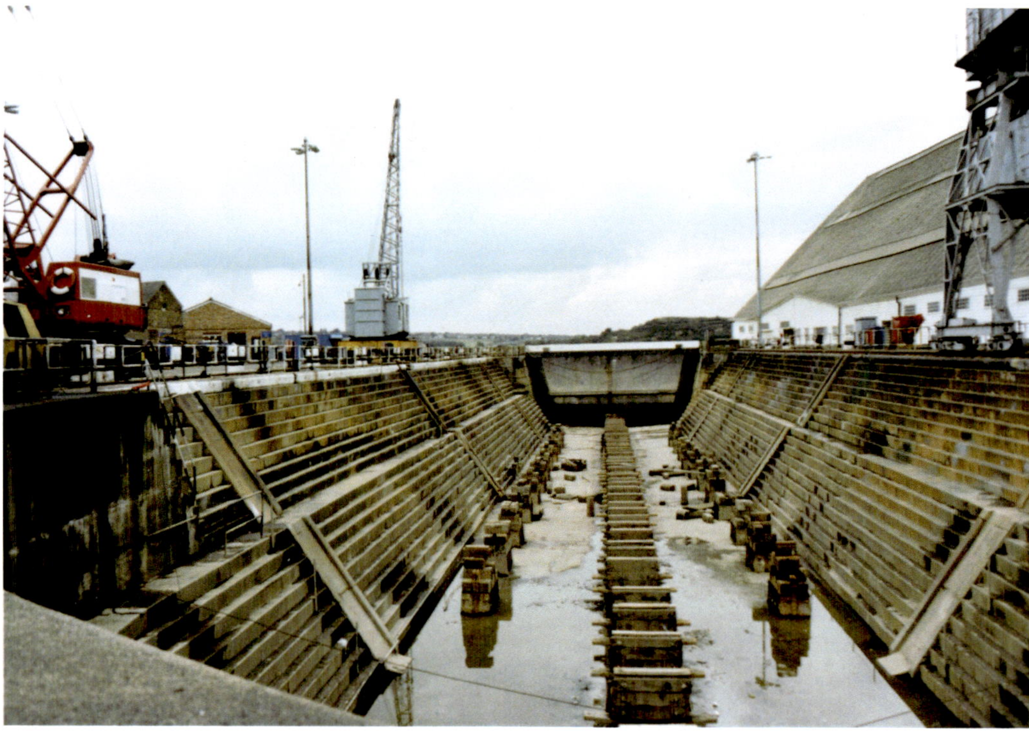

Among the most obvious facilities at Chatham, and used both for the repair and construction of warships, were the dry docks. No. 4 Dock is seen here shortly after the closure of the yard in 1984.

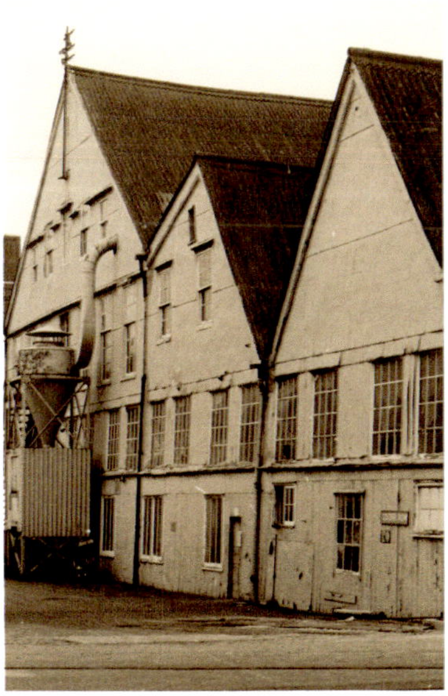

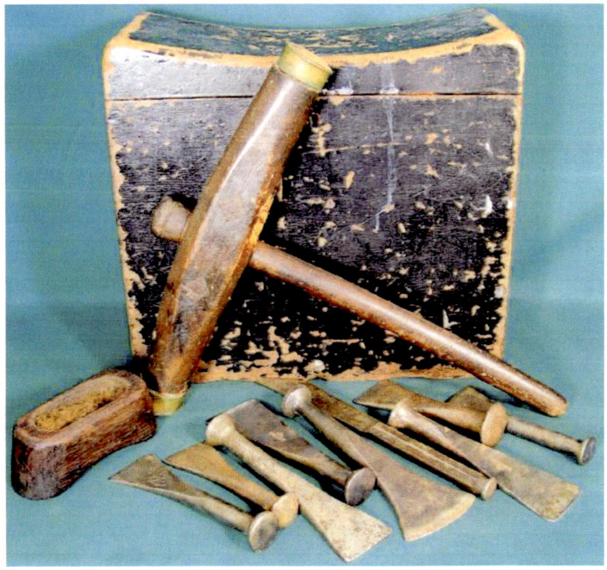

Above left: The mast houses seen here when Chatham was a working yard. Now given a somewhat more attractive appearance, the mast houses had been covered with asbestos cladding during wartime years to protect them from fire in the event of enemy bombing.

Above right: The tools of the trade. These were once the essential requisites of the caulker, an artisan skilled in caulking or making waterproof, through sealing the gaps between the timber planking on the hull of a ship and through which water would otherwise seep. Once caulked, the hull would be tarred to complete her water tightness.

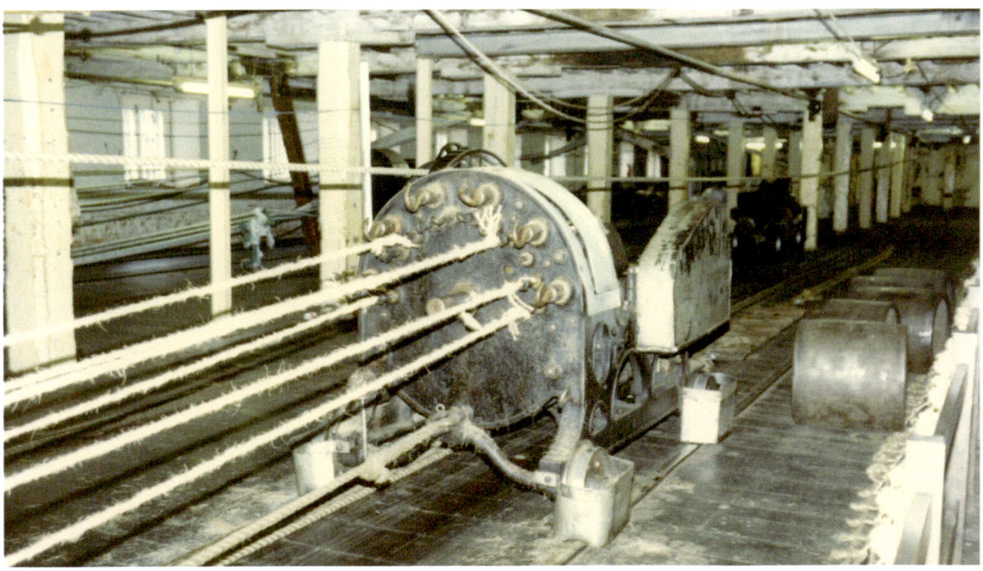

A large wooden warship of the eighteenth century required between 20 and 30 miles of rope, primarily for the standing and running rigging as well as for hauling the anchors. All of these ropes were manufactured in the ropery and from the mid-nineteenth century, saw the introduction of steam power to make the rope-making process more efficient.

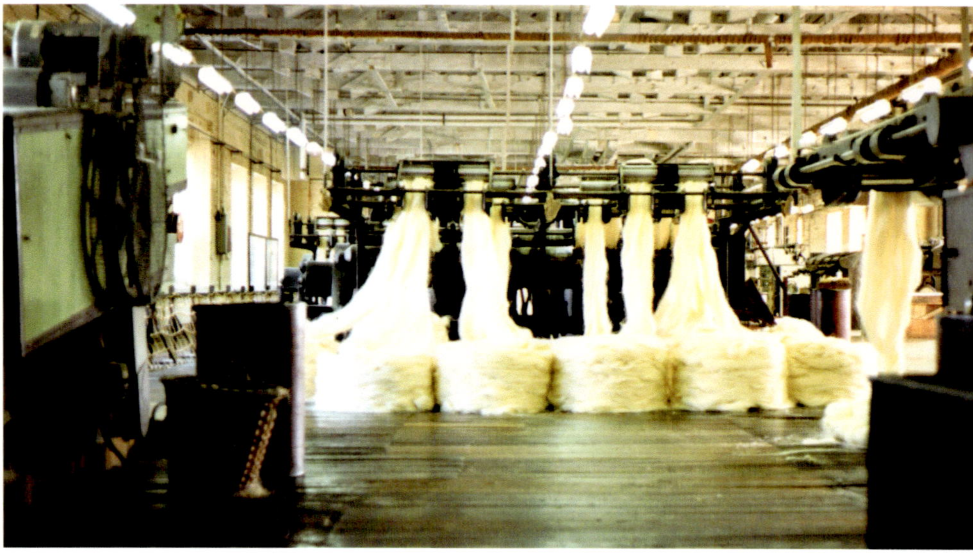

To manufacture rope, the basic raw material, hemp, was once brought into the yard, mainly from Russia, in bales that were first stored, before hatchelling – the combing of the fibres. Once a process carried out by hand, powered machinery, as seen here before the closure of the yard, was introduced during the nineteenth century.

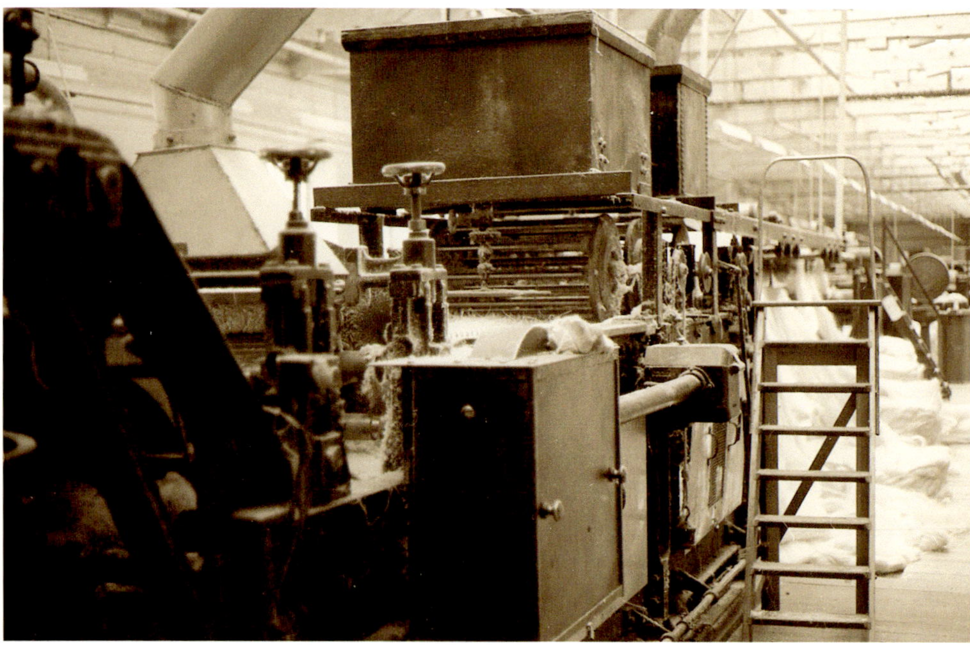

A further view of the hatchelling process as conducted in the Chatham dockyard ropery when in the days of the navy. Once hatchelled, the combed fibres were spun into yarn, before being tarred and then laid into rope. All were procedures carried out in the ropery. As with hemp, the main supplier of tar during the eighteenth century was again Russia. The importance of Russia as a supplier of naval stores such as hemp, iron and mast timbers is a subject fully explored in this writer's book entitled *The Anglo-Russian Naval Alliance of the Eighteenth Century and Beyond* published in 2022.

From the mid-nineteenth century onwards, women were employed in the ropery, but had their own separate point of entry, preventing them mixing with the men of the yard. They were also given different times in which they entered and left the yard.

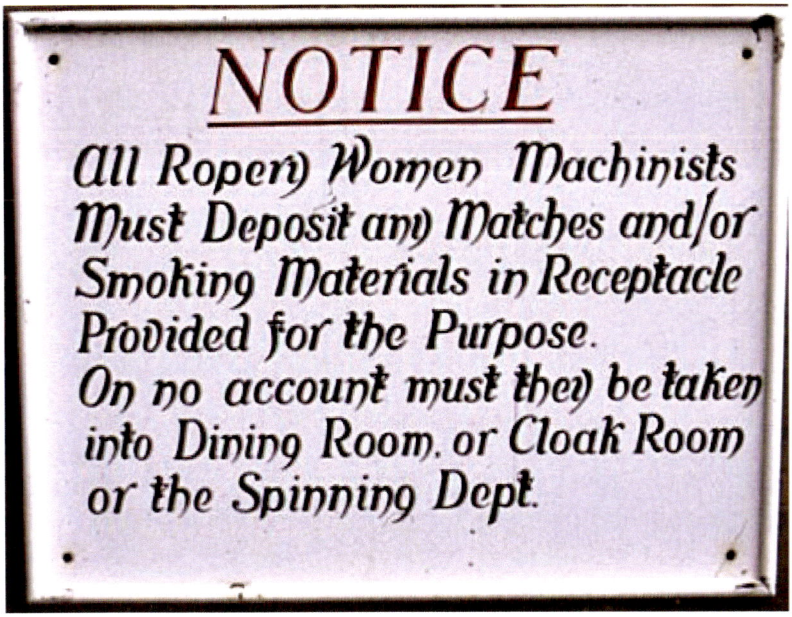

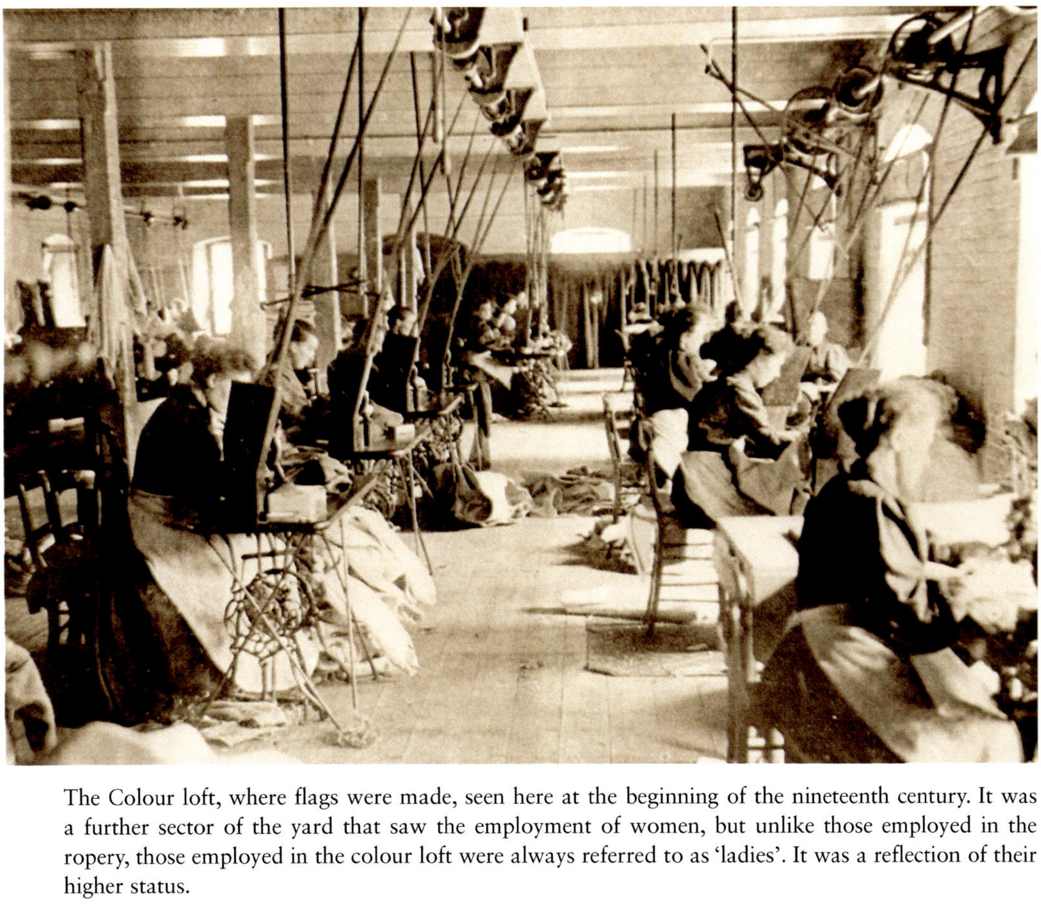

The Colour loft, where flags were made, seen here at the beginning of the nineteenth century. It was a further sector of the yard that saw the employment of women, but unlike those employed in the ropery, those employed in the colour loft were always referred to as 'ladies'. It was a reflection of their higher status.

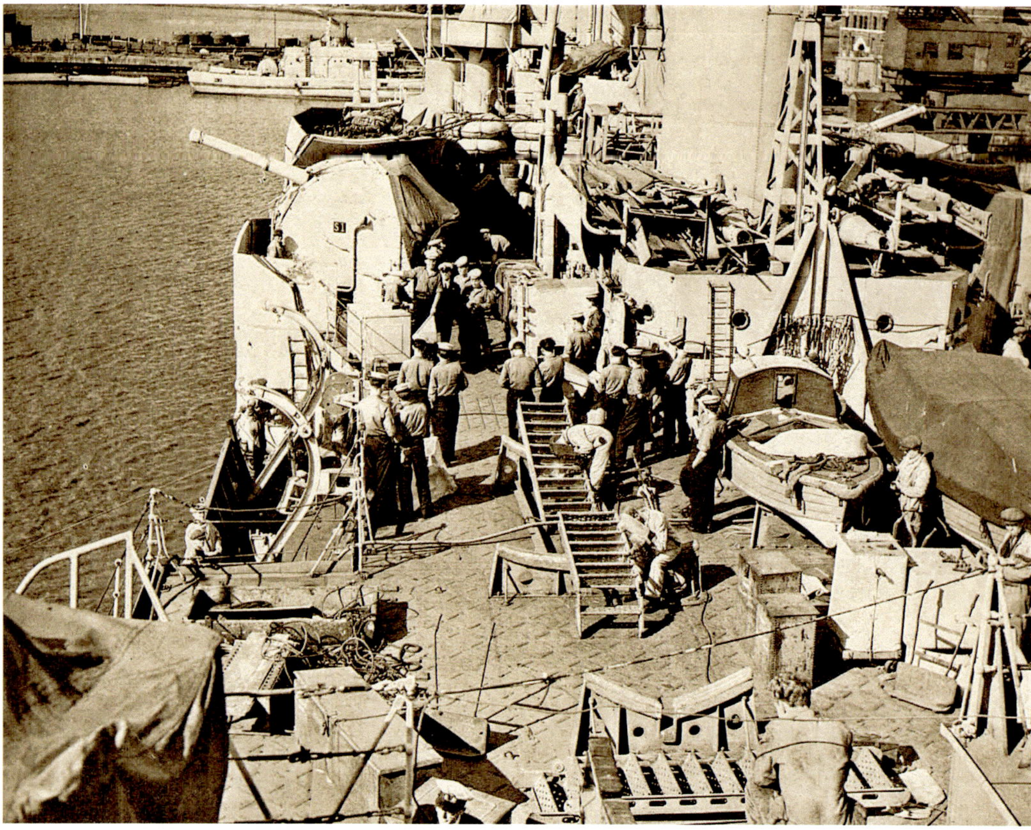

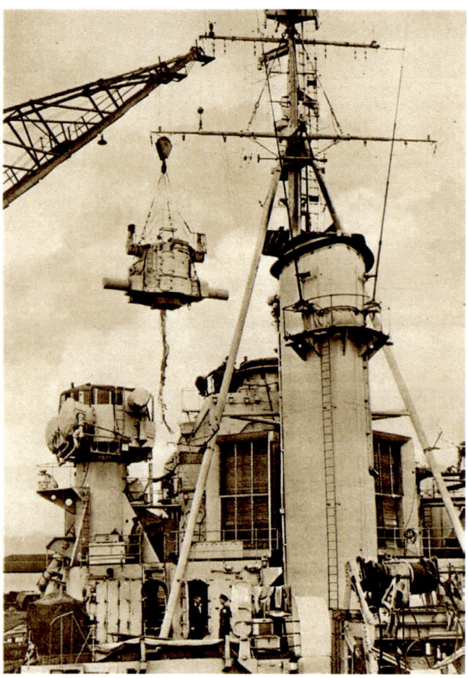

Above: Refitting work underway at Chatham on *Superb*, a 'Tiger' class cruiser. In 1948, when this photograph was taken, the dockyard at Chatham employed a workforce of 13,000, of which around 2,000 were women.

Left: Here, work continues on *Superb*, where the 8,000-ton cruiser is receiving her main armament gun director.

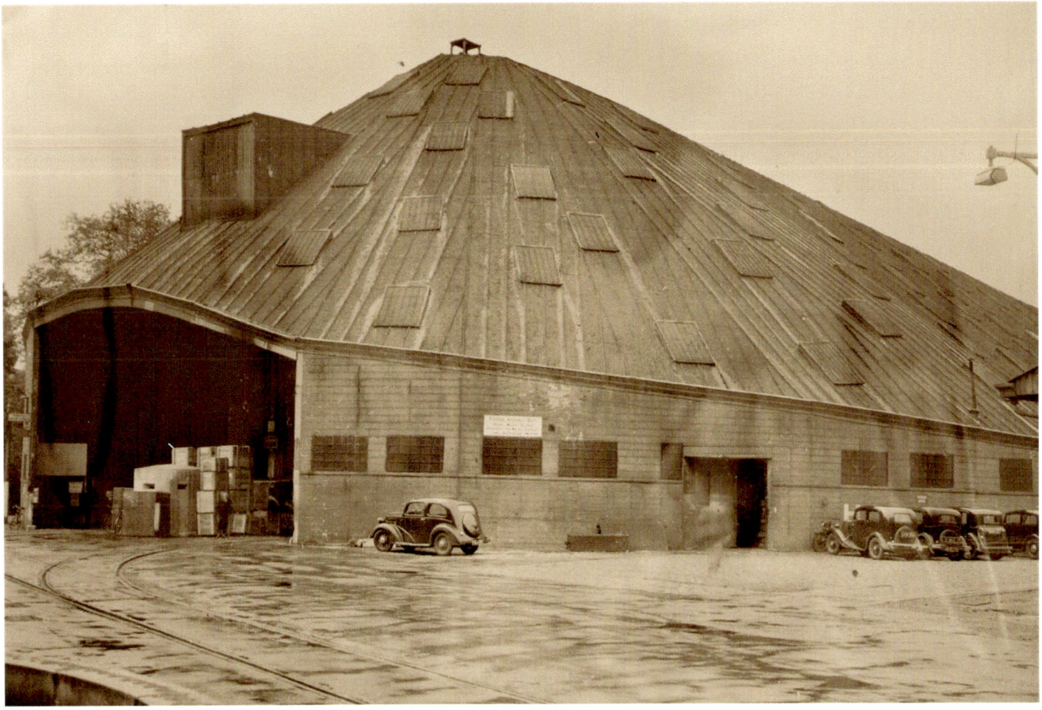

Above: While today Chatham Historic Dockyard has a fine collection of covered slips from the nineteenth century, the earliest of those massive structures, the No. 2 Covered Slip erected in 1817, no longer exists, destroyed by fire in July 1966. The covering given to the No. 2 slip not only rose to a considerable height but swept out grandly on each side, this to provide a sheltered working area for those employed on constructing new vessels.

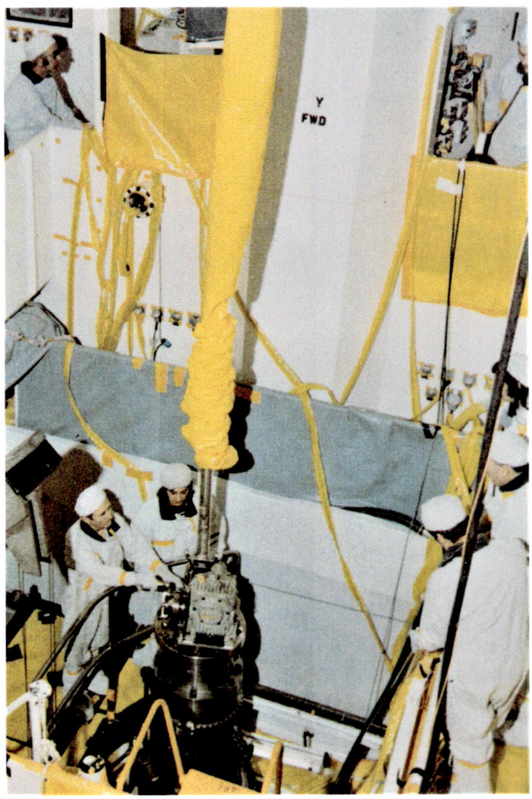

Right: Re-fuelling a nuclear submarine within the now demolished Nuclear Refit Centre that was built in the dockyard and officially opened in June 1968. The Nuclear Refit Centre continued to operate until shortly before the yard closed with many believing that the verry existence of this important facility at Chatham would ensure that the naval dockyard at that time would not face closure.

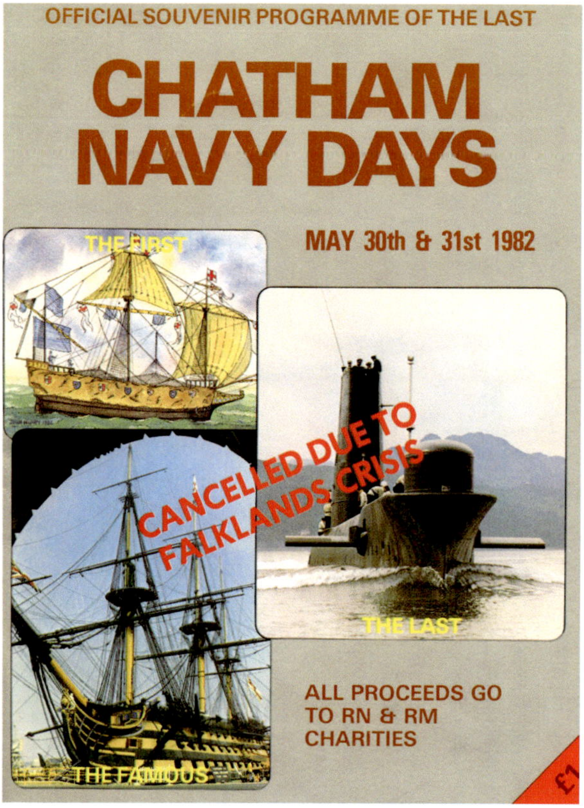

Left: The last of the Navy Days at Chatham. A one-time annual event that demonstrated to the public both naval warships and the work of the yard, the last was to have been held in May 1982 but had to be cancelled because of the Falklands War.

Below: Following the closure of the yard in 1984, the area of the yard created during the seventeenth century, but fundamentally a naval yard reflecting the Georgian era, was turned into a tourist attraction run by the Chatham Dockyard Historic Trust. Particularly popular with visitors is the Chatham-built submarine *Ocelot*, seen here being towed up the Medway on the day she returned to the yard.

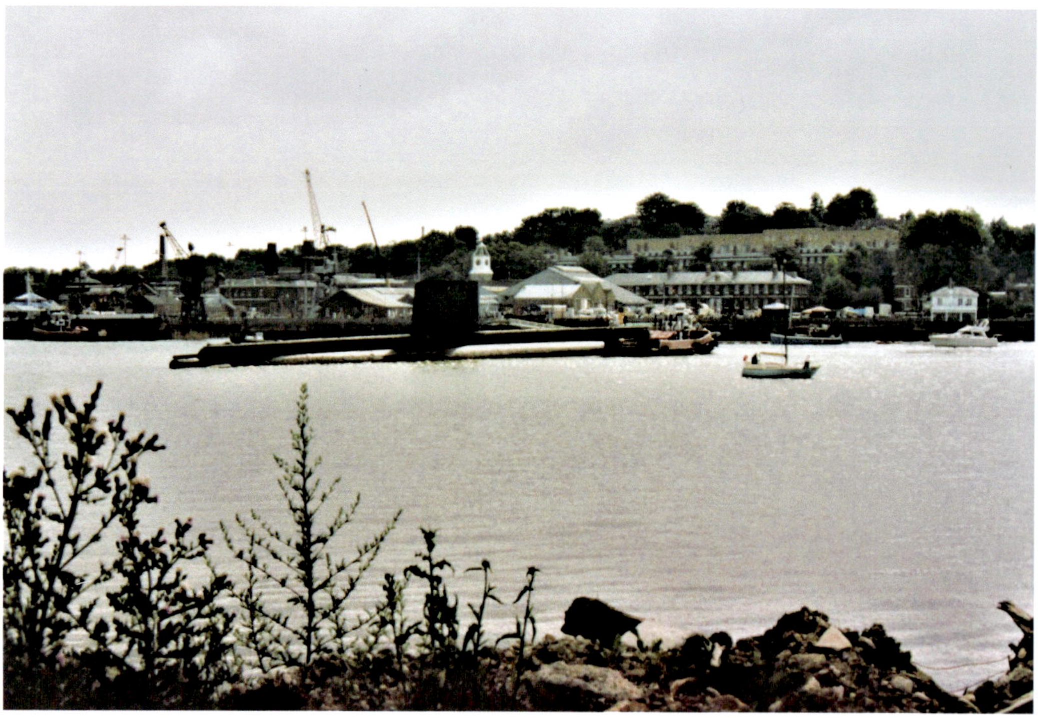

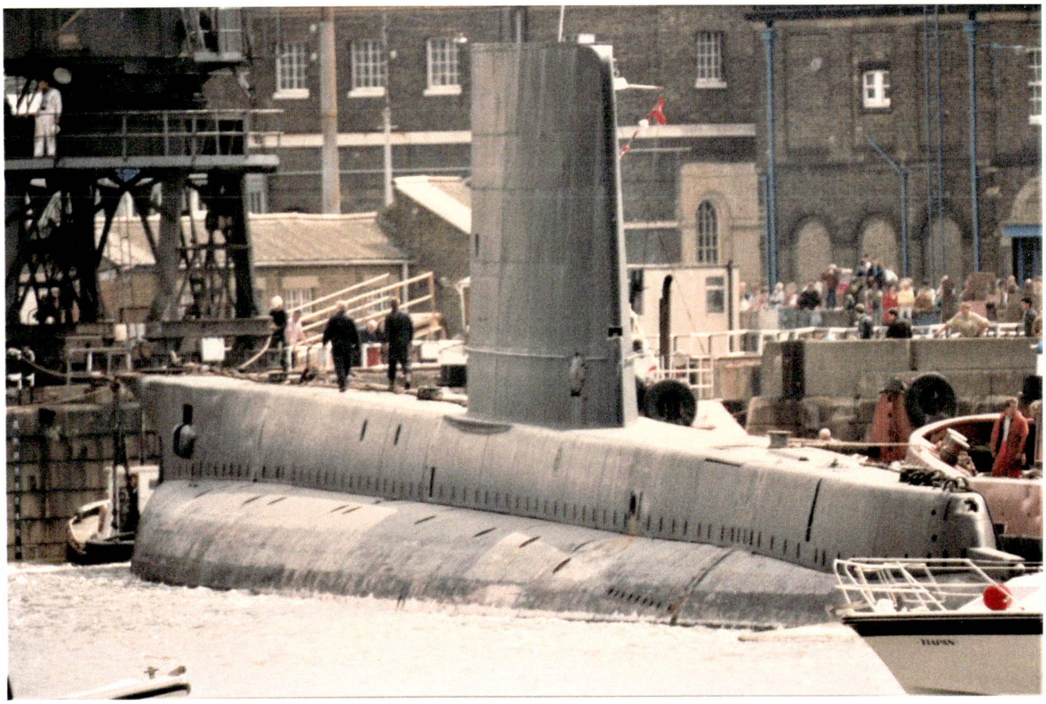

Above: *Ocelot* being carefully manoeuvred into the No. 3 Dock.

Right: Later the same day, 12 July 1992, *Ocelot* is seen secure in the No. 3 Dock.

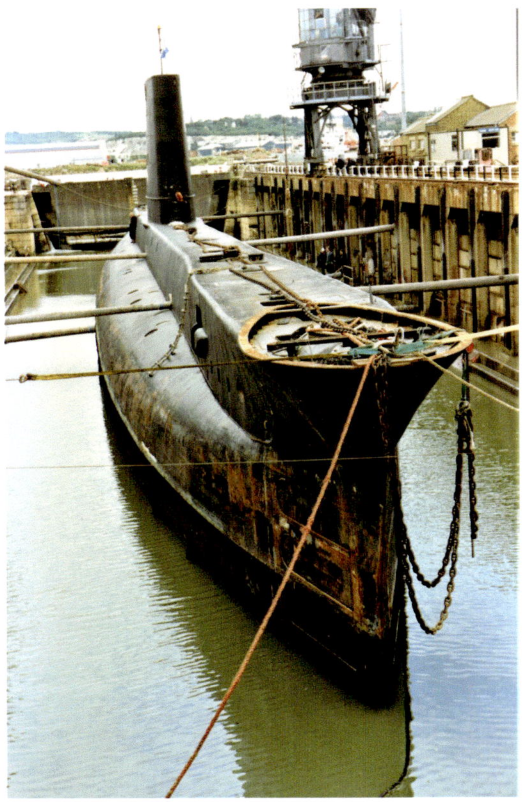

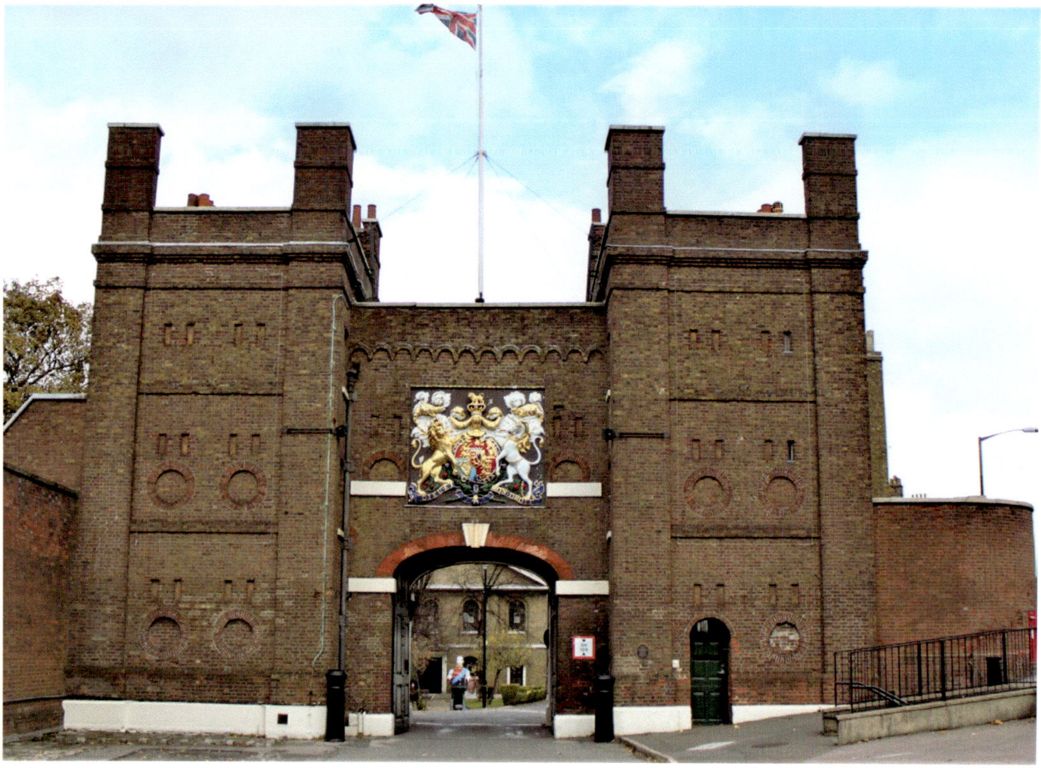

A further reminder of what Chatham has lost. Through this, the Main Gate into the dockyard and completed in 1720, passed for more than 250 years many of the labourers and artisans employed in what was for so many years one of the largest industrial enterprises in the country.

4

Street Scenes

Chatham as a town has been subject to much piecemeal development over the centuries, much of this to accommodate changes in methods of transport and a general increase in traffic. Once the main road to London from the coast ran through the High Street, causing frequent log-jams of horse-drawn carriages, but this was relieved by the construction of New Road, effectively a by-pass that relieved Chatham of this congestion. In later years a fly-over was built and then demolished while horse buses gave way to trams and eventually buses. Much has changed and continues to change.

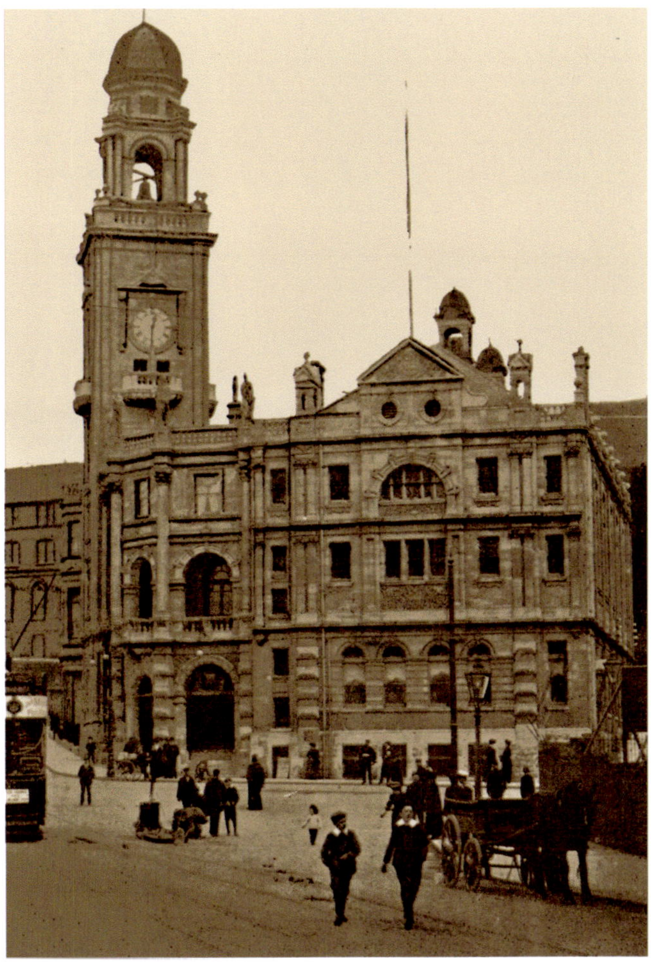

The Town Hall was once the hub of Chatham's tramway system, trams first operating in the town during the summer of 1902. From the Town Hall it was possible to travel not just across Chatham, but also onward to Frindsbury, Rochester, Gillingham and Rainham.

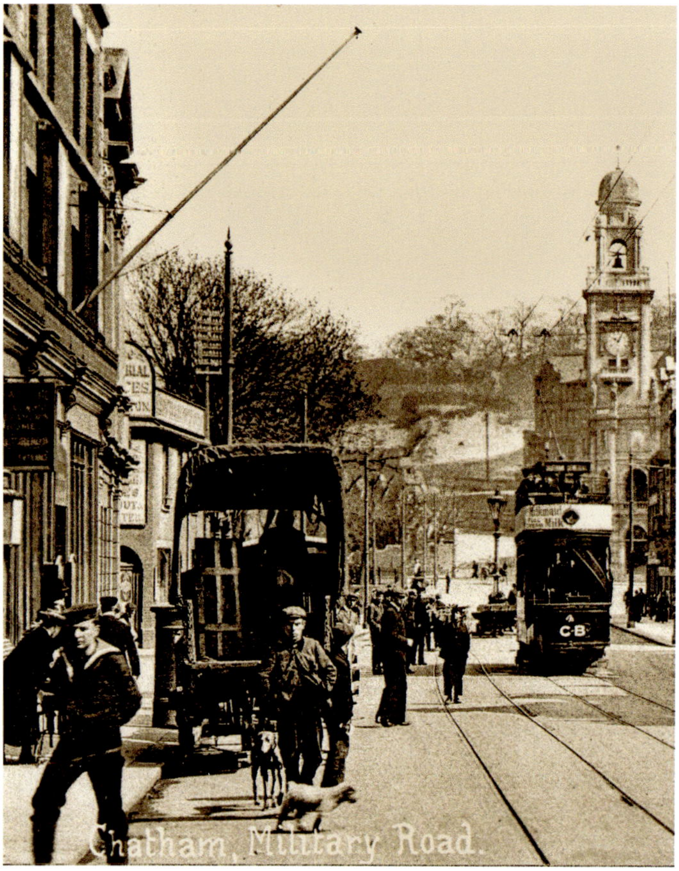

Left: A tram on route C-B seen here in 1905. Route C-B, marked on the tram in white with a purple background, ran from Gillingham (Victoria Bridge) via Brompton to Chatham Cemetery in Maidstone Road.

Below: Intermingling with trams and slowing the passage of the new transit system was the continuing use, for many years, of horse-drawn carts. This postcard would have found itself on sale for many Christmases during the first and second decades of the twentieth century.

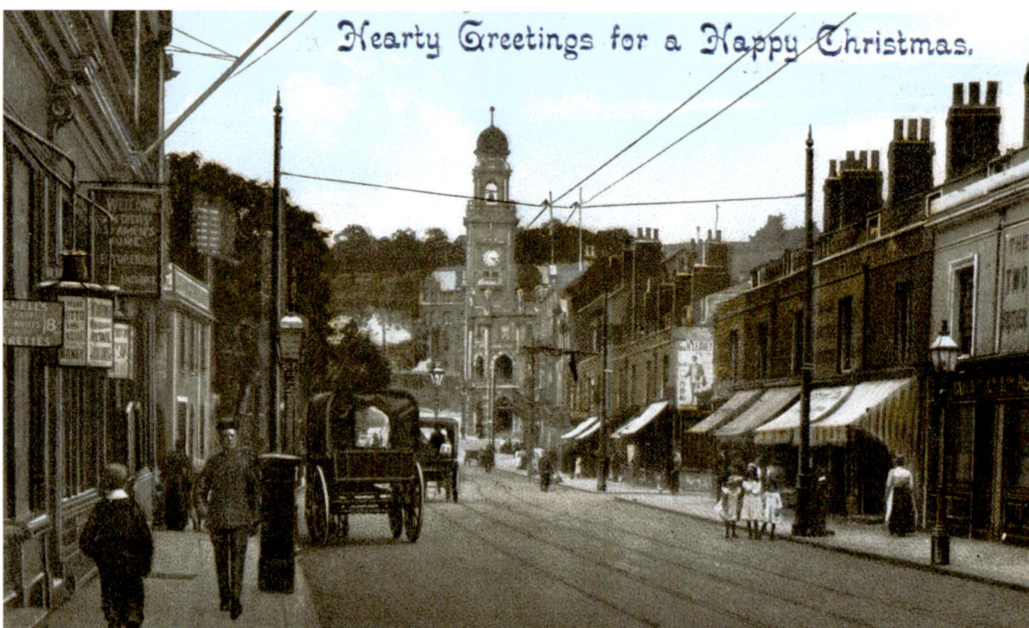

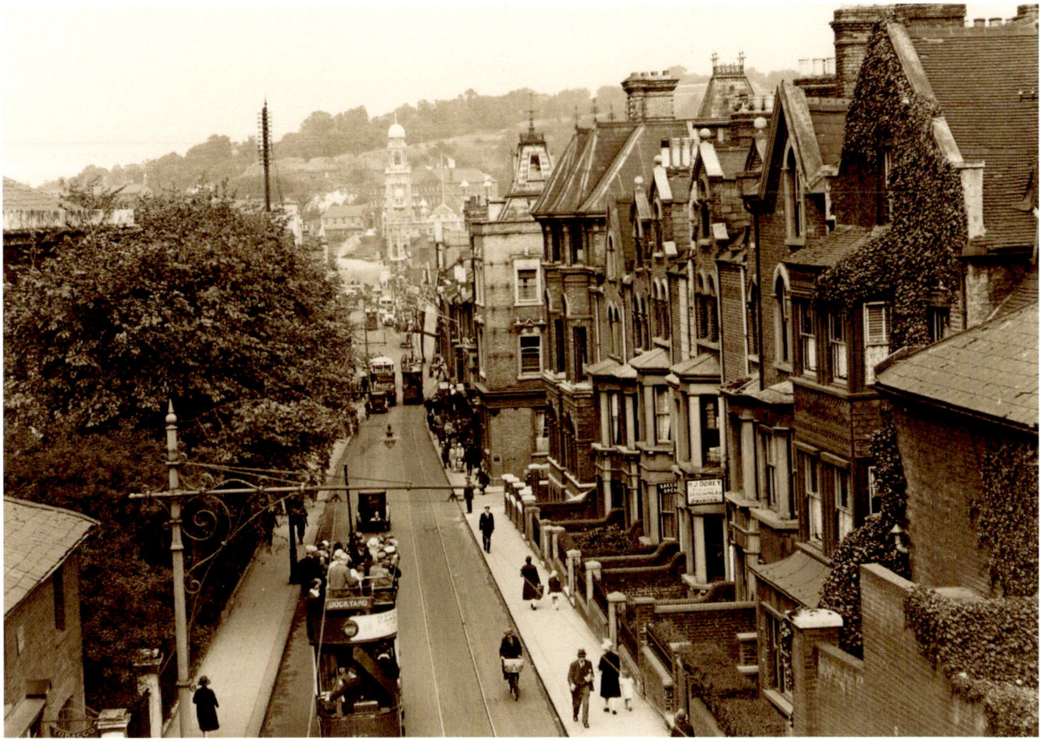

Above: Trams continued to operate in Chatham until 1930, with this 1920s view of Military Road, as seen from the New Road viaduct, depicting a tram on route L-D, heading first to the Town Hall before travelling along Dock Road to its final destination, the Dockyard. The starting point of trams on route L-D was the Hen & Chickens at Luton with L-D (Luton-Dockyard) emblazoned in black on a yellow background.

Right: A tram seen at Luton Arches and heading for the Town Hall from Gillingham having passed along Canterbury Street and Chatham Hill. This is route TH-G (Town Hall-Gillingham), with the lettering in white on a red background. The Arches date to 1858 and form the eastern entry into the town of Chatham.

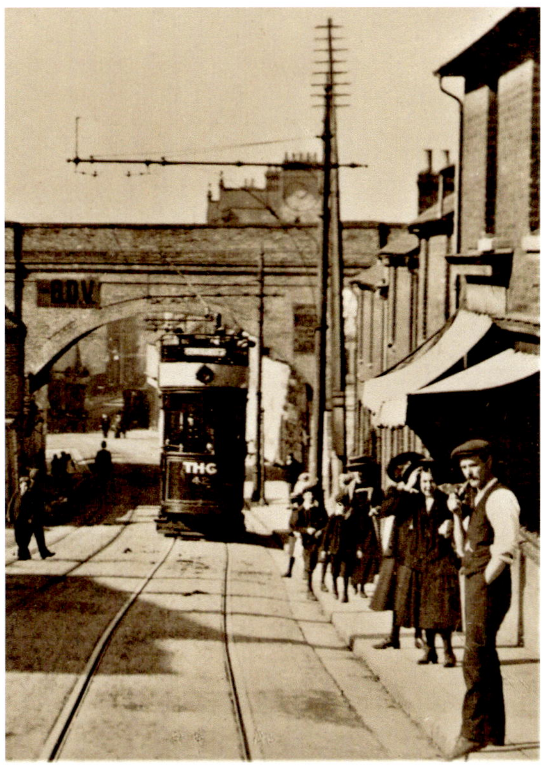

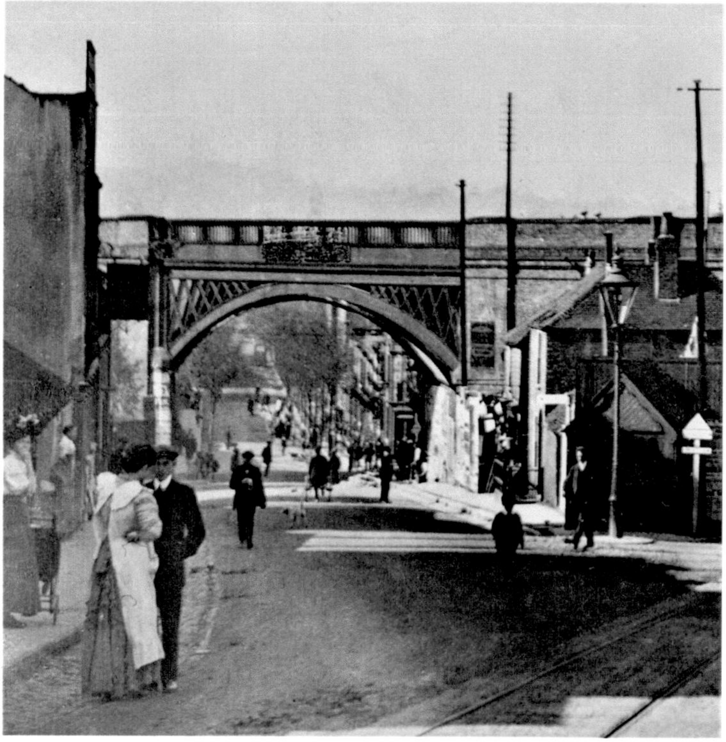

Left: A *c.* 1910 view of Luton Arches looking towards Chatham Hill.

Below: Travelling along Chatham Hill, a Gillingham-bound tram on route TH-G can be seen on a dismal wet and rainy winter's day.

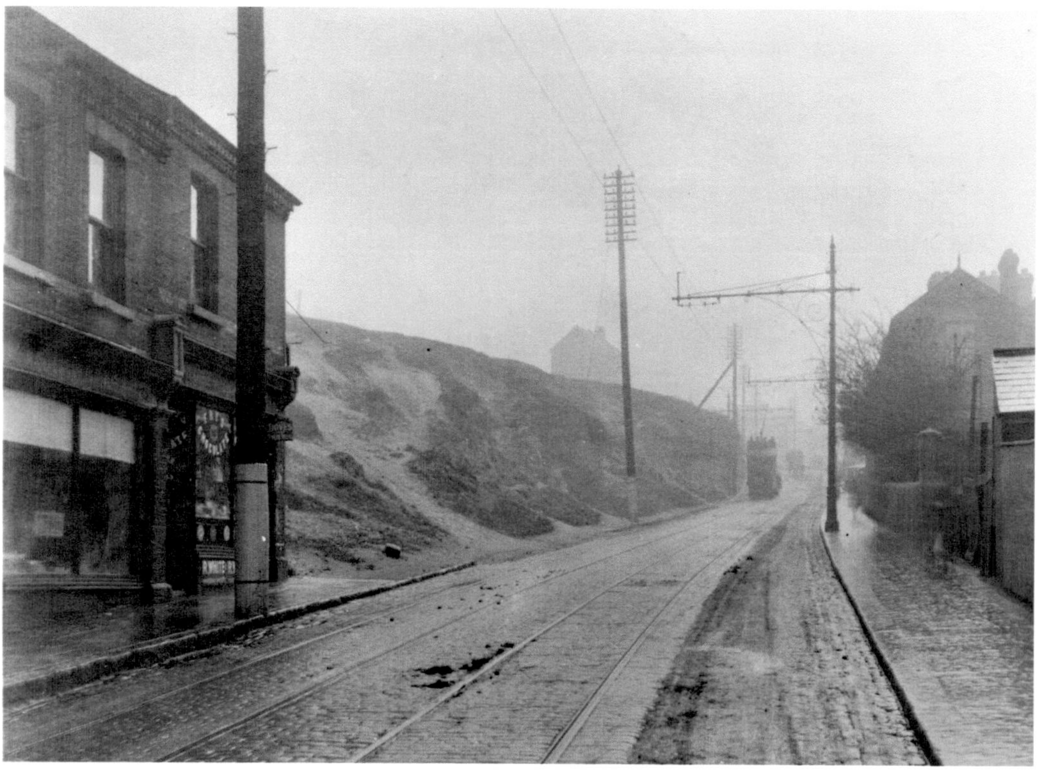

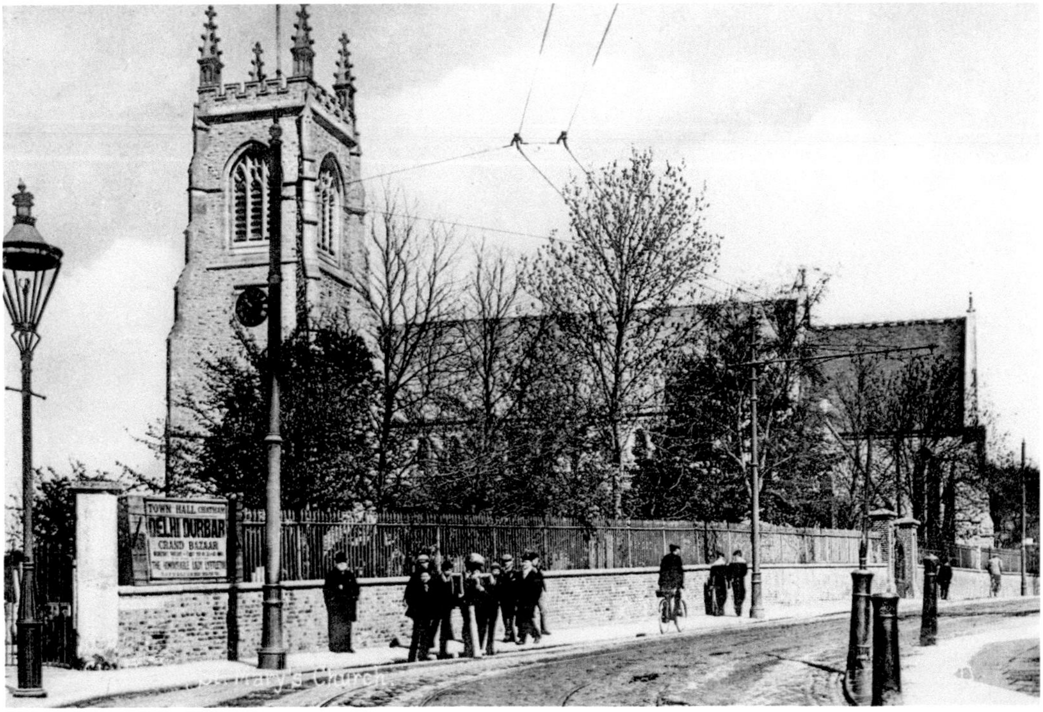

Above: St Mary's Church, Dock Road, *c*. 1910. On the railings is an advertisement for an event at the Town Hall, a bazaar entitled the Delhi Durbar.

Right: At the corner of Medway Street and the High Street a police officer is seen directing traffic.

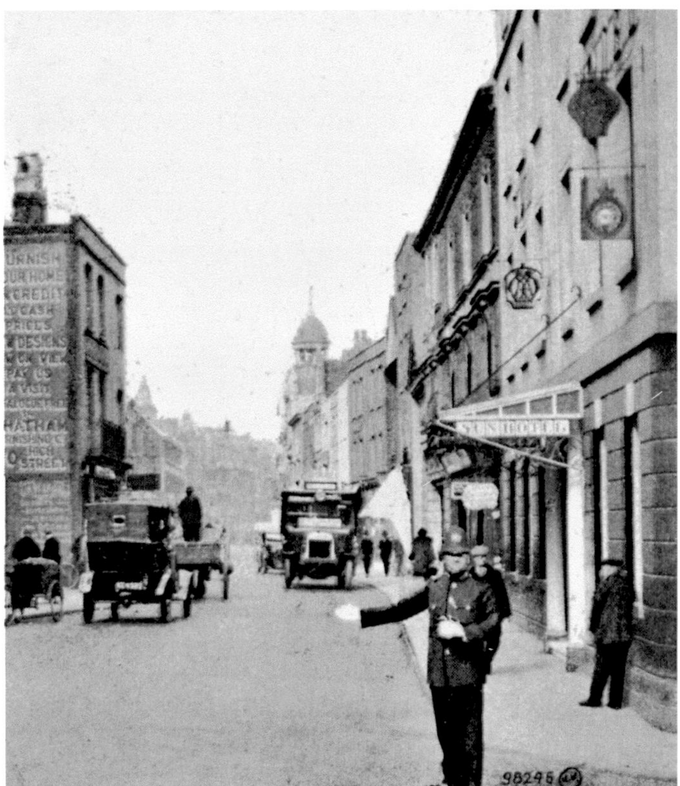

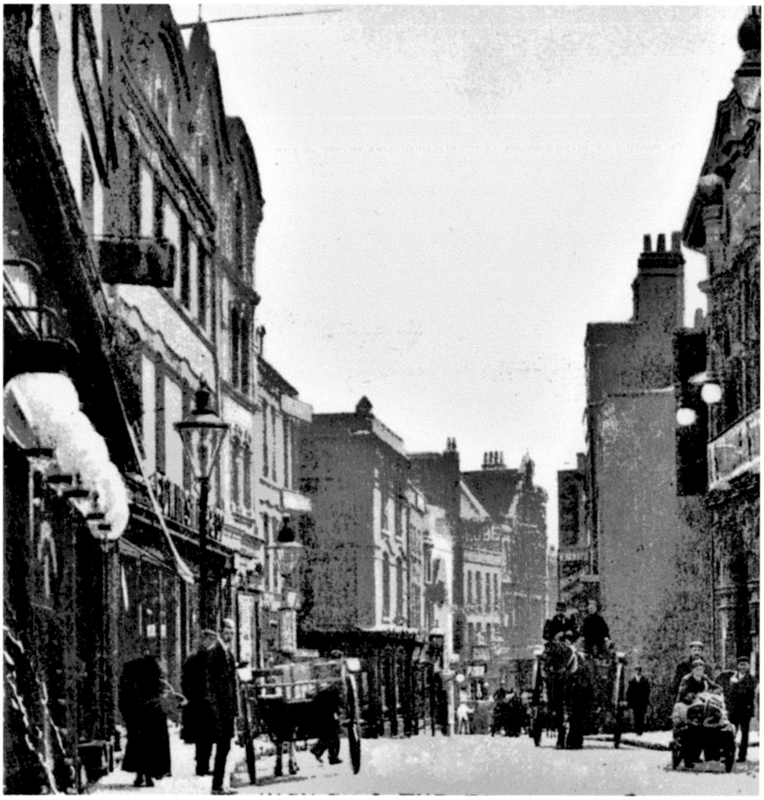

Left: More horses and carts in the Edwardian period High Street.

Below: New Road today is never this quiet nor as picturesque. The road itself dates to the late eighteenth century and was built to ease traffic congestion in the High Street.

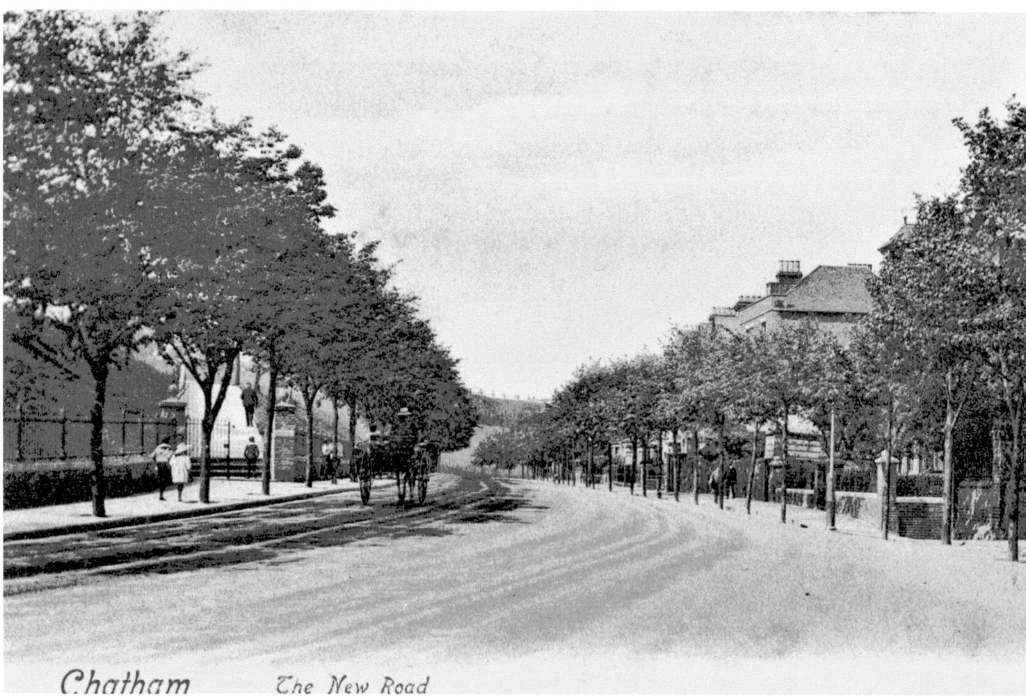

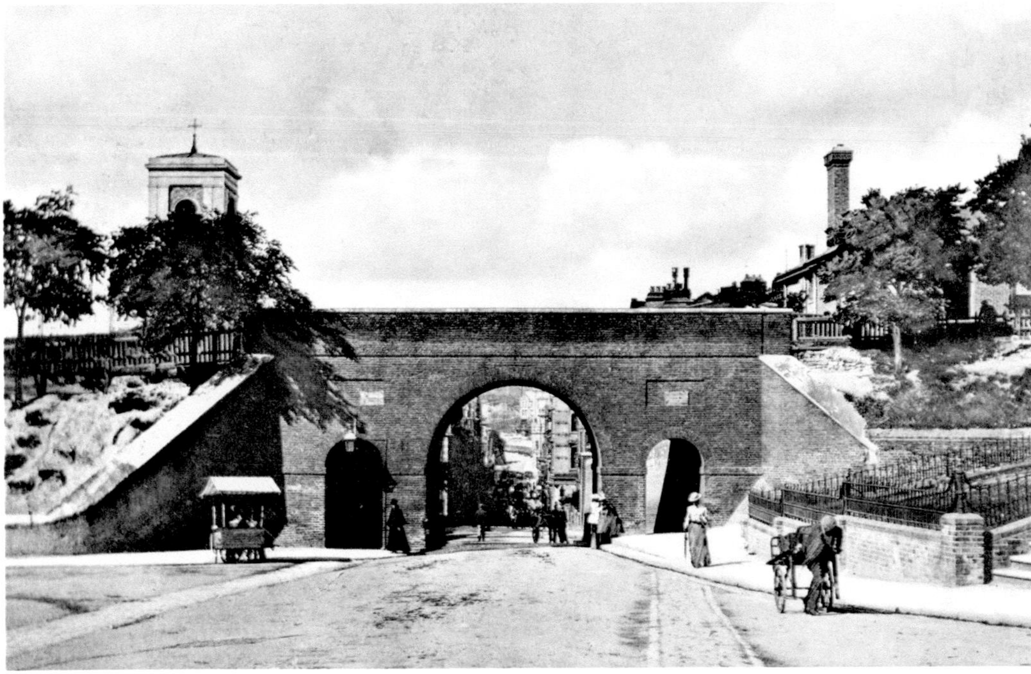

The viaduct that carries New Road over what was once Rome Lane. Built of red brick, with the foundation stone laid on 17 August 1779, it also served as a military gateway into the town.

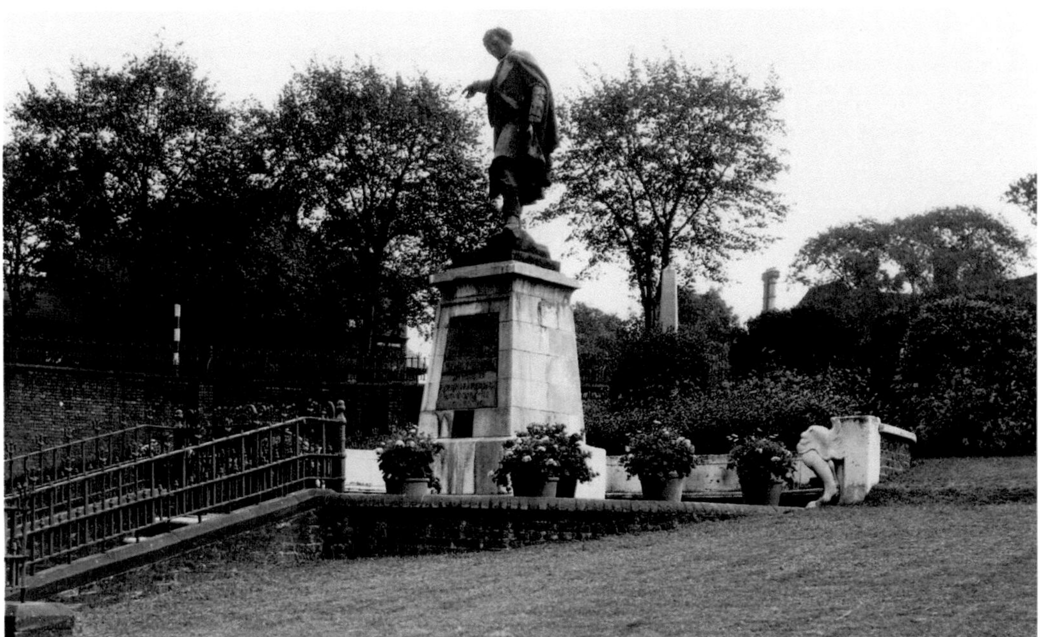

Seemingly once given much more care and attention than it ever receives in this day and age, this image shows the memorial statue to Thomas F. Waghorn, a naval officer who developed the first practical overland route to India.

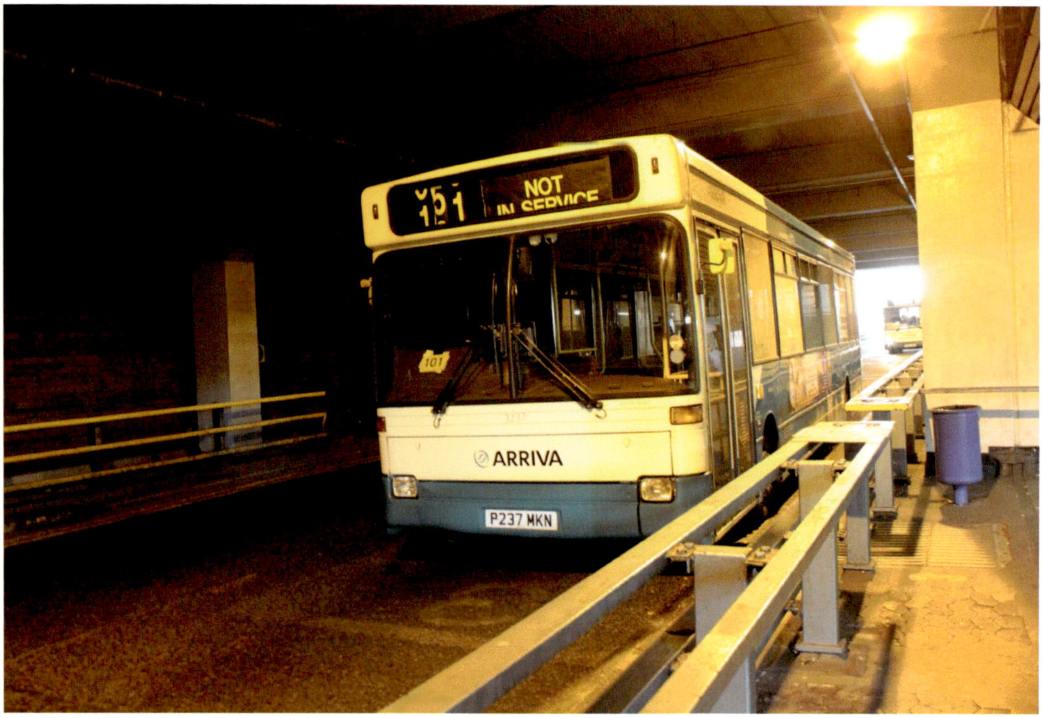

For just over three decades the interior of the Pentagon served as the town's main location for buses. It was not an especially pleasant experience for bus users – dark and fume ridden, it was not exactly the best that the twentieth century could have offered.

5

The Quieter Side of Town

While Chatham has long been a vibrant community, busy, industrious and hard-working, there are areas within the boundaries of the former borough where restful moments were possible and where the hustle and bustle of everyday life could be forgotten. To begin with, there was extensive farmland and open fields, but as the demand for housing for dockyard workers increased, much of that land was lost. In search of the quieter pleasures in life, away from commotion of the town, parks and gardens were created by the town council, while in the summer river cruises were a popular pastime.

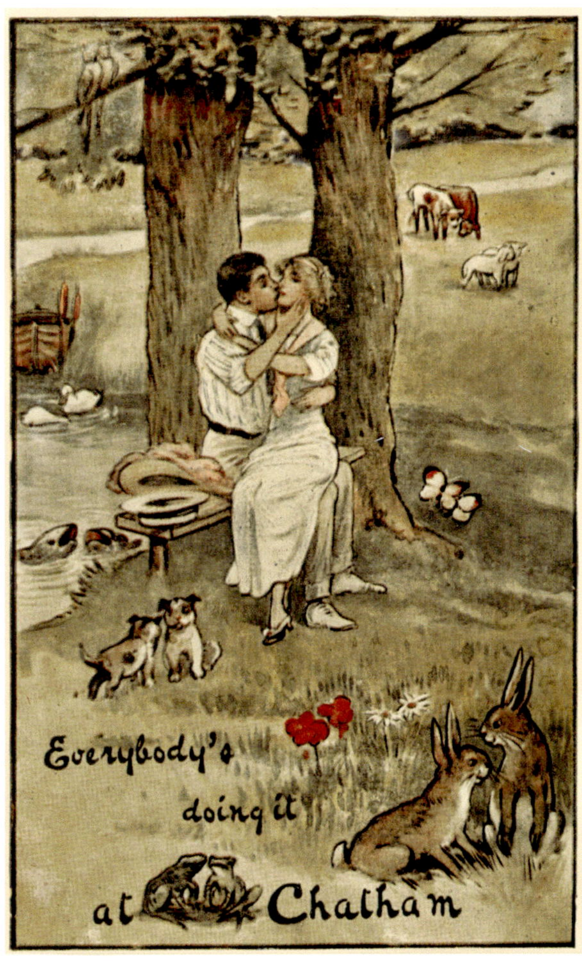

A somewhat fanciful depiction of the less urbanised areas of Chatham that during the mid-1920s, when this picture card was posted, were still to be found in abundance within the borough.

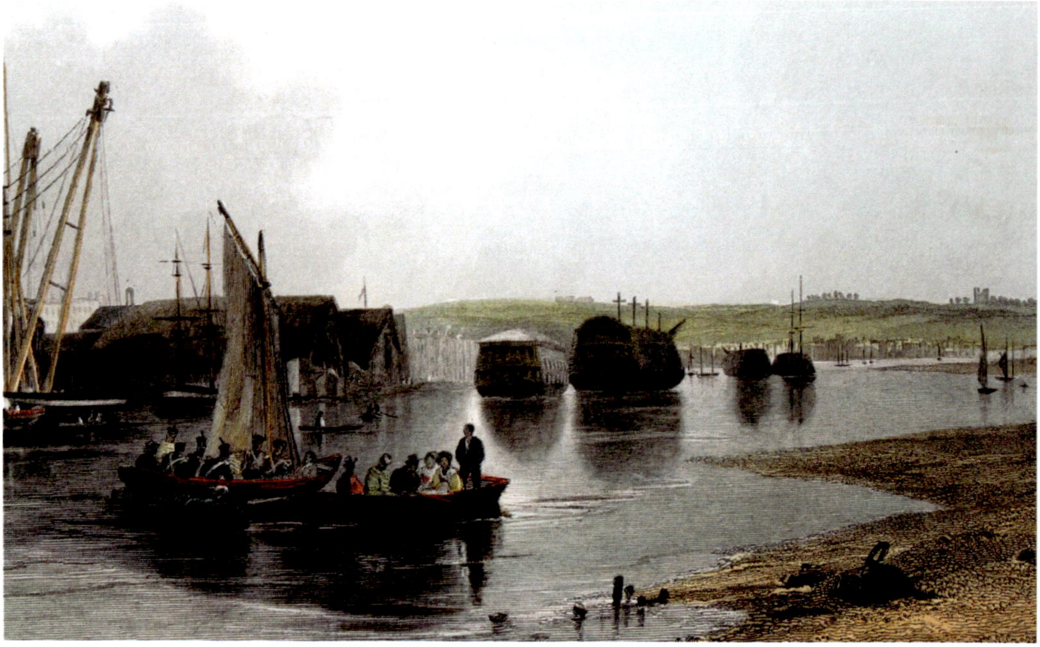

Going back to the 1820s, another idyllic and peaceful scene, but this time somewhat more realistic. In the foreground, a party of gaily dressed women and their male companions are taking a leisurely boat ride along the Medway, passing several hulks that were then lying off the dockyard. The town of Chatham is to be seen in the distance, while a party of soldiers are also relishing the joys of the river as, presumably, they head back to their barracks.

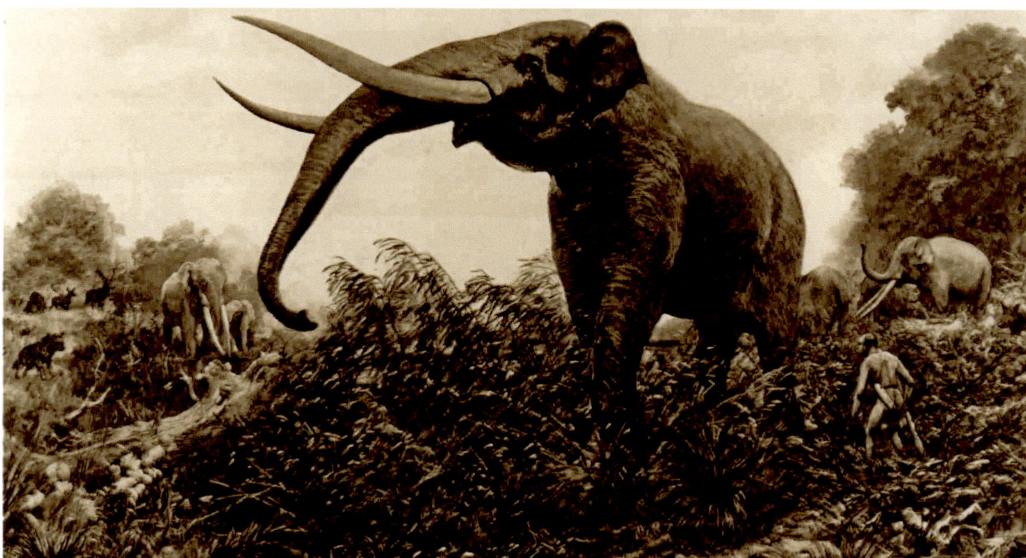

Going back even further in time, the area now called Chatham took on a very different appearance. This early twentieth-century drawing is based on a sensational discovery made near Chatham in 1913, the fossilised remains of a 400,000-year-old giant elephant. Such beasts were then a common sight in southern England, hunted by the ancestor of modern-man, *Homo Heidelbergensis*.

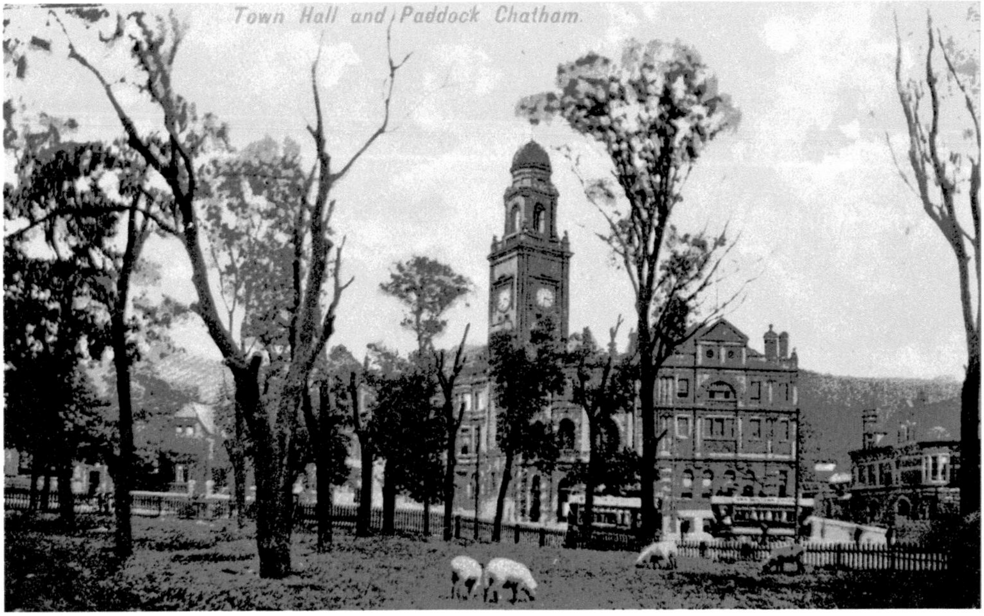

While trams, newly introduced at the time of this picture, had made of the Town Hall stop a busy inter-change, sheep still grazed on the Paddock. Once owned by the War Department, the Paddock was soon to be developed as a public open space. Medway Council is currently planning landscaping that will see a restructuring of the Paddock to create a more vibrant public space for residents and visitors to enjoy.

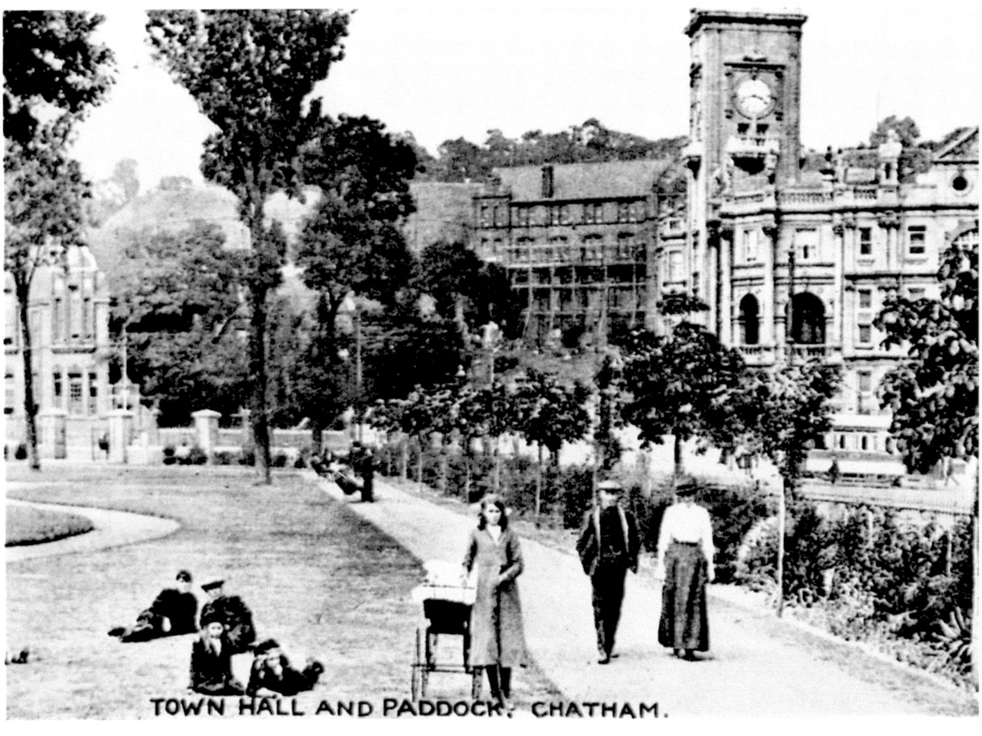

The Paddock during the early 1900s following its redevelopment as a public open space.

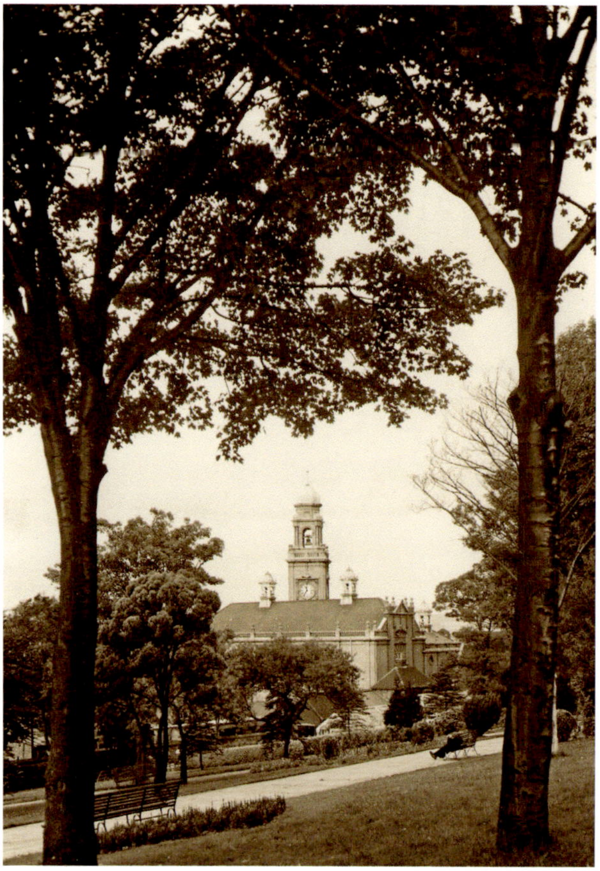

Left: The Town Hall Gardens seen here during the interwar years. The Town Hall Gardens were purchased by the borough council in 1905 and soon after landscaped for public use.

Below: The bandstand in Victoria Gardens where, during the summer, a weekly programme of music was held, military bands always proving especially popular. Within the bandstand can be seen a small fence and, within this area concert-goers could purchase a seat priced at one penny; for those outside this seating area there was no charge.

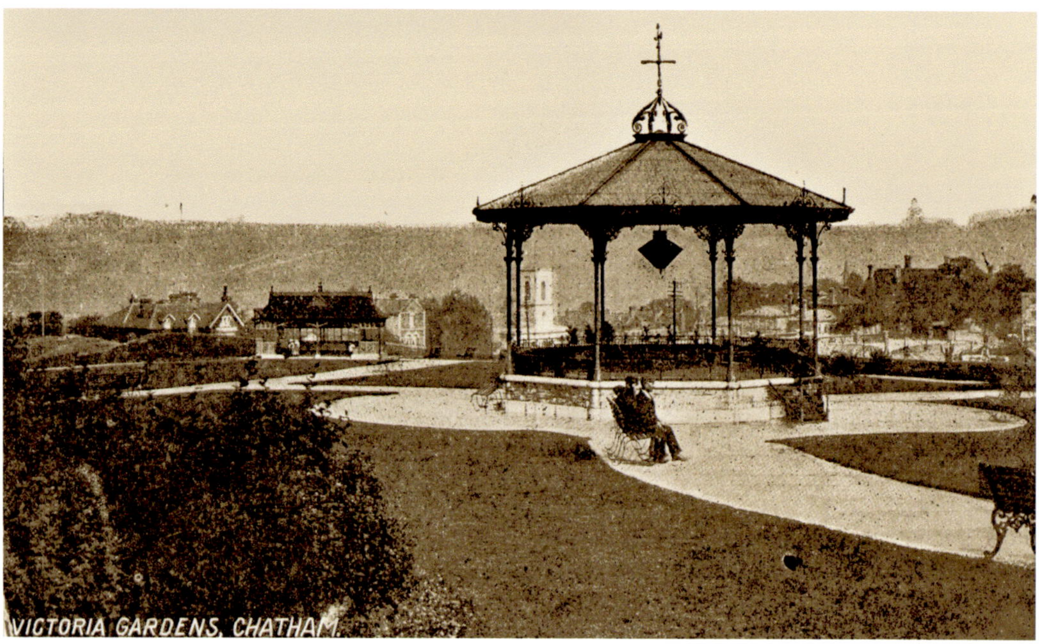

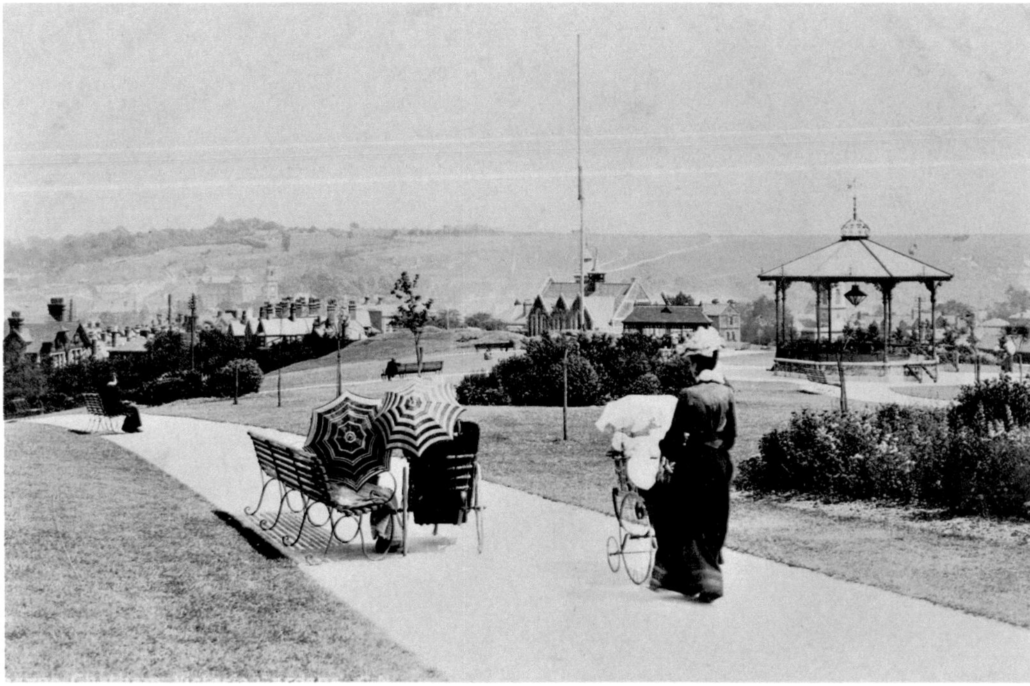

Victoria Gardens, created out of land owned by the Ordnance Department, had at first been leased to Chatham Town Council. Formerly laid out as a public park in 1897, it was so named to mark the diamond jubilee of Queen Victoria. In total, the project cost £1,420, with the gardens opened by the then Mayoress, Mrs H. T. Brown, on 15 September 1897.

Returning to the river, residents of Chatham, throughout the early years of the twentieth century, could board steamers either for a cruise along the Medway or a means of reaching a holiday destination during the summer. Southend and Margate, with their extensive beaches and world-famous piers, were especially popular destinations.

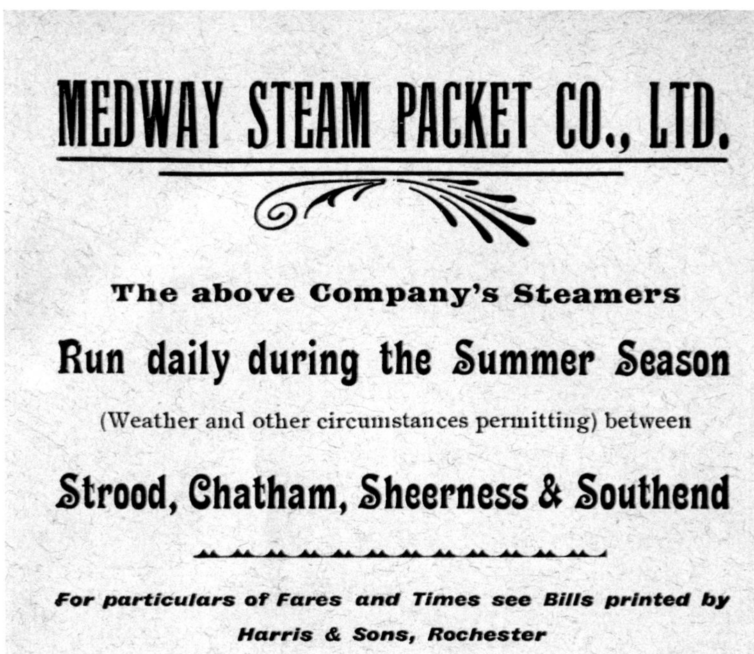

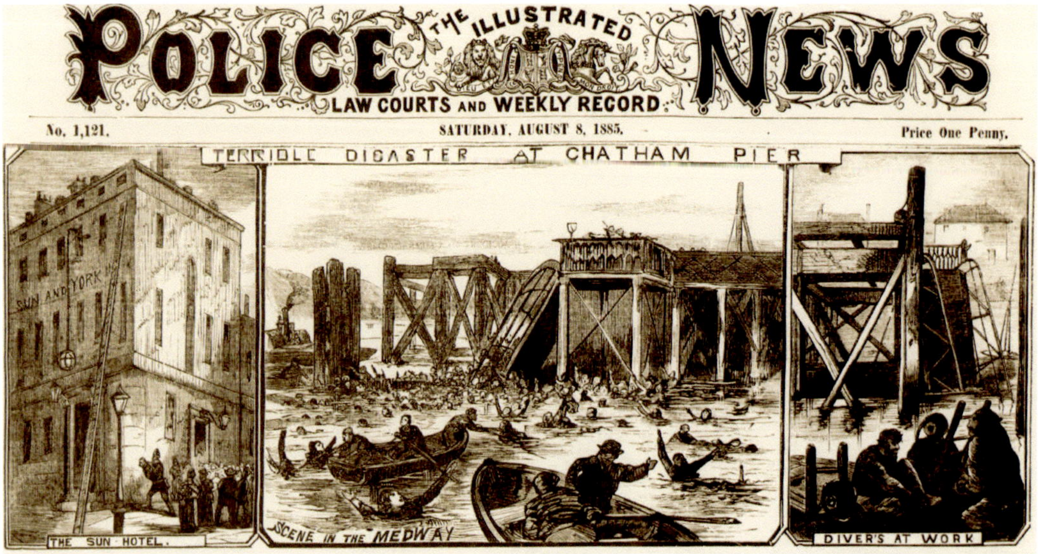
THE ILLUSTRATED POLICE NEWS LAW COURTS AND WEEKLY RECORD

No. 1,121. SATURDAY, AUGUST 8, 1885. Price One Penny.

TERRIBLE DISASTER AT CHATHAM PIER

THE SUN HOTEL.

SCENE IN THE MEDWAY

DIVER'S AT WORK

It was from Sun Pier that steamers could be boarded, long queues often assembling on the hottest days of the year. In July 1885, with work in hand to replace an earlier and smaller pier, a temporary iron angle gangway had been put in place, this attached to the pier and a floating barge moored in the river. On Sunday 26th, the weather being particularly hot, large crowds descended upon the pier to board one of the waiting steamers. With so many passing along the gangway, the weight was too much and it gave way. As can be seen from this contemporary newspaper depiction, many were thrown into the river, but miraculously no lives were lost with only a few sustaining injury and taken to the nearby Sun Hotel.

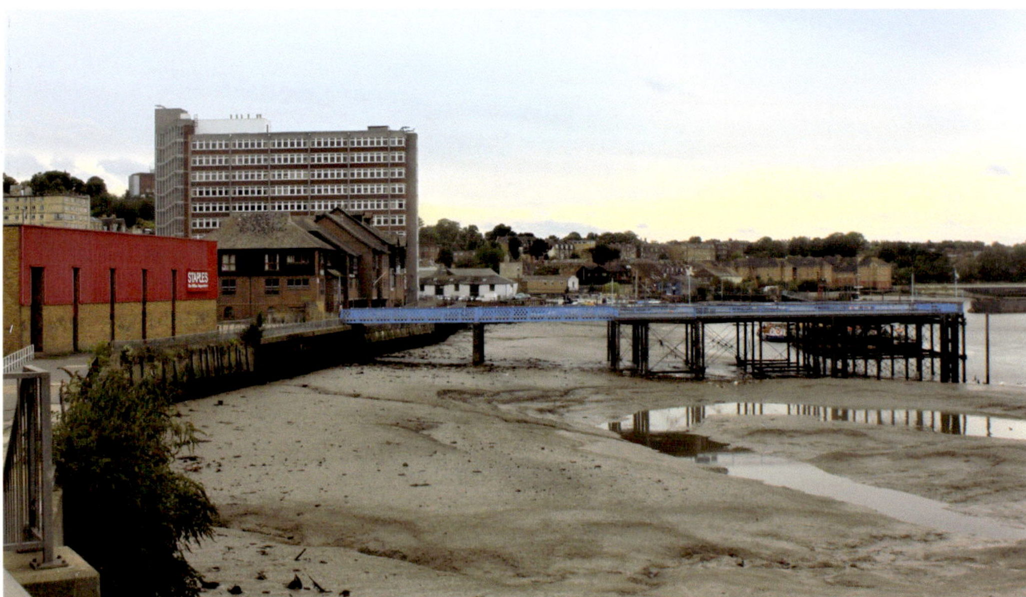

The new pier, as finally completed in 1886, was provided with a more substantial floating gangway to allow for the boarding of steamers at any state of the tide and a covered waiting room. The pier today, as seen here, still exists, but no longer has a covered waiting room.

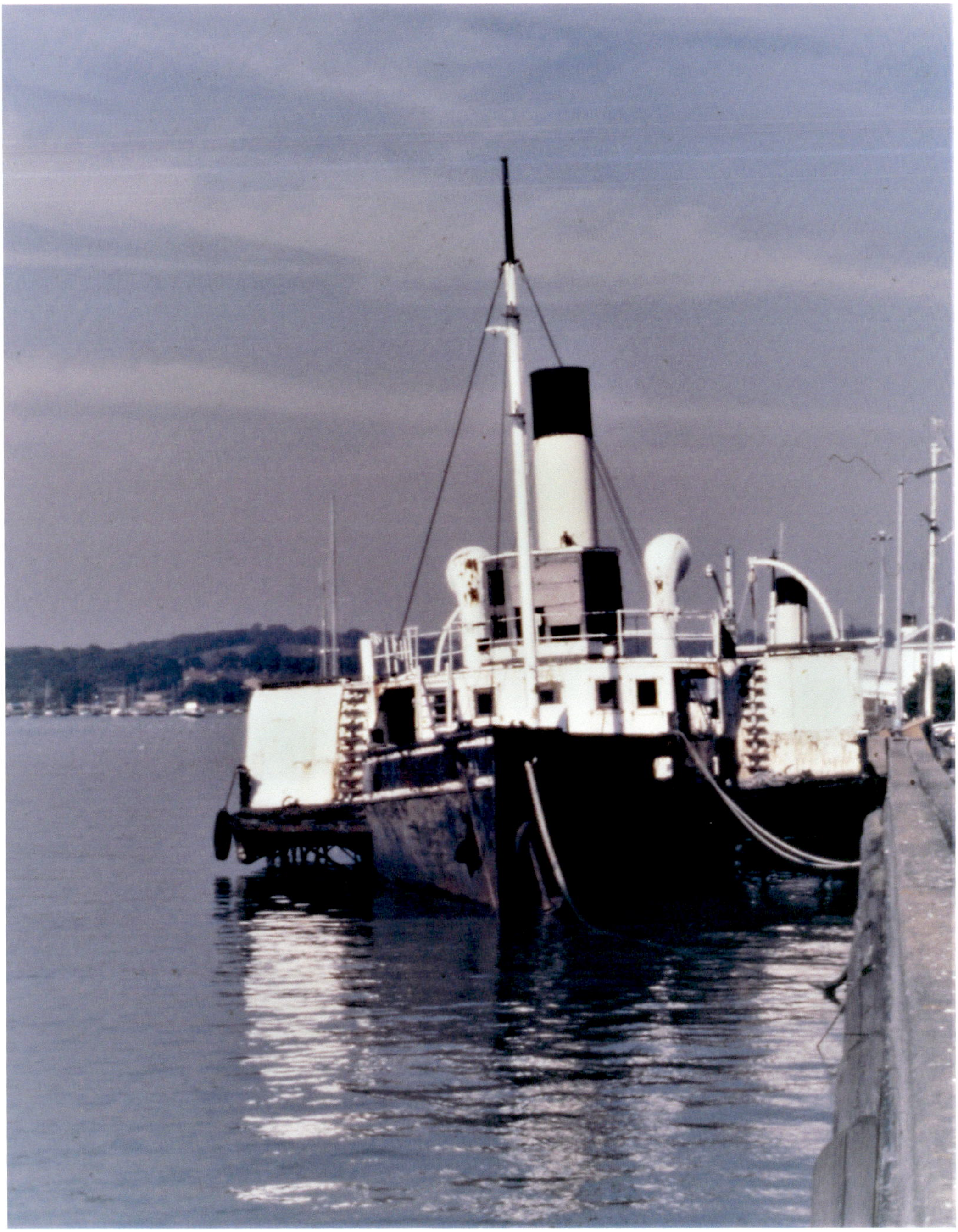

The paddle steamer *Medway Queen*, operated for many years by the New Medway Steam Packet Company, was a regular visitor to Sun Pier. Remarkably, the *Medway Queen* survives to this day. A one-time seemingly abandoned hulk, she is seen here alongside Chatham dockyard during the 1980s. Since that time the 'Medway Queen Preservation Society', based in Gillingham, have been on a tireless mission to restore the vessel. Eventually it is intended that the *Medway Queen* will once more become seaworthy.

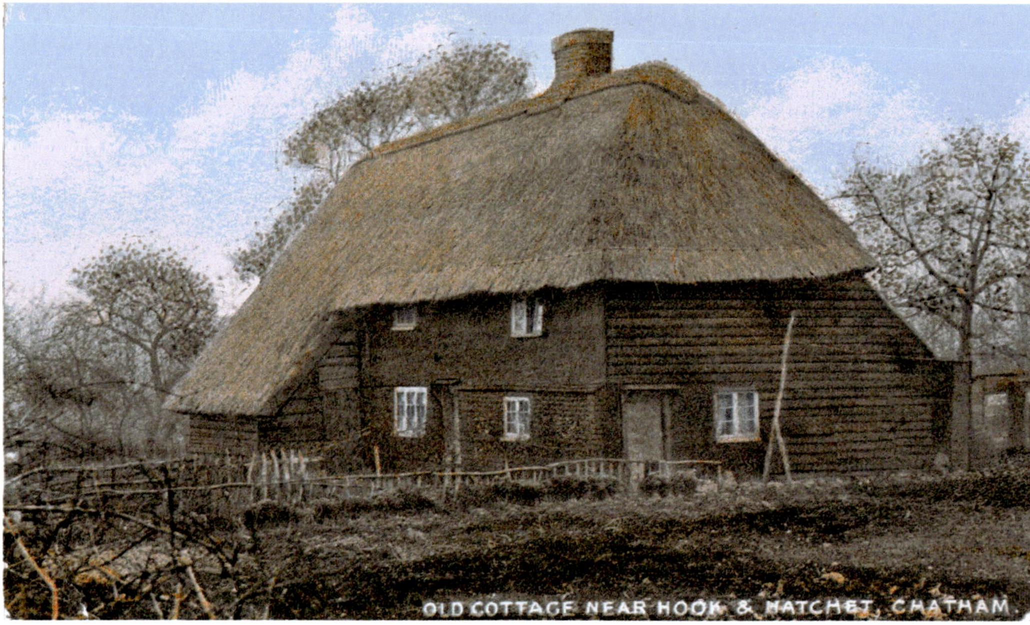

Captioned 'Old Cottage near Hook & Hatchet, Chatham', this postcard picture, dating to the early 1900s, is probably the long-demolished house belonging to Brown's Hill Farm, an area, as with much of Waldeslade, now covered by extensive housing.

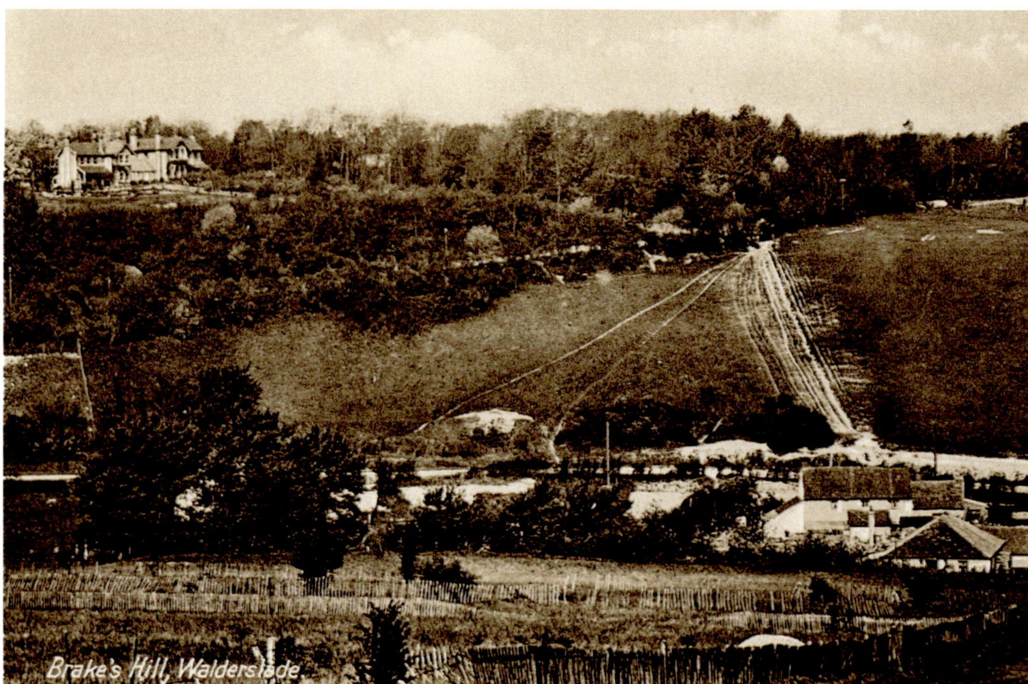

Brake's Hill, Waldeslade, seen before the development of Walderslade, a process that really began after the First World War, but fundamentally continued throughout the twentieth century.

6

Military Barracks

Chatham, through the existence of its naval dockyard and ordnance wharf, was, from the seventeenth century onwards, following the establishment of the dockyard in the previous century, a major military-industrial complex essential to the needs of the Royal Navy. In turn, it was the navy that was the first line of defence against overseas invasion while securing, during wartime, the safe passage of commercial shipping. It was trade, especially overseas trade, upon which the wealth of the nation had become increasingly dependent. Without the dockyard at Chatham, the navy would be much weakened, unable to carry out the important work with which it was tasked. Therefore, it was essential that Chatham should be prioritised in matters of its own defence, secure against either capture or destruction by an enemy. The Dutch had attempted its destruction in 1667, and the government as a result was determined that such an opportunity must never again be allowed to occur. Defending Chatham from land attack was, during the eighteenth and early nineteenth centuries, the role of the Lines, with large numbers of troops brought into the area to man them, and in turn needing barrack accommodation. The presence of so many soldiers also had a massive impact on the town in general.

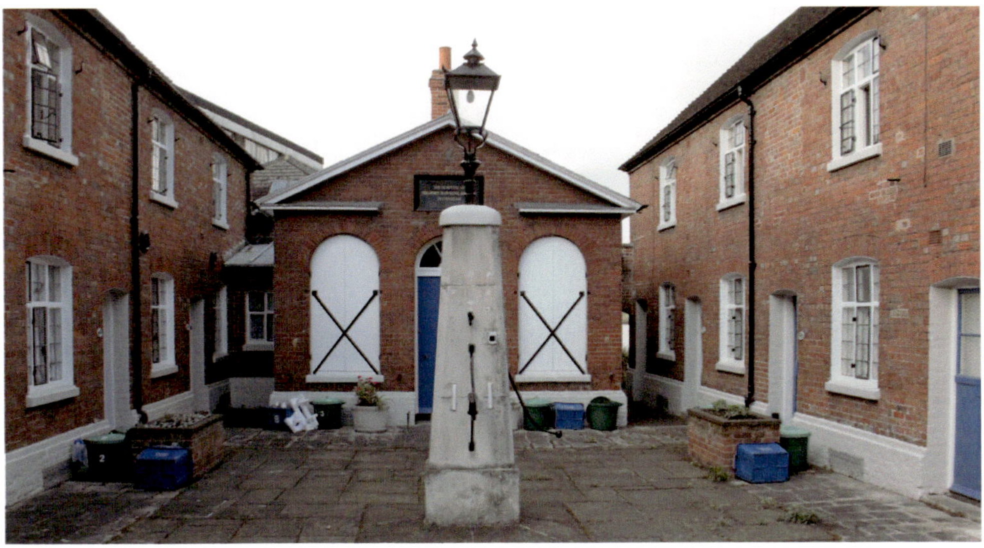

Pre-dating any of the military barracks, but still an element of that military-industrial complex was the Hospital of Sir John Hawkins, Knight, which stands at the extreme west end of the High Street. It was established by Sir John Hawkins, the one-time slave trader and Treasurer and Controller of the Navy under Elizabeth I. It is an almshouse intended to support destitute seamen and shipwrights, with Hawkins at the time having in mind those who had served the nation against the Spanish Armada of 1588. It still provides accommodation for a small number of residents, but following the closure of Chatham dockyard in 1984, the hospital has been opened to men and women of all three services using a selection criterion based on need.

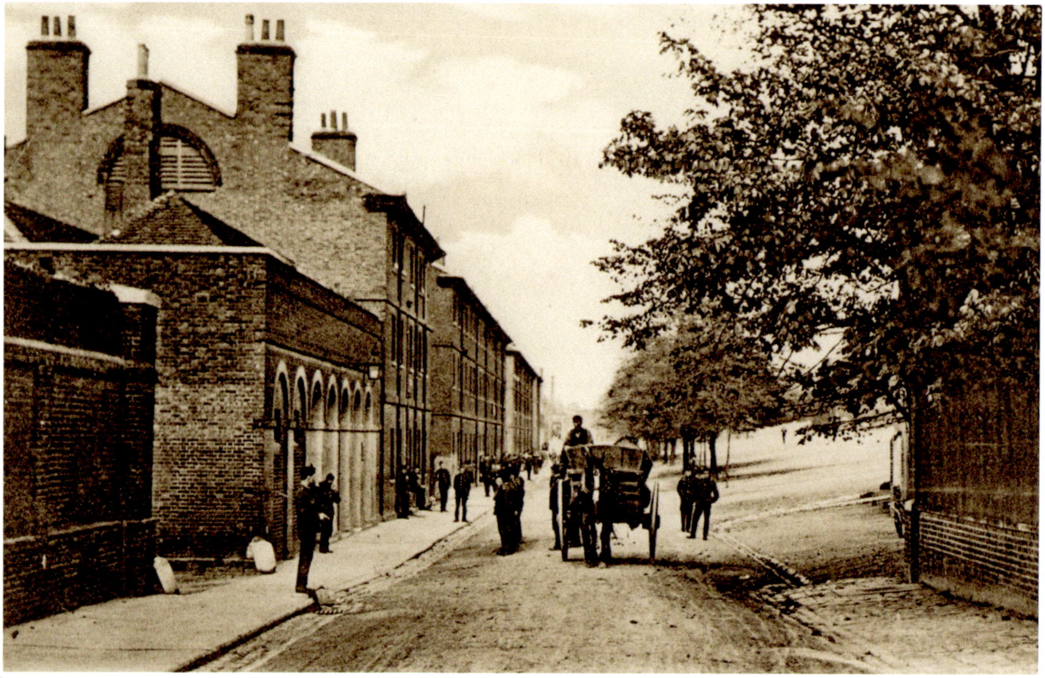

To accommodate troops required to defend Chatham and man the Lines, Chatham Infantry Barracks was constructed during the 1750s. Seen here are the original barrack buildings that, when first built, accommodated nearly 2,000 men. With but a few exceptions, the original buildings were demolished during the 1930s, replaced by much more modern accommodation blocks.

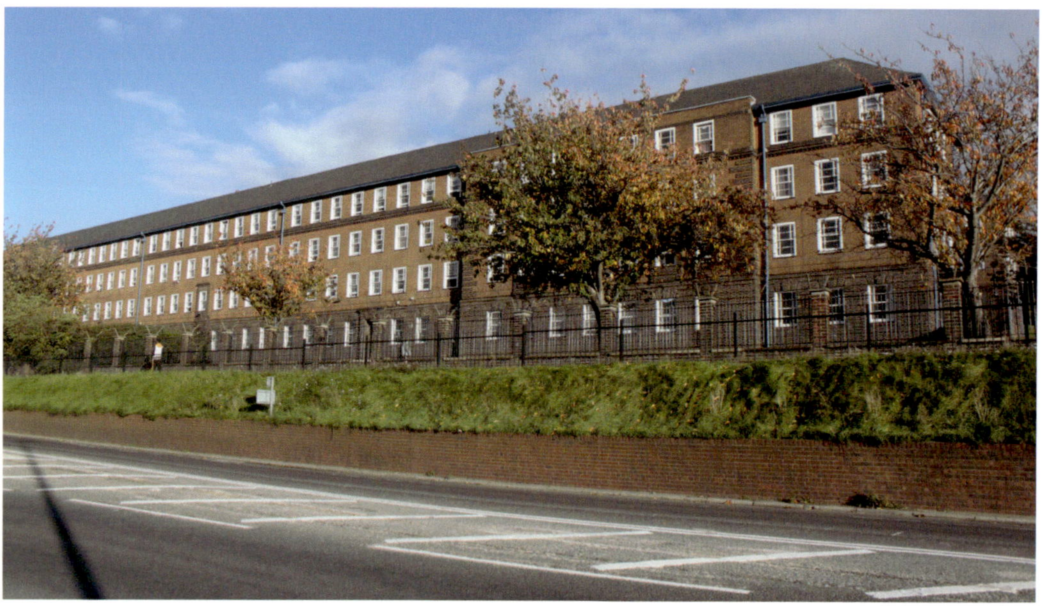

Renamed Kitchener Barracks in 1928 following the taking over of the former Chatham Barracks by the Royal Engineers, this is how the barracks looked in 2010, just eight years before these buildings were themselves demolished.

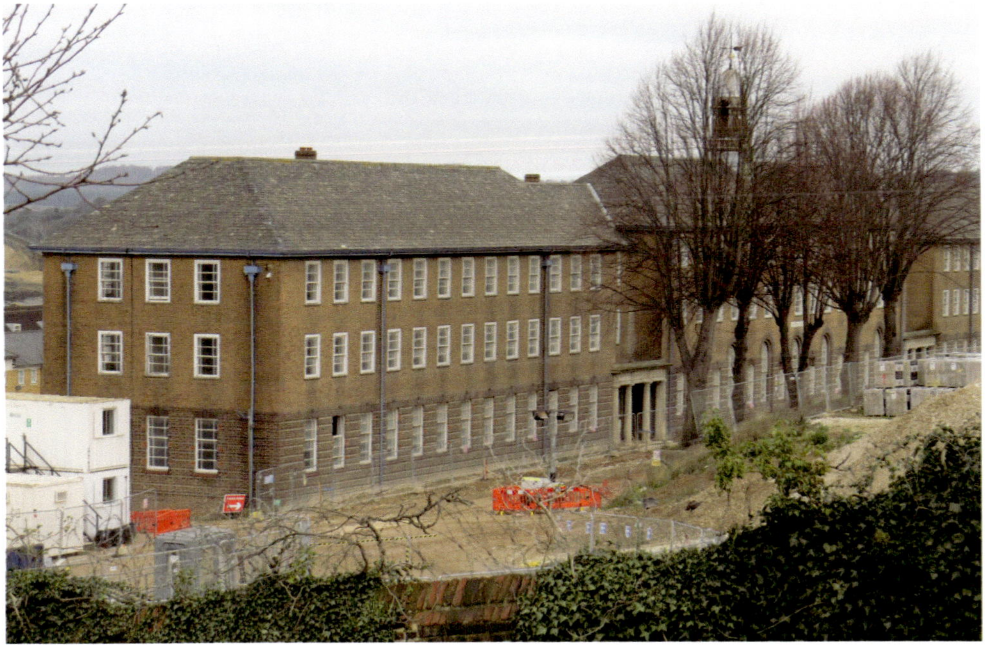

It was in 2015 that the site of Chatham/Kitchener Barracks, having been sold to a property developer, saw permission given for the building of 295 homes. Some of the 1930s buildings were to be retained, along with those that had remained from the eighteenth century. Seen here in 2018, work is about to commence on the barrack buildings that once fronted onto Dock Road.

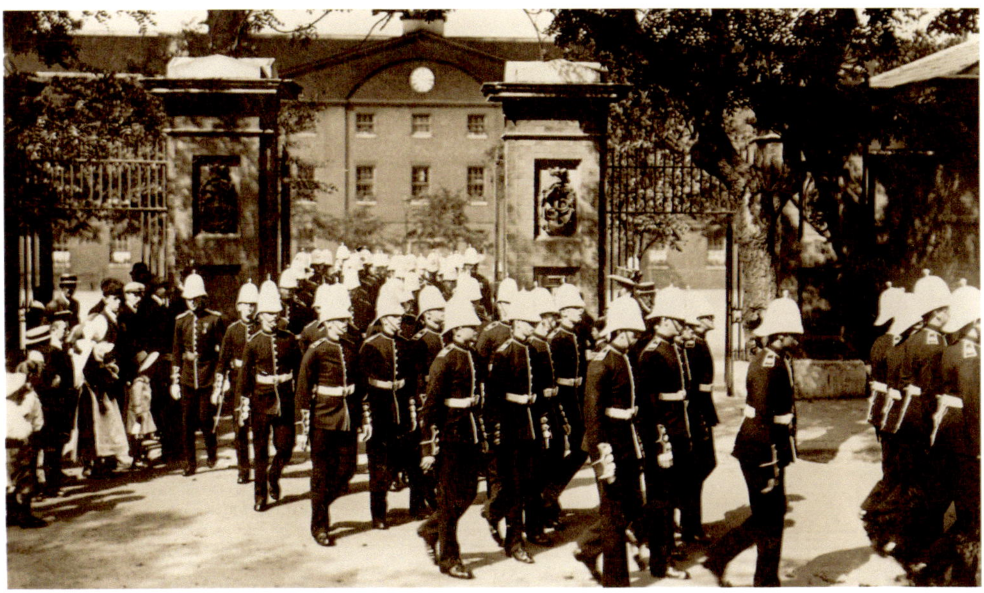

While an obvious need existed for barracks to properly accommodate men brought to Chatham to guard the Lines, the Royal Marines also required barrack accommodation. Their barracks in Dock Road was the first such accommodation built in Chatham, completed sometime around 1779. In this early twentieth-century photo, a parade of Marines is leaving from the main gate of the barracks.

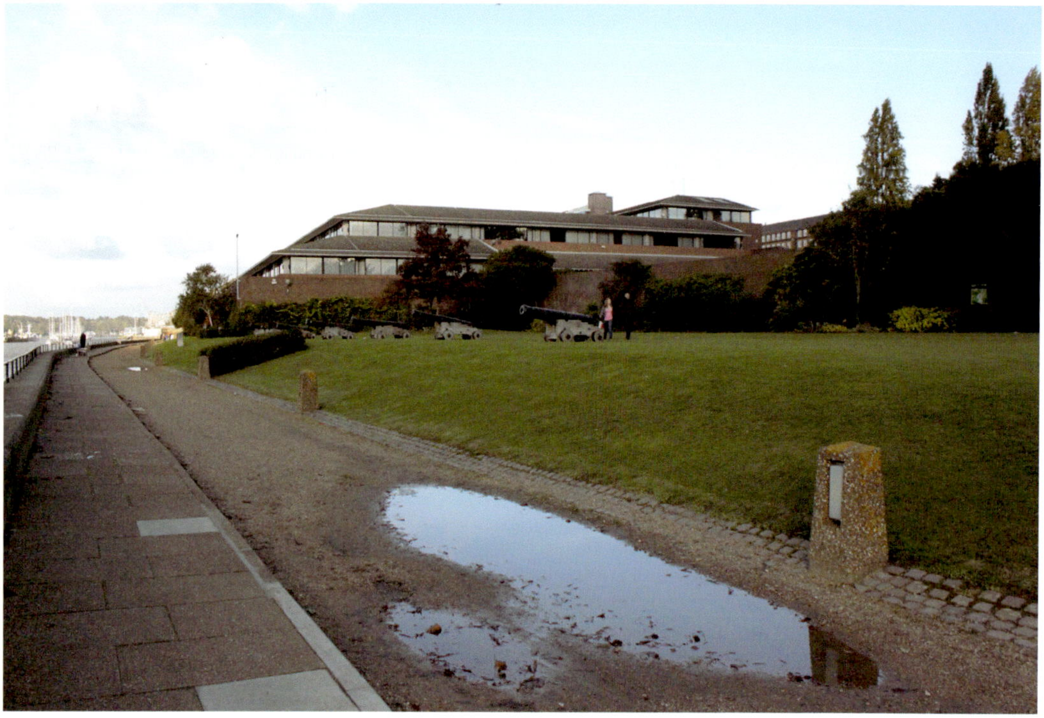

No longer required, the Royal Marines ceased occupying their barracks in Chatham during the 1950s, and the buildings were demolished in 1960. With the site cleared, Lloyds, the insurance company, built an office complex on the site, a block that is now occupied by Medway Council.

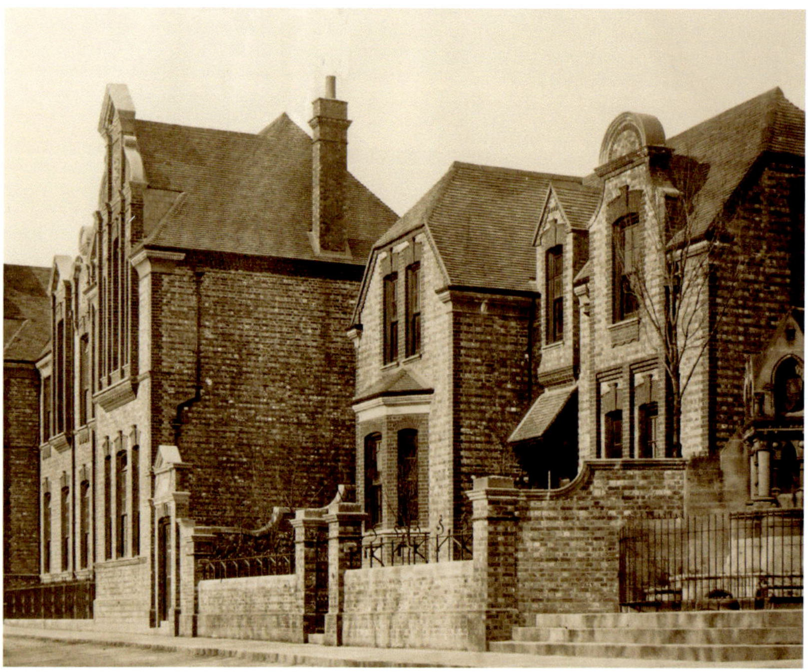

While now an Armed Forces Careers Office (1–3 Dock Road), the building, in the 1930s when this picture was taken, served as a Royal Marine School, doubling also as a recruiting office for the Royal Navy and Royal Marines.

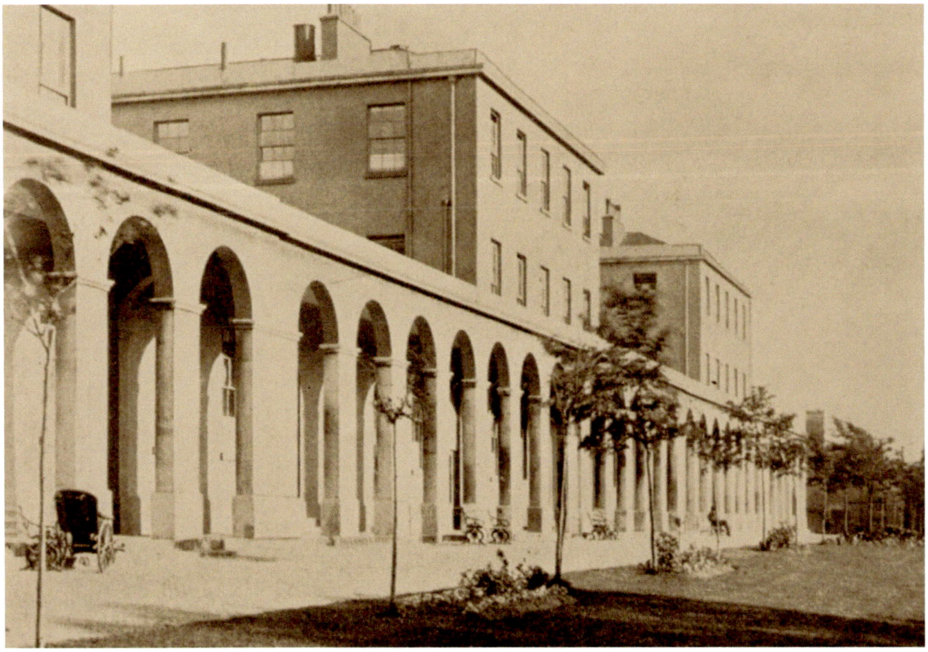

Also falling into the hands of the Royal Marines was the Melville Naval Hospital building which once stood opposite the Main Gate of the Dockyard on the grounds of the present-day Melville Court. The naval hospital had been opened during the early nineteenth century but was closed as a hospital in 1905 following the opening of the much larger naval hospital in Gillingham (now Medway Maritime Hospital). For the Royal Marines, the former hospital building was used for physical training and gunnery.

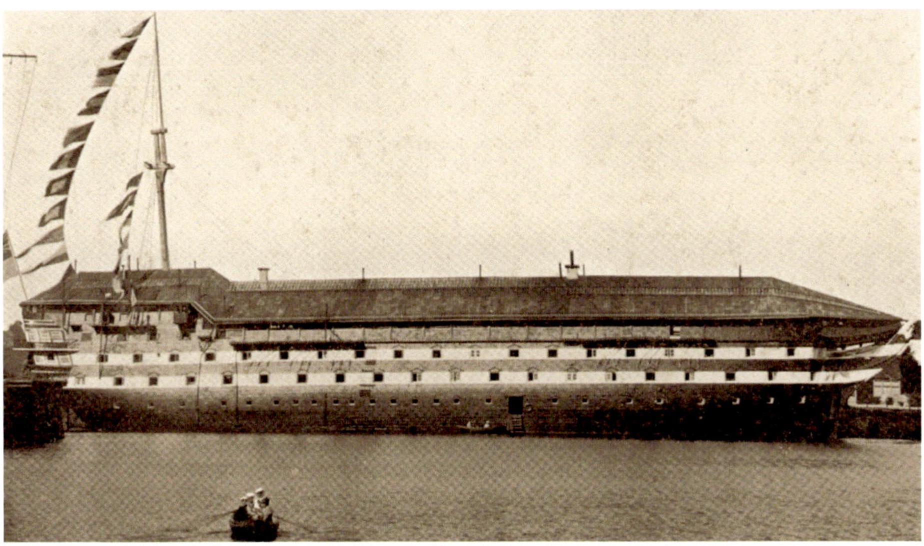

For seamen of the Royal Navy brought to Chatham during the nineteenth century, and while awaiting transfer to a seagoing ship, they too required accommodation. At that time, the housing offered was on board hulks – warships long out of commission – that were moored along the banks of the Medway. Here is one such hulk, HMS *Pembroke*.

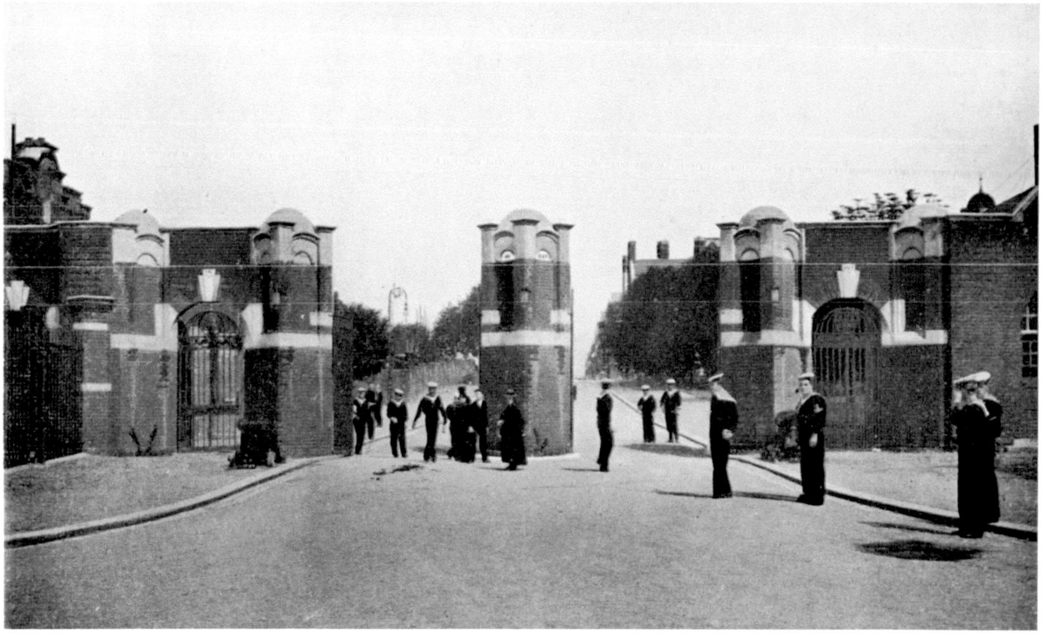

It was *Pembroke* that came to bestow its name on the Royal Naval Barracks and was first opened in 1903. This is the main entrance, seen here shortly after the opening of the barracks which, although always known as the Royal Naval Barracks, Chatham, lay within the borough of Gillingham.

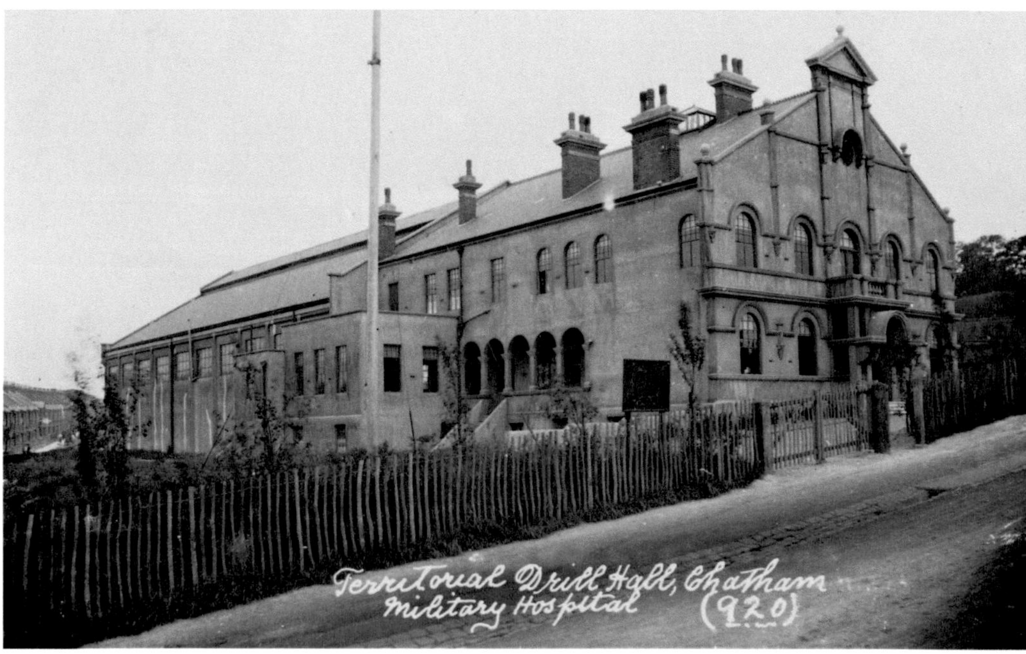

Once standing on Fort Pitt Fields close to Victoria Gardens, the Volunteer Drill Hall, demolished in February 1933, served the purpose of providing a training venue for the locally formed volunteer battalion of the Royal West Kent Regiment. Those who joined the battalion were only required to undertake military service, other than training alongside the regular army, if the country was threatened with invasion.

7

Life Outside the Barracks

With so many soldiers and sailors having been brought to Chatham, the central area of the town became a magnet to which these soldiers and sailors were drawn as a break from the monotonous life that the barracks otherwise inflicted upon them. This explains why the town had so many pubs. Barnard's Palace of Varieties also played an important role, putting on two performances each evening, the first beginning at 6.30 p.m., timed to allow those from the military services to return to barracks before the gates were shut. However, by the later years of the nineteenth century there was considerable concern that more needed to be done to provide entertainment that did not expose new and younger recruits to the evils of alcohol.

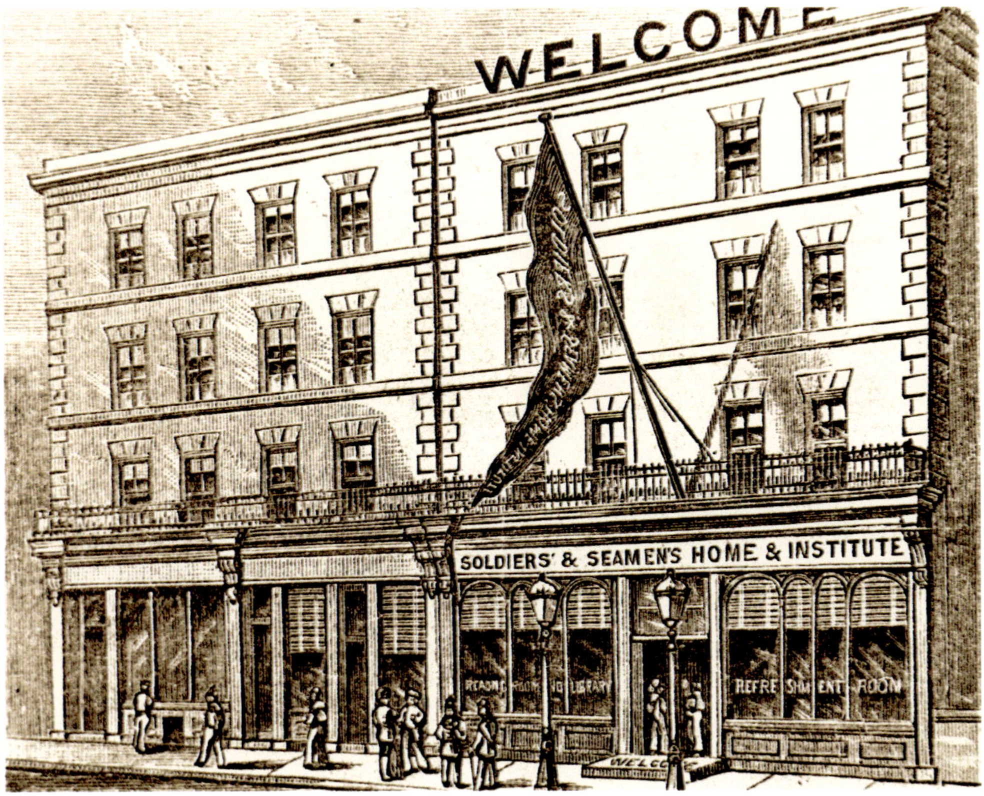

One of the earliest buildings within the town to provide more wholesome entertainment for off-duty servicemen was the 'Welcome Soldiers' and Seamen's Home and Institute' in Military Road that was first opened in October 1877. Financing the setting up of the 'Welcome' had come through voluntary subscriptions raised by the Wesleyan chaplain of the Garrison, the Revd J. Burgess, with the Institute open to all ranks.

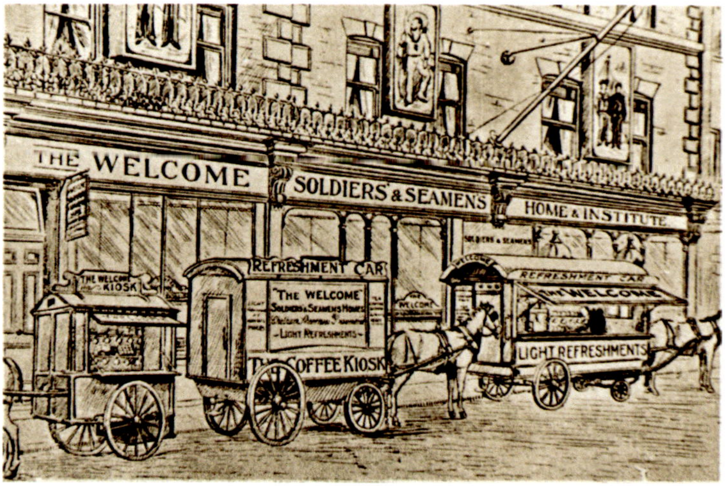

Over time the Welcome Soldiers' and Seamen's Home developed an outreach service, taking into the dockyard non-alcoholic drinks for those employed within the yard.

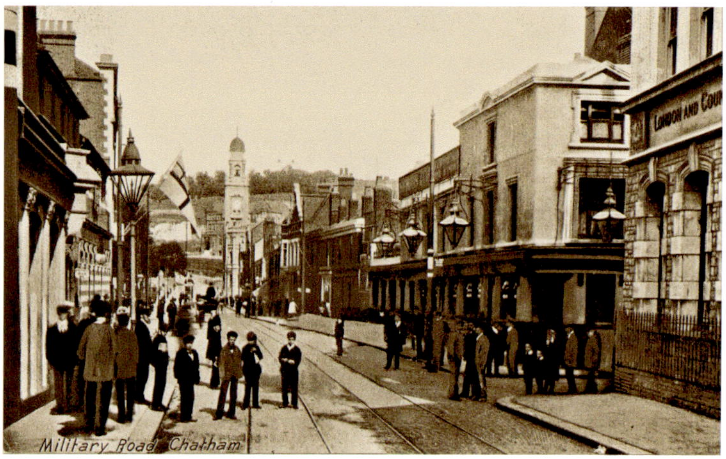

The location of the Welcome Soldiers' and Seamen's Home can be readily appreciated from this *c.* 1910 view of the building (on the left) and by which time it had considerably extended the services it offered, having 120 beds for overnight accommodation, a lecture theatre, library and reading room.

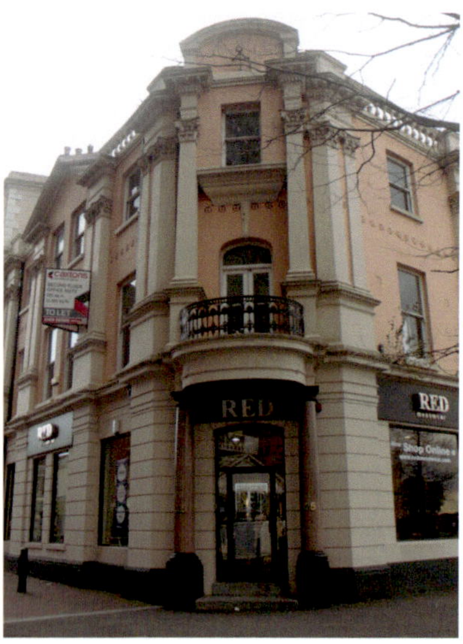

The former Welcome Soldiers' and Seamen's Home building today, now a small boutique shop.

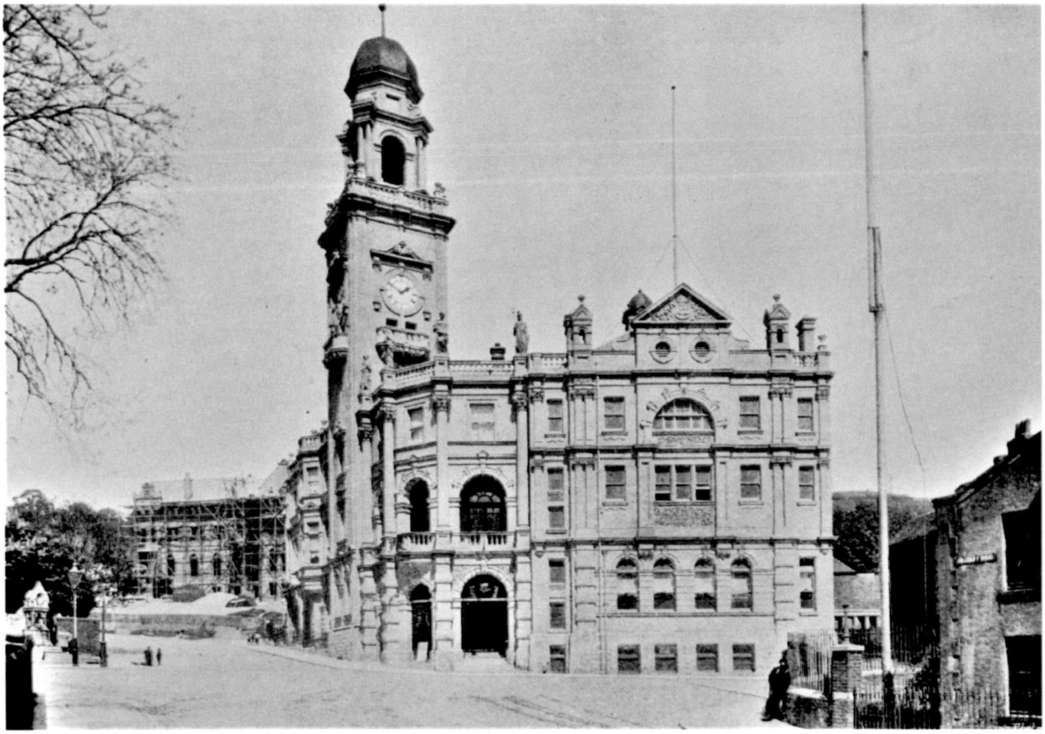

Behind the Town Hall in 1901 construction work is underway on the Royal Sailors' Home on a site provided by the War Office. A further institute that provided an alternative to the many pubs in Chatham, it was designed by George E. Bond, the accomplished local architect. It was mainly financed from contributions given by the men and petty officers of the fleet with some money also provided by the Admiralty. Beginning business on 18 January 1902, but not officially until the following month when it was formally opened by Lord Selborne, the First Lord of the Admiralty, it had at that time overnight accommodation for ninety-four men, alongside a dining room, billiard room and a recreation room.

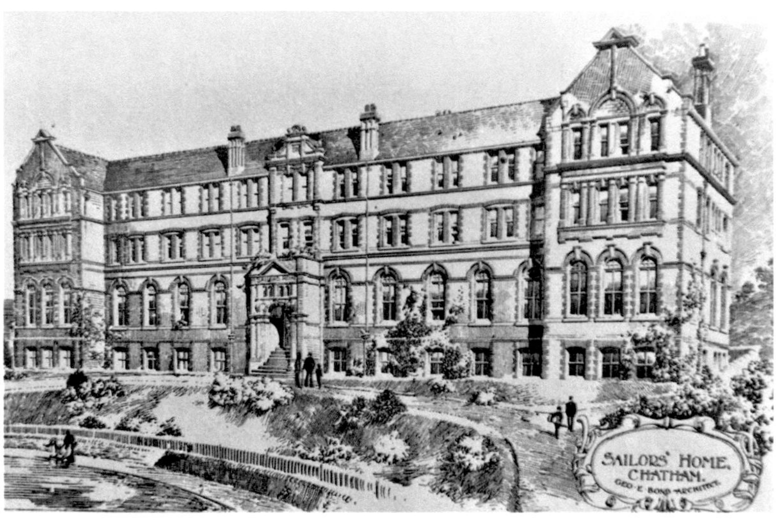

An artist's impression of how the Royal Sailors' Home would look upon completion. The drawing includes a never-completed west wing.

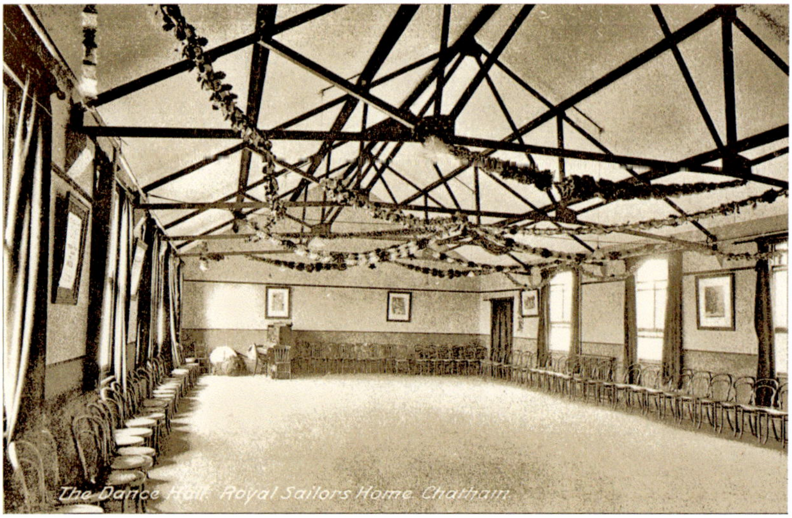

The dance hall within the Royal Sailors' Home. The building was demolished at the beginning of the present century.

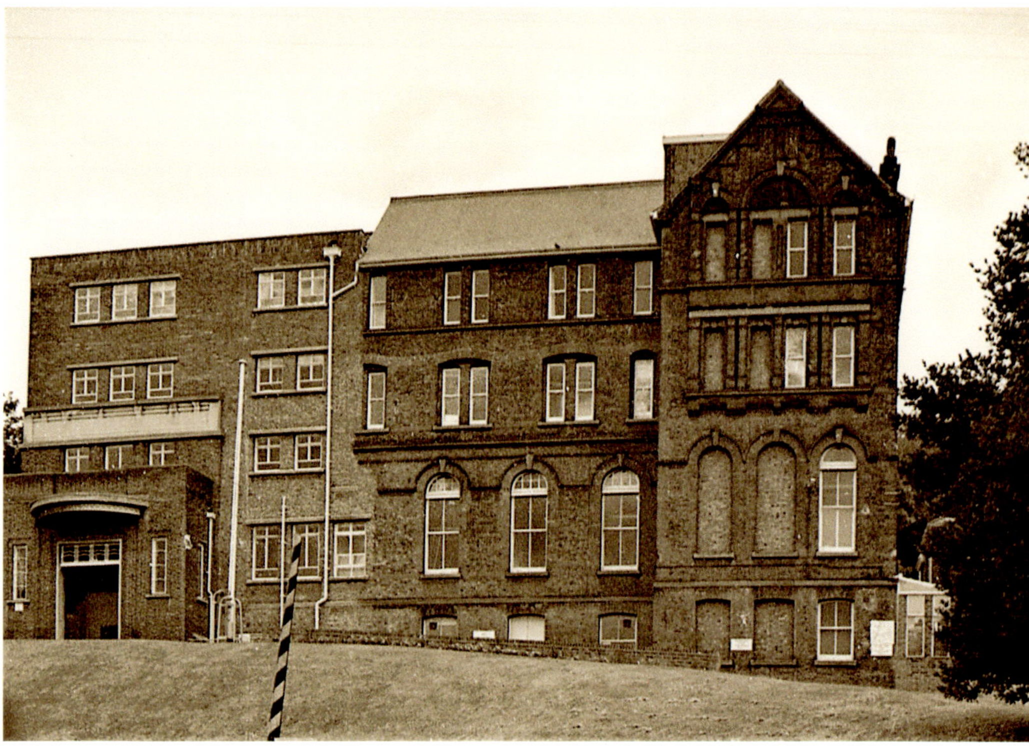

A 1970s view of the Royal Sailors' Home, by then no longer serving its original purpose and known then as Barrier House. While the west wing was never completed to its original design, a much later and less attractive extension had been added on the west side of the building. The failure to construct that west wing meant that the building was of insufficient size to meet the demands placed upon it. This was especially felt on Sunday nights when men arrived in Chatham by late trains to join their ships early on Monday morning and as a result were constantly seen loitering about the streets, not knowing where to find a decent sleeping place. In those times, the limits of the home made it impossible to receive them.

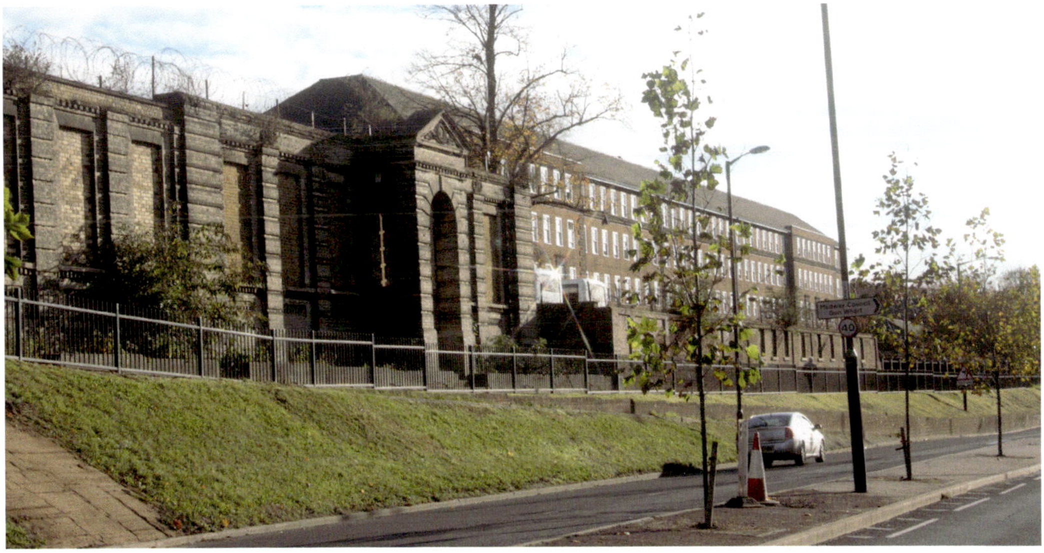

The War Office was also concerned that recruits into the army should have more uplifting entertainment, Chatham Barracks as it was then, gaining in 1861 an off-duty venue, the Soldiers' Institute and Garrison Club. While the Institute building has long since been demolished, its colonnaded entrance is still visible on Dock Road. Behind can also be seen the barrack block which was demolished in 2015.

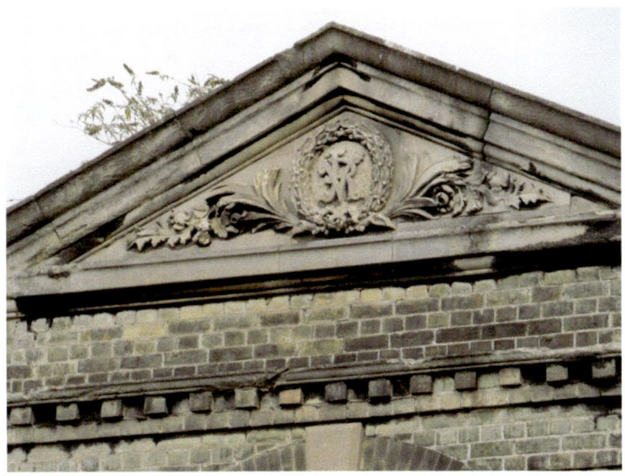

Detail of the pediment that sits over the now disused entrance to the Soldiers' Institute and Garrison Club in Dock Road.

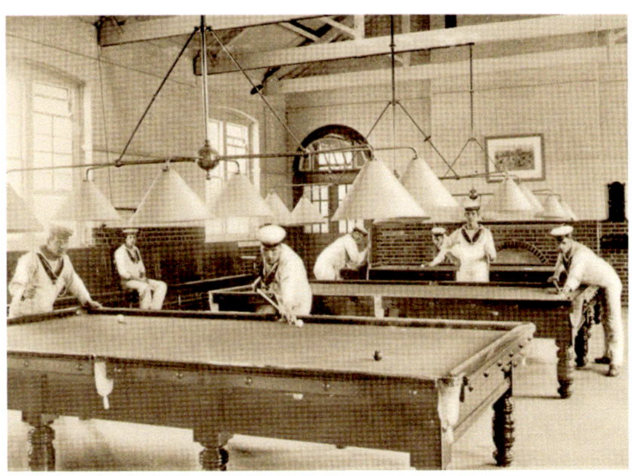

The Royal Naval Barracks, Chatham, otherwise known as HMS *Pembroke*, from the very outset provided ratings with various recreational facilities including this billiard room. While situated within the boundary of Gillingham, but always known as The Royal Naval Barracks, Chatham, those seamen billeted here looked upon Chatham as their real home, and would descend upon Chatham most evening before returning to the barracks. Through its location in Gillingham however, more on the Naval Barracks will be found in my soon to be published *Lost Gillingham*.

8

Mine's a Pint

Pubs, inns and tap houses in Chatham were numerous and varied considerably in size. At one end of the spectrum were simple houses converted into a tap house and run, most frequently, by the wife of a dockyard worker, helped by the husband once he had returned from earning his daily wage. For such an enterprise, the clientele was quite minimal, possibly no more than handful of customers, fellow dockyard workers, drawn to the hostelry to spend an evening in the company of fellow shipwrights, caulkers or anchor smiths. At the other end of the spectrum were the pubs closest to the barracks, and regularly meeting the needs of countless numbers of soldiers and seamen whose capacity for drink, especially when returning from an overseas posting or many months at sea, was almost unquenchable. Fights were not uncommon, often continued in the bye-ways of Chatham, with such incidents regularly broken up by the local constabulary, the dockyard police or the military police attached to each of the barracks. Such a high level of policing in the past often resulted in Chatham being seen as safer in those days than it is today – providing of course you were prepared to step over a bruised, battered and intoxicated servicemen who had fallen to the ground.

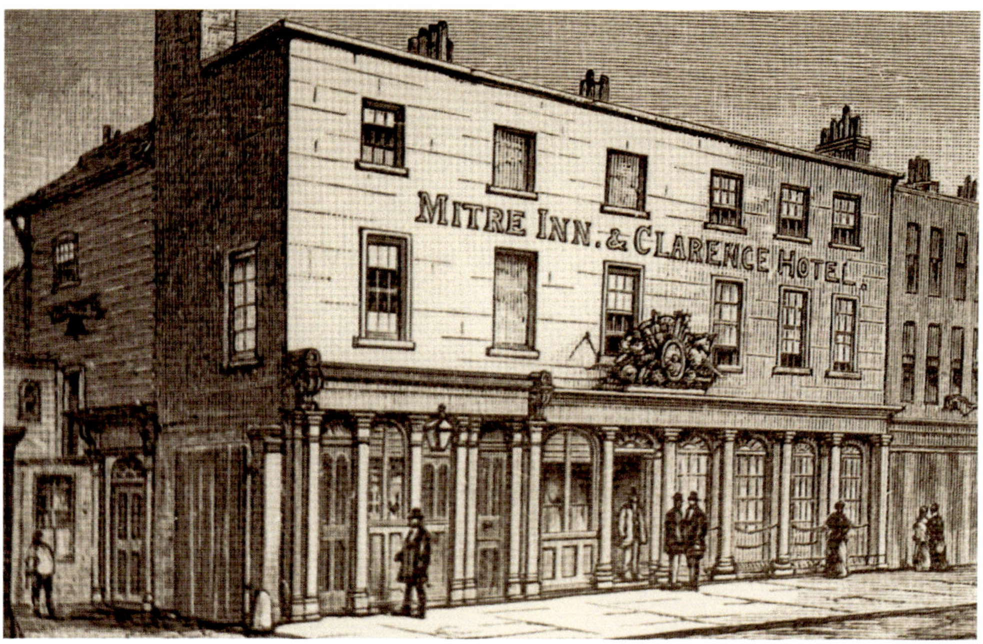

The Mitre Inn and Clarence Hotel (198 High Street) dates back to 1768 and was once the classiest of all the drinking establishments, being Chatham's coaching inn and from where each day the London coach, the *Blue-eyed Maid*, set out on its journey that took no less than five hours. Among those known to have stayed here were Charles Dickens, Horatio Nelson and the future King William IV.

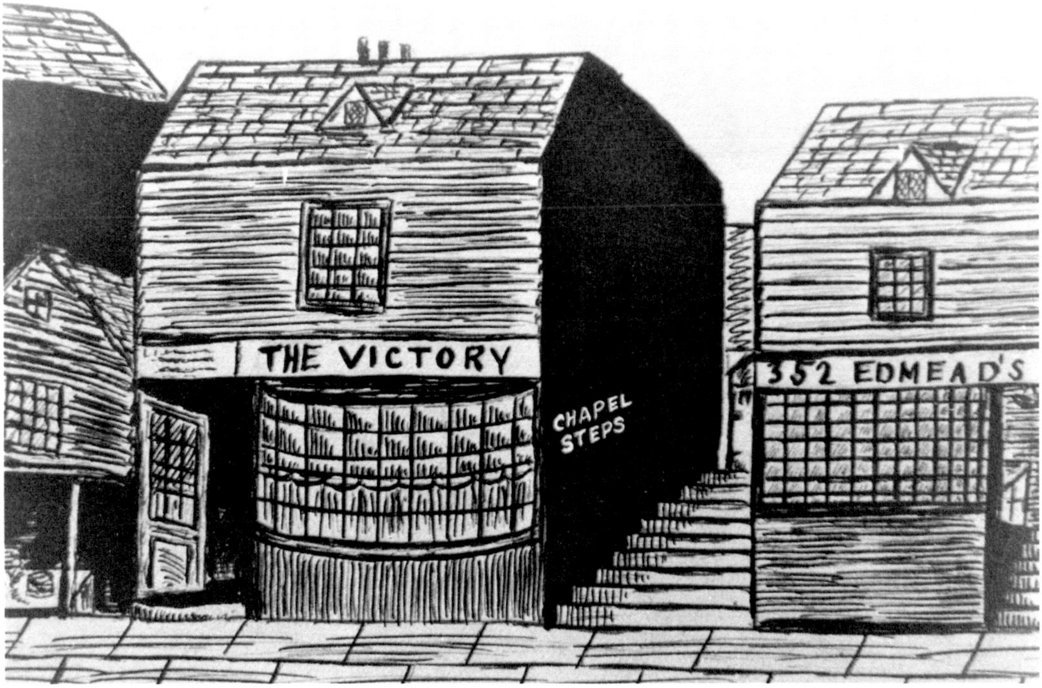

Above: In contrast with The Mitre and Clarence was this small beer house, the Victory (350 High Street), depicted sometime around 1870, but despite its diminutive appearance, it probably did a roaring trade.

Right: The United Services Hotel (188 High Street) was especially renowned because of the numerous fights that broke out, it attracting, as it often did, a service clientele that was often more disunited than united. It can be identified in this early twentieth-century photograph from the sign by the horse and cart which reads 'Long Bar'.

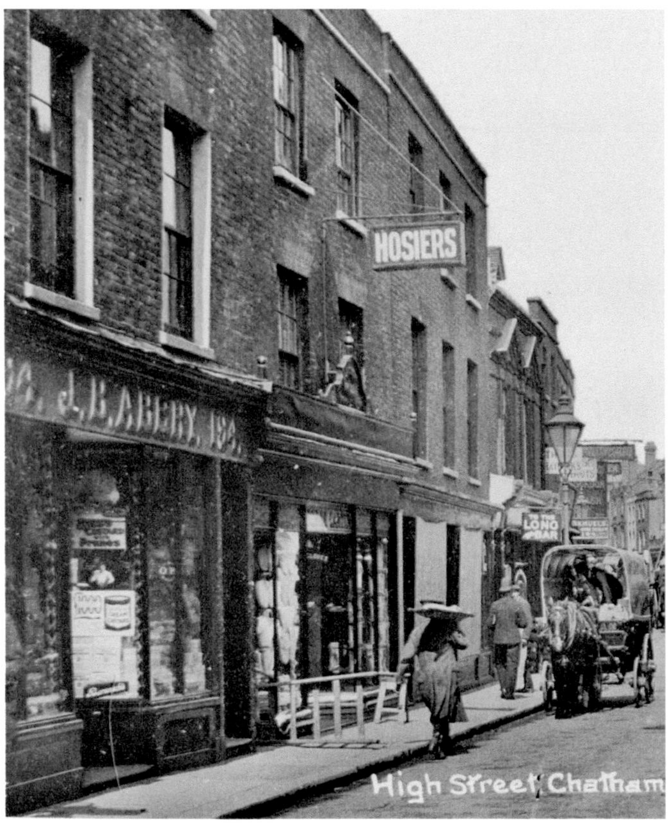

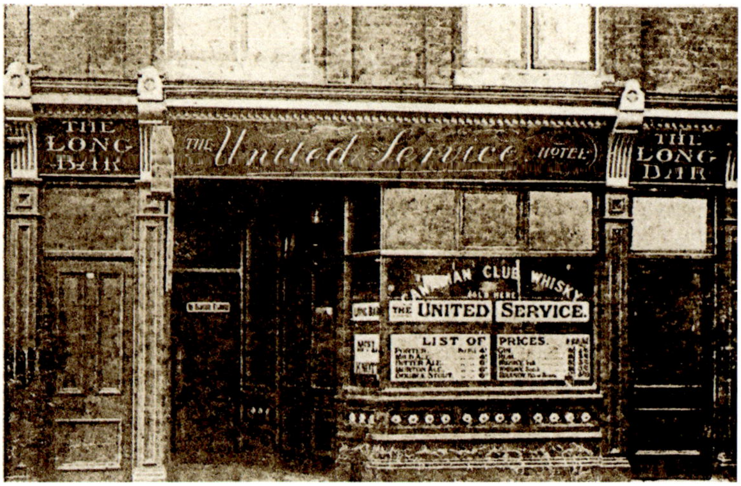

A closer view of The United Services Hotel, and which as a marketing ploy, clearly boasted of possessing a long bar – effectively the longest in the town. This, in itself, made it an especially popular rendezvous for those in military service.

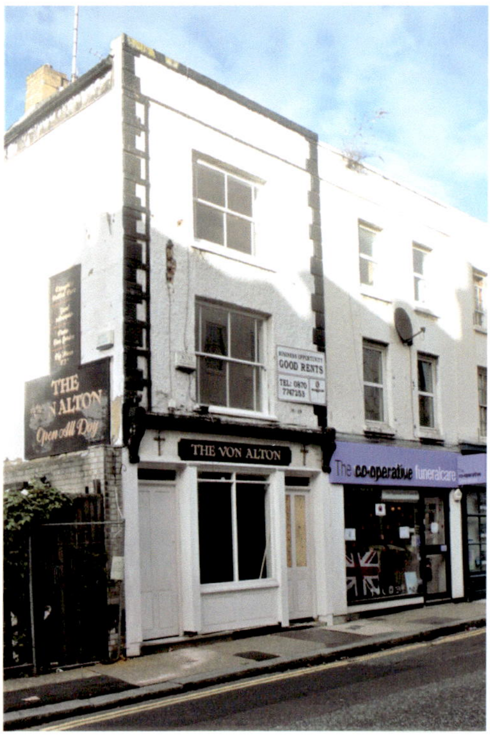

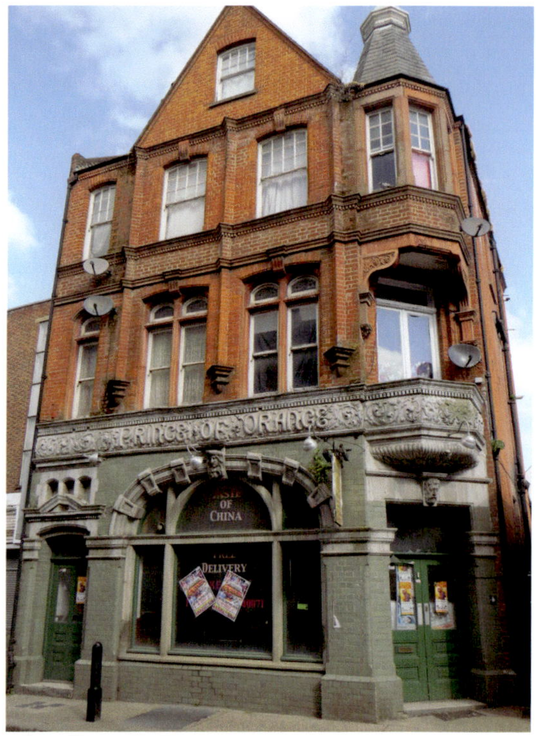

Above left: Von Alton (63 High Street). Once known as the Von Alten, being named in honour of a German general who fought alongside the British during the Peninsular War. It seems it might have dropped this name as a patriotic gesture during the First World War, being listed in the immediate post-war period as 'a beer retailer'. However, the name had reappeared, but with the change from 'Alten' to 'Alton' by 1936 and under which name it continued until closing as a pub in 2004.

Above right: Prince of Orange (21 High Street) goes back to at least the early nineteenth century, although the building itself has a later appearance, possibly a result of essential rebuilding following a serious fire that broke out in March 1859.

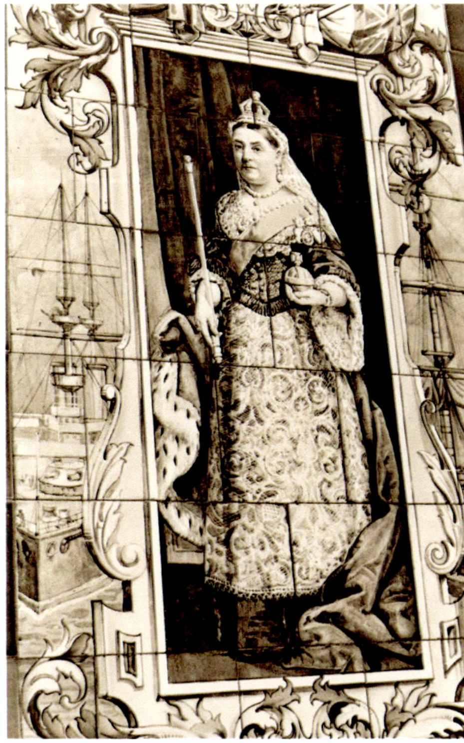

Right: An outstanding feature of the British Queen (330 High Street) was the tiled entrance with its representation of Queen Victoria which itself dated to the nineteenth century. Unfortunately, the image as seen here either no longer exists or has been completely covered over when the building ceased as a High Street pub.

Below left: Only a short way along the High Street from the British Queen stood, until 2017, The Little Crown (346 High Street), the building itself dating to 1892.

Below right: The Fountain (248 High Street), now a betting shop, goes back much further than the building itself would suggest. While the building seen here is late nineteenth century, a record of The Fountain, possibly on the same site, goes back to at least the final decade of the eighteenth century when the licensee was William Dadd, a member of a family with considerable connections to Chatham.

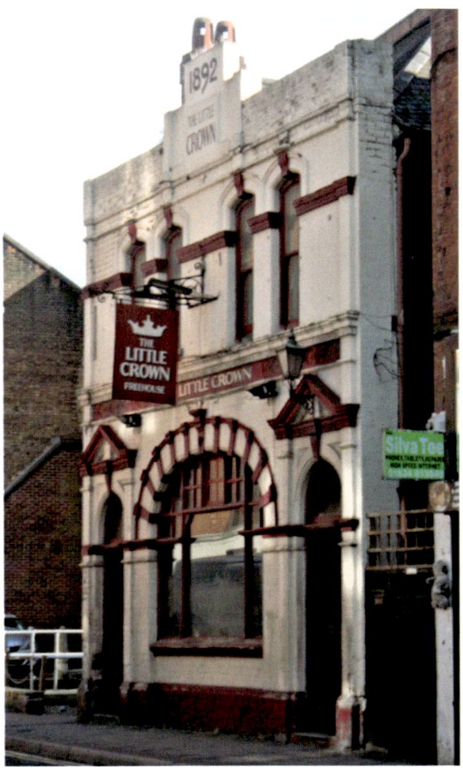

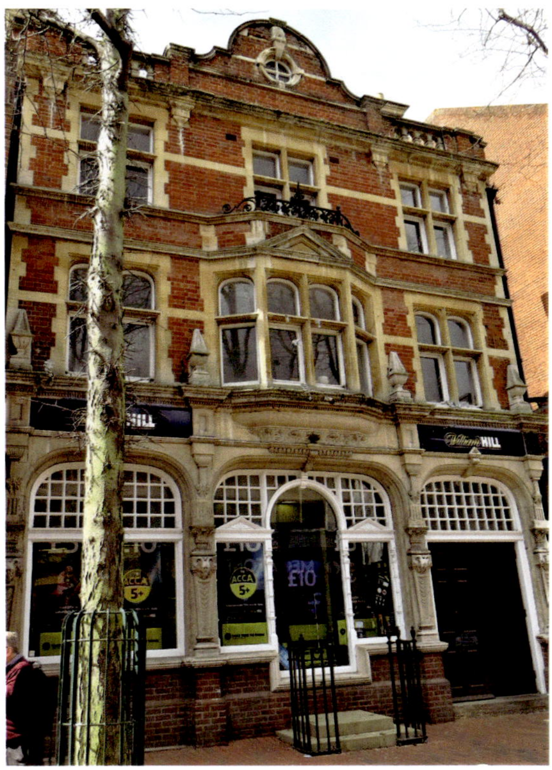

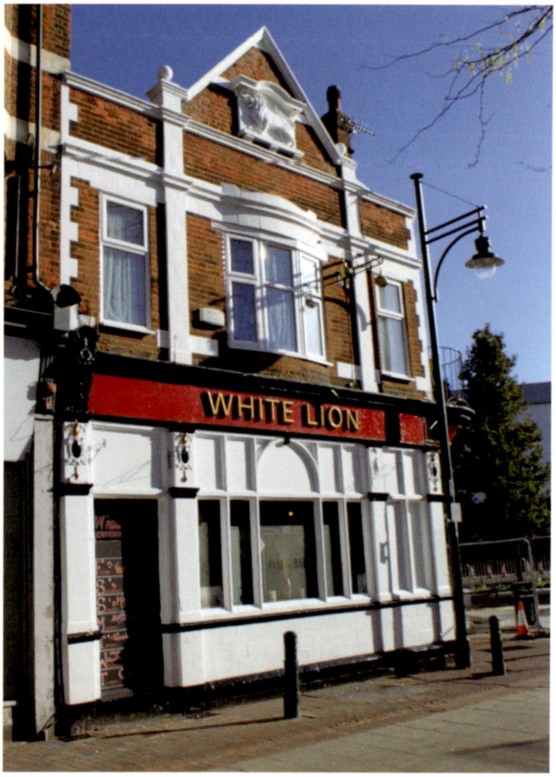

A late nineteenth-century building, the White Lion (325 High Street) is a rarity, a Victorian pub that still survives, rather than having been transformed into some alternative function. That this pub, in common with most others in the High Street, was popular with servicemen during the nineteenth century is partly demonstrated by the appearance in court of Gunner Richard Evans of the Royal Artillery in December 1861. He was found guilty of stealing three shillings from the till of the White Lion having spent much of the day 'lurking about the bar', leaving in the afternoon with the money.

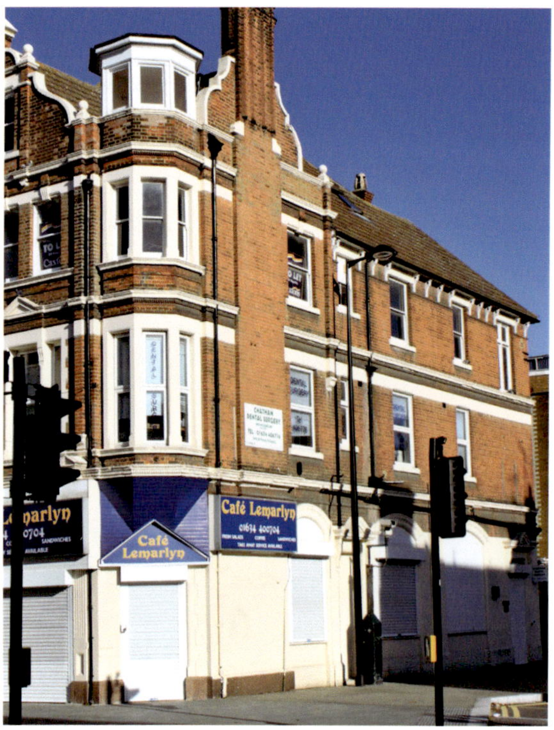

The Globe (131 High Street) on the corner of Globe Lane is yet one more once popular public house that was forced to close with subsequent conversion to other use. While the building is Victorian, sale particulars for The Globe Inn on this site date back to 1819. Less than a stone's throw away from The Globe could once be found the Old George Inn (9 Globe Lane), which also dated back in time to at least 1819. Demolished during the 1970s, the Old George Inn's interior featured several ornate mirrors and a bar piano. In 1863 the landlord of the Old George was warned that if he opened his pub on Sunday during unlawful hours, he would lose his licence. It seems that pubs in Chatham at that time were prepared to serve drinks beyond the permitted hours, adding to the high levels of intoxication in the High Street.

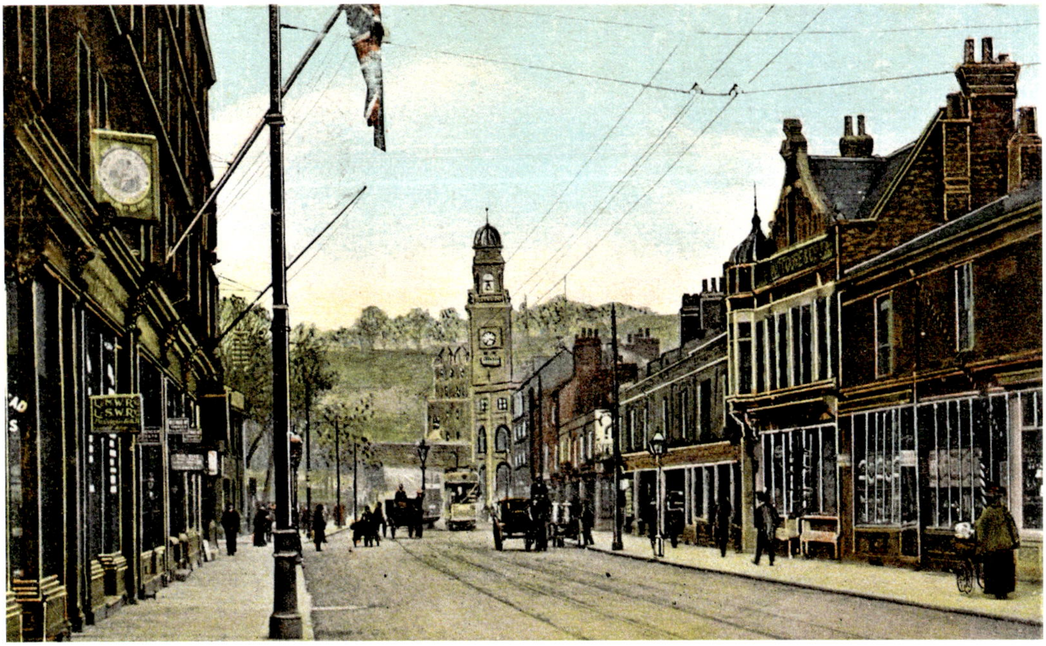

Above: An ongoing battle between temperance groups and purveyors of liquor saw Military Road at the heart of this battle, for on the left-hand side, as viewed here, was the 'Welcome Soldiers' and Seamen's Home and Institute' which deliberately did not serve alcoholic beverages. On the opposite side of the road were positioned the Eagle Tavern (54 Military Road) and the Naval and Military Arms (26 Military Road), both situated in the block nearest to the Town Hall. Nearer the camera, but not so far from the previous two pubs, is the Two Brothers (16 Military Road) while also on the same side of Military Road, but at the junction with the High Street, was the Red Lion.

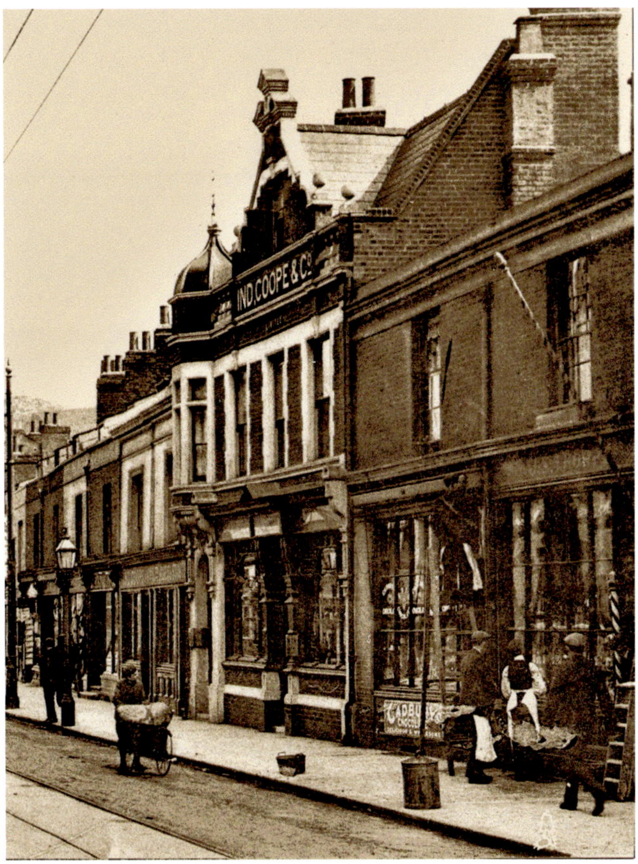

Right: The Two Brothers in Military Road.

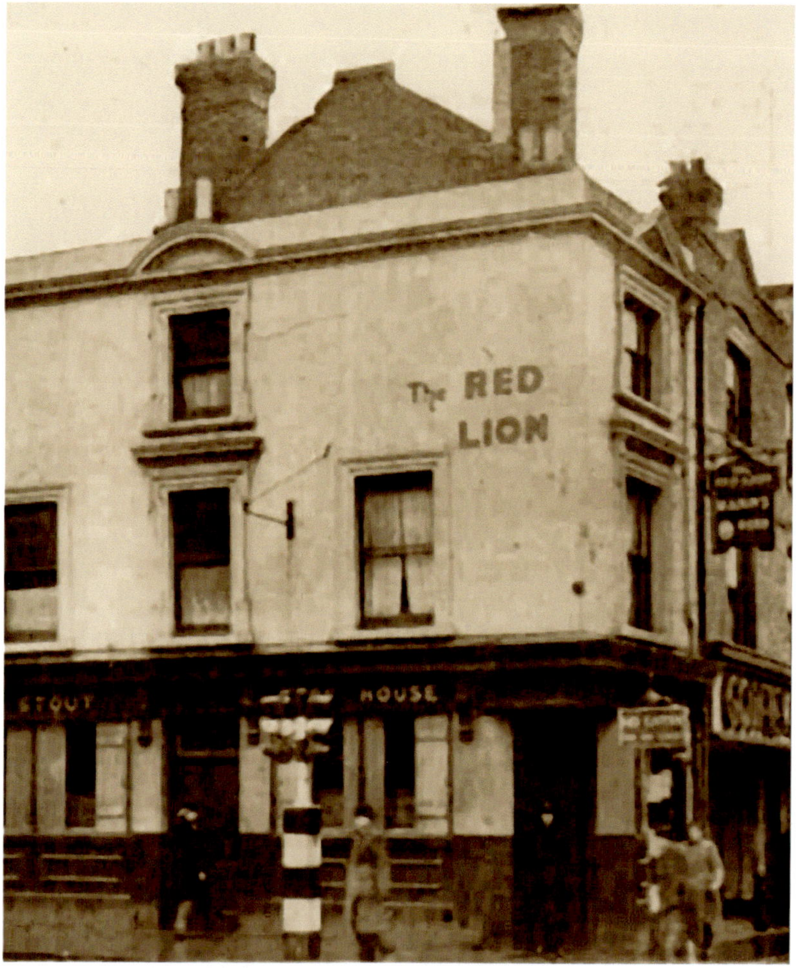

The Red Lion (145 High Street) on the corner of the High Street and Military Road with an entrance on both streets is seen here in 1945. It closed in 1961, and was subsequently replaced by a new building which currently is home to the jewellers H. Samuel.

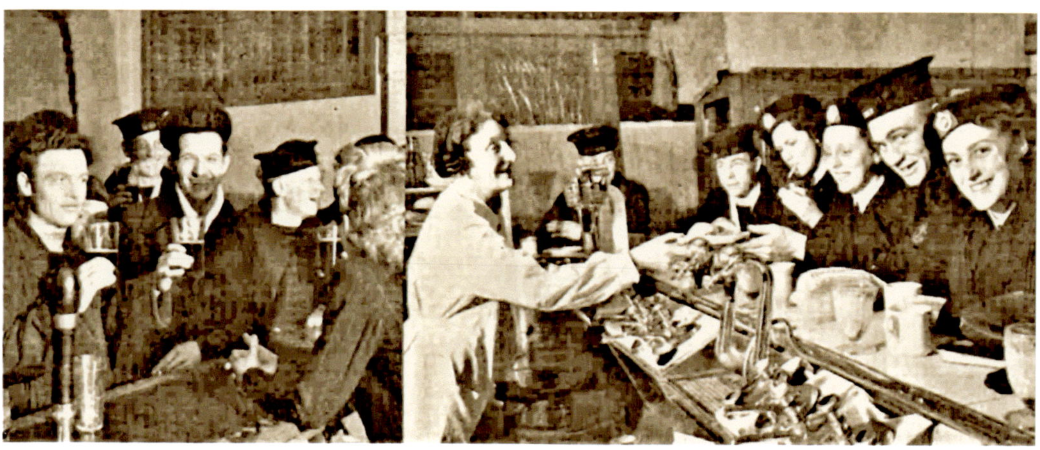

Inside the Prince of Wales in 1945, bustling with seamen, most of whom would have served in the recently ended war. The Prince of Wales is in Railway Street and is another survivor from the past.

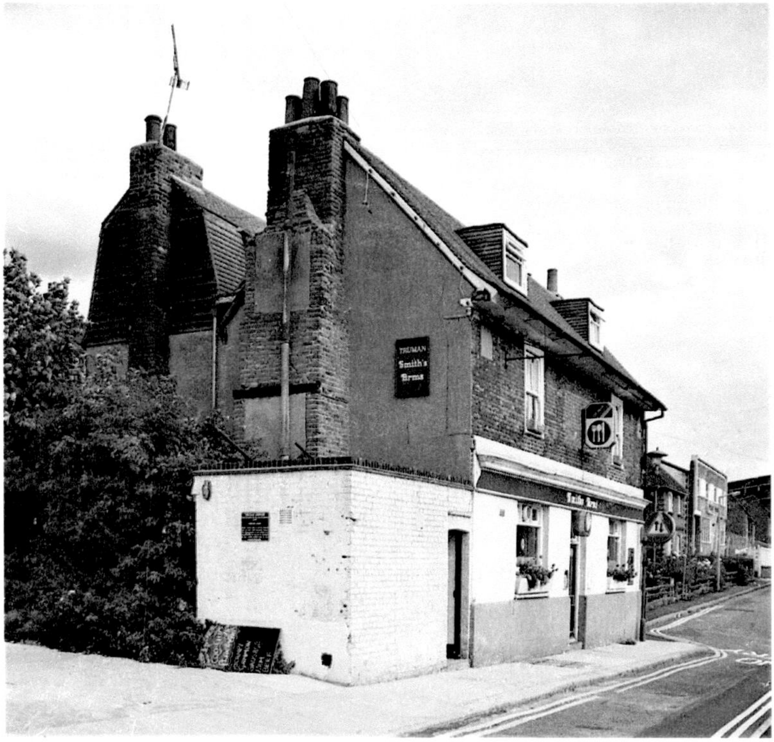

The Smiths Arms (9 Cross Street). Following closure this became a luncheon club, but in 2016 the building was demolished with planning consent given for construction of a now completed four-storey residential block.

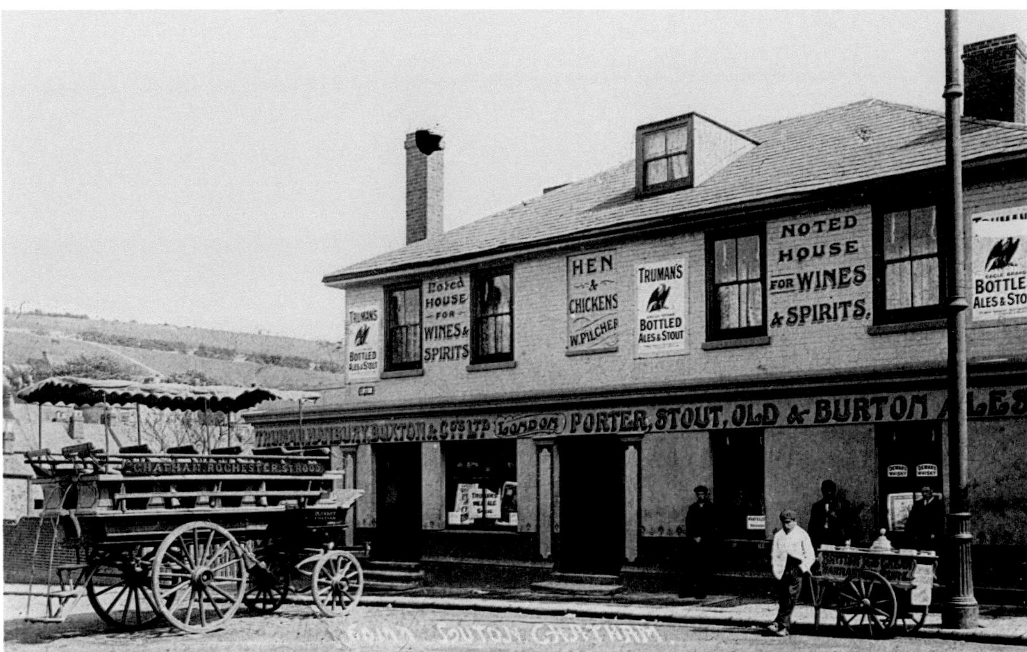

The Hen and Chickens, Luton, once the final stop on the tram route that ran between the Town Hall and the village of Luton where an increasing number of dockyard workers took up residence once the tram route had been created.

9
Memorable Events

Like any town, Chatham has witnessed many a memorable occasion, but due to its importance as a naval and military town, many have also been memorable to the nation as a whole. After all, it was from the dockyard that Nelson's flagship at Trafalgar, *Victory*, was launched together with a succession of cruisers, submarines and battleships. The town has also seen many British visiting monarchs, while in 1698, Peter the Great, the Tsar of all Russia, made a point of visiting Chatham, touring the dockyard and boarding several of the ships in the river.

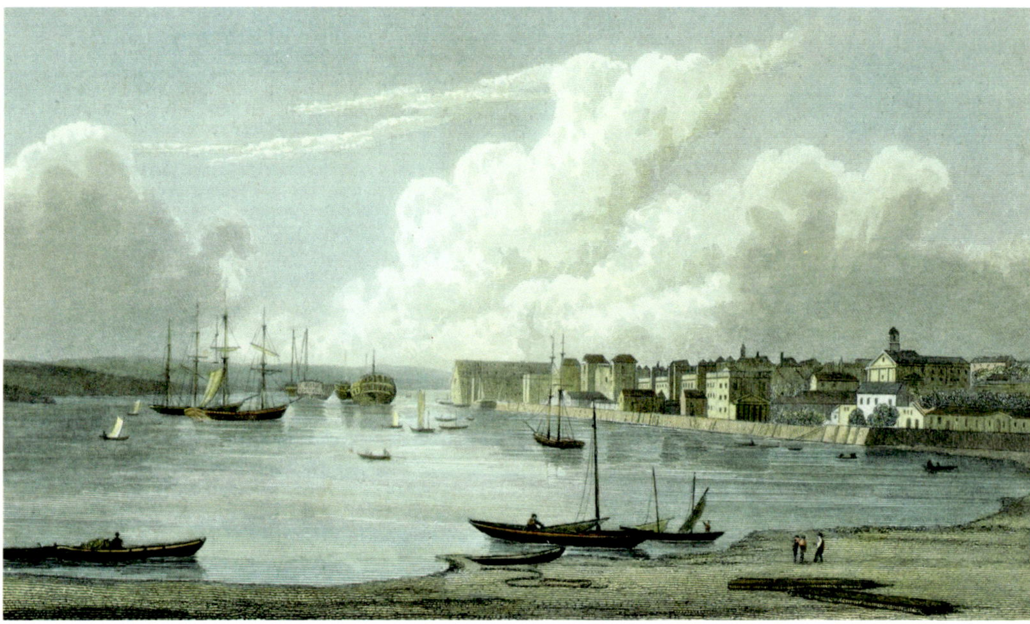

Perhaps the most important of those memorable events, through its impact on the future development of Chatham, was the purchase and raising in 1571 of the flag of St George on the site of the newly created dockyard. Admittedly a low-key event, it was this formal recognition of Chatham as a dockyard that must be seen as the first stepping stone in the development of the town (by then only a village) as a sizeable military-industrial complex. The site of the dockyard at that time was immediately below St Mary's Church, with what later became the Ordnance Wharf below the church on the edge of the water. The present-day Historic Dockyard was itself founded as a naval dockyard in the early seventeenth century.

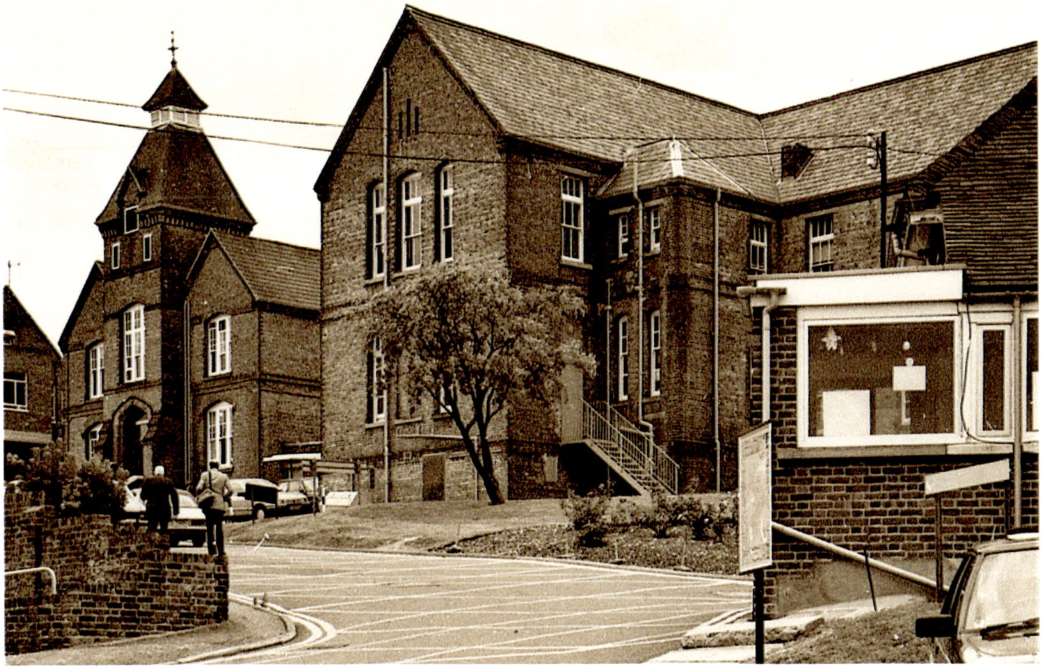

All Saints' Hospital in Magpie Hall Road, seen here prior to its closure and subsequent demolition. The opening of this building in 1859 was itself a memorable event for some, but one to be forgotten by others. This was because when it first opened it was the workhouse, financed by the Medway Union, and even in the 1970s, because of its long-time association with being a workhouse, older residents of Chatham feared going there even though it was, by then, a highly competent NHS facility.

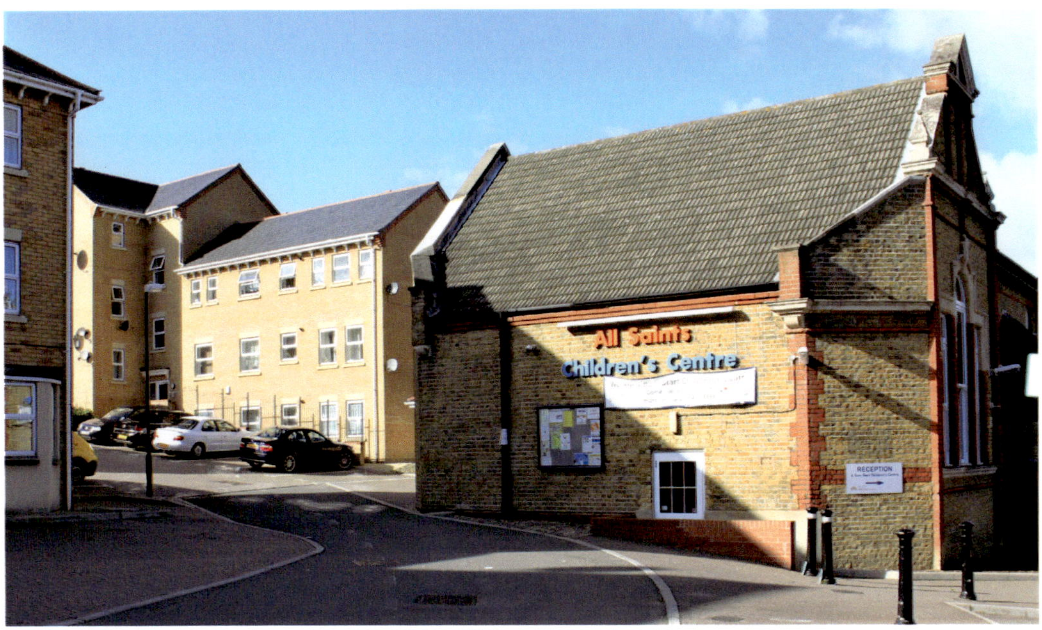

Today little remains of the former hospital.

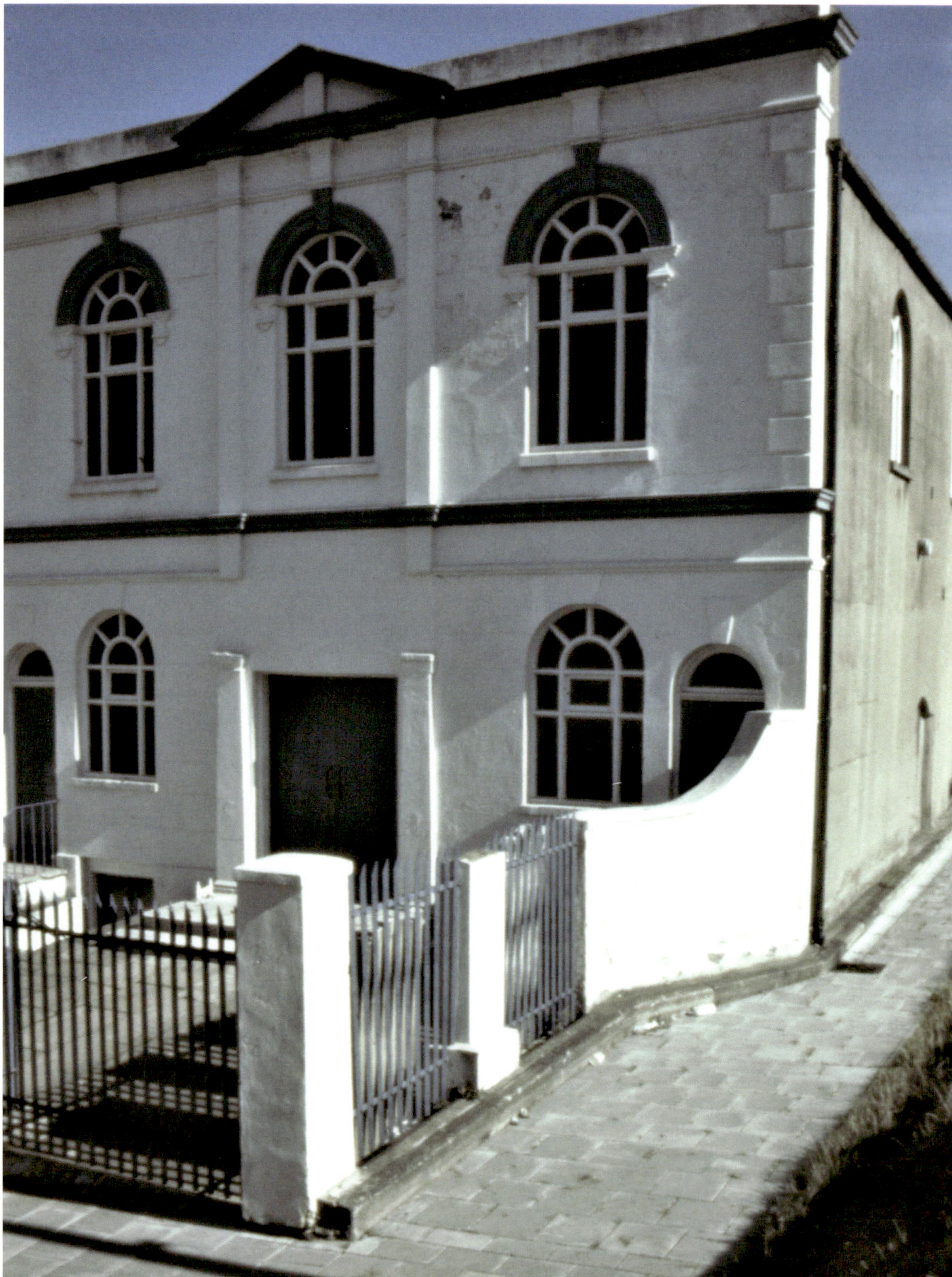

The now demolished chapel in Clover Street, removed to make way for the extensive realignment of roads in and around the town. Completed in 1821, it was one particular important event for the Zion Baptist community.

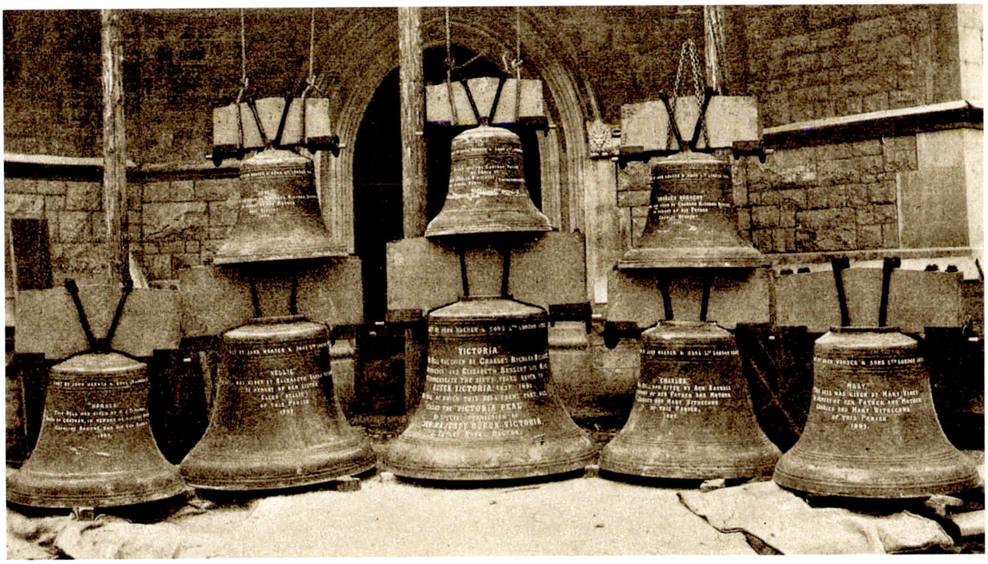

In February 1898 a special service was held at the then parish church of St Mary the Virgin in Dock Road to dedicate the completion of Victoria Tower, the church bell tower. Indeed, the entire church, at that time, had undergone a complete rebuilding in a mock-Gothic style. Here you can see the church bells ready for hoisting, each bell given a separate name and an inscription to indicate the name of the person who had gifted it to the church.

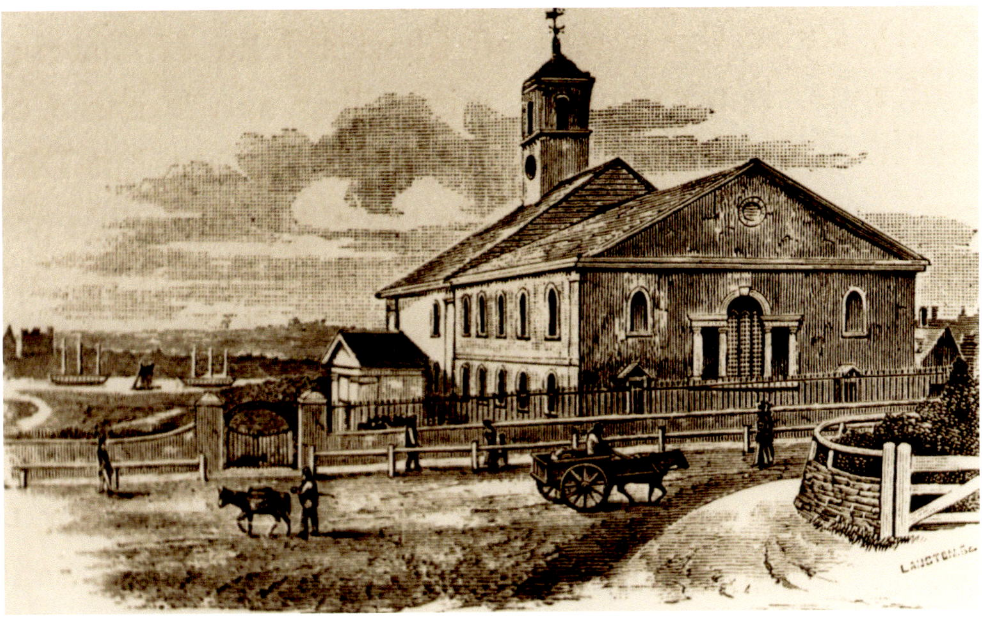

The Church of St Mary the Virgin, with foundations going back to the Normans, had been rebuilt in 1788 in the Classical style of architecture. Indeed, the church has gone through a surprising number of rebuilds, being originally Saxon but rebuilt by the Normans. Following a devastating fire it was again rebuilt in the fourteenth century. As for the rebuilt church of 1788, this saw a substantial rebuilding in the Early English style during the 1880s with Victoria Tower added in 1897.

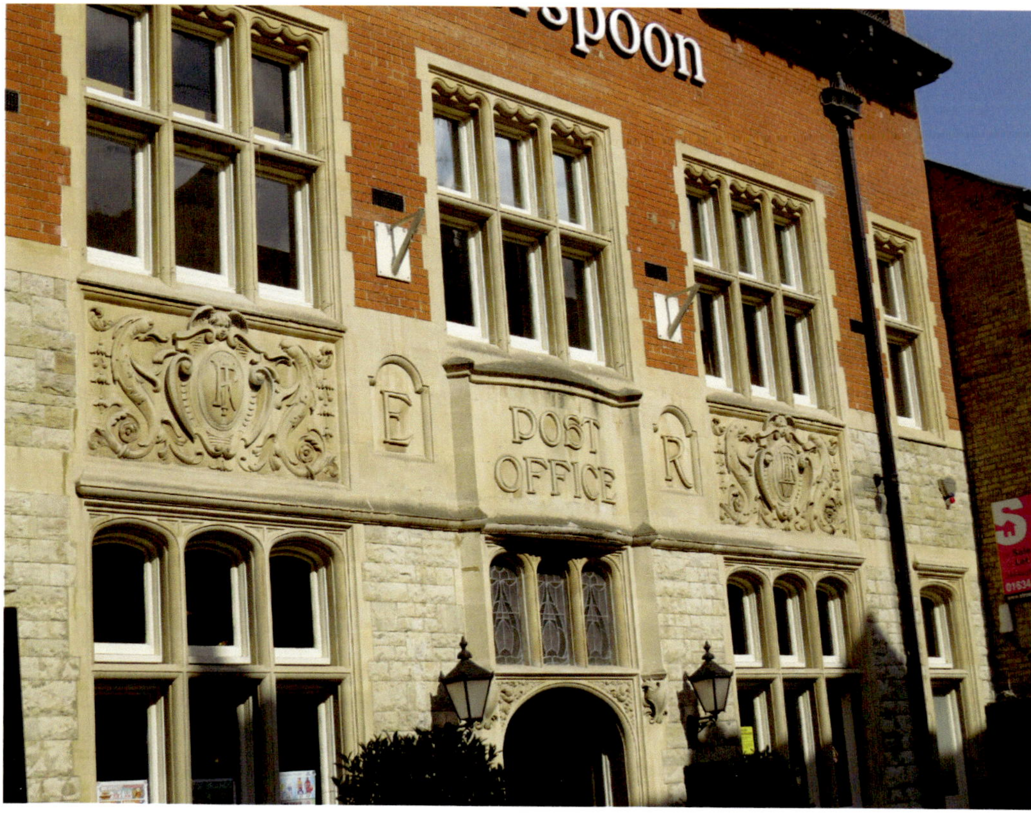

The impressive Post Office building that once served Chatham, now a Wetherspoons pub, was officially opened with considerable ceremony in 1902, its design and size fitting Chatham as a major naval town. Now known as the 'Sir Thomas Waghorn', the building makes an interesting connection between the former use of the building as a post office and Waghorn, the man who pioneered a land route to India as once used by the early postal service. Waghorn's statue, of course, is only a short distance from the old Post Office building.

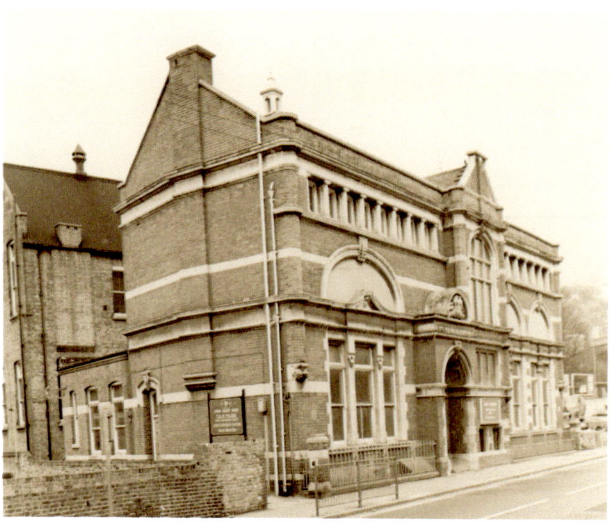

Chatham's first public library was opened in October 1902. It once stood at the east end of New Road, but was demolished in mid-1984.

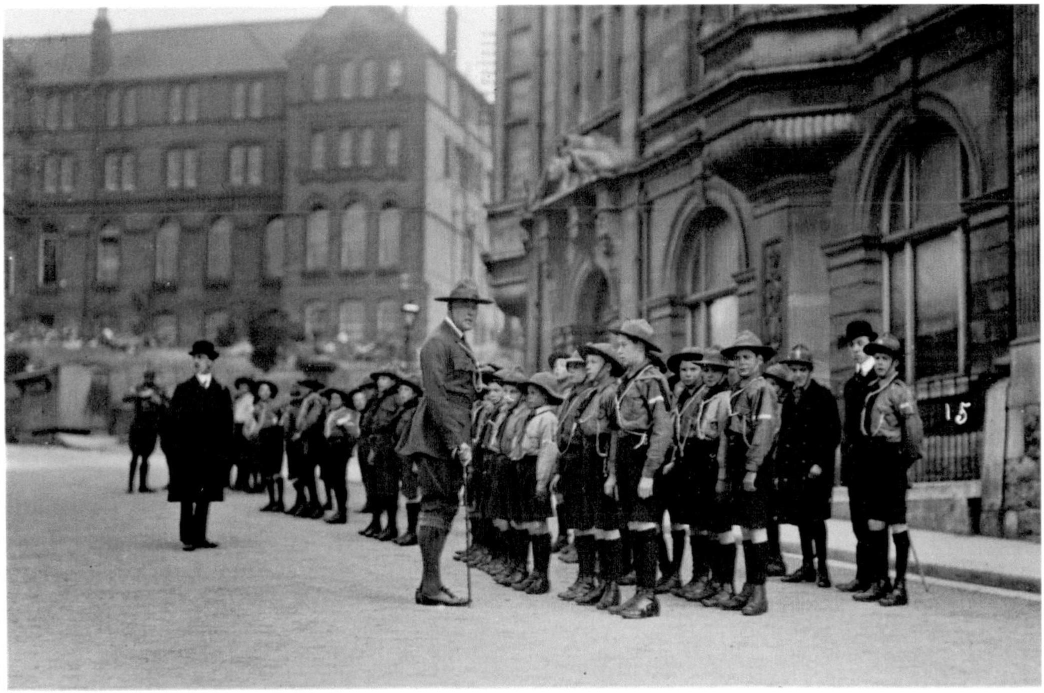

St George's Day Parade, 20 April 1913. Scouts assembled outside the Town Hall, with the now demolished Royal Sailors' Home also to be seen.

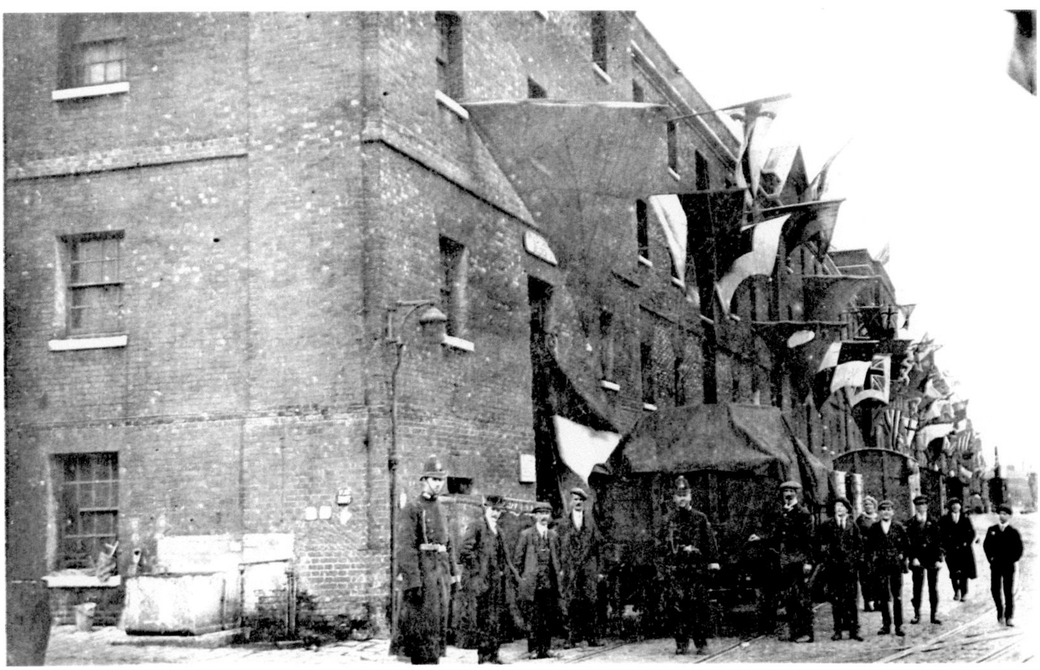

Armistice Day, 11 November 1918. A memorable and much-anticipated event was suitably celebrated at the dockyard with an outbreak of flags.

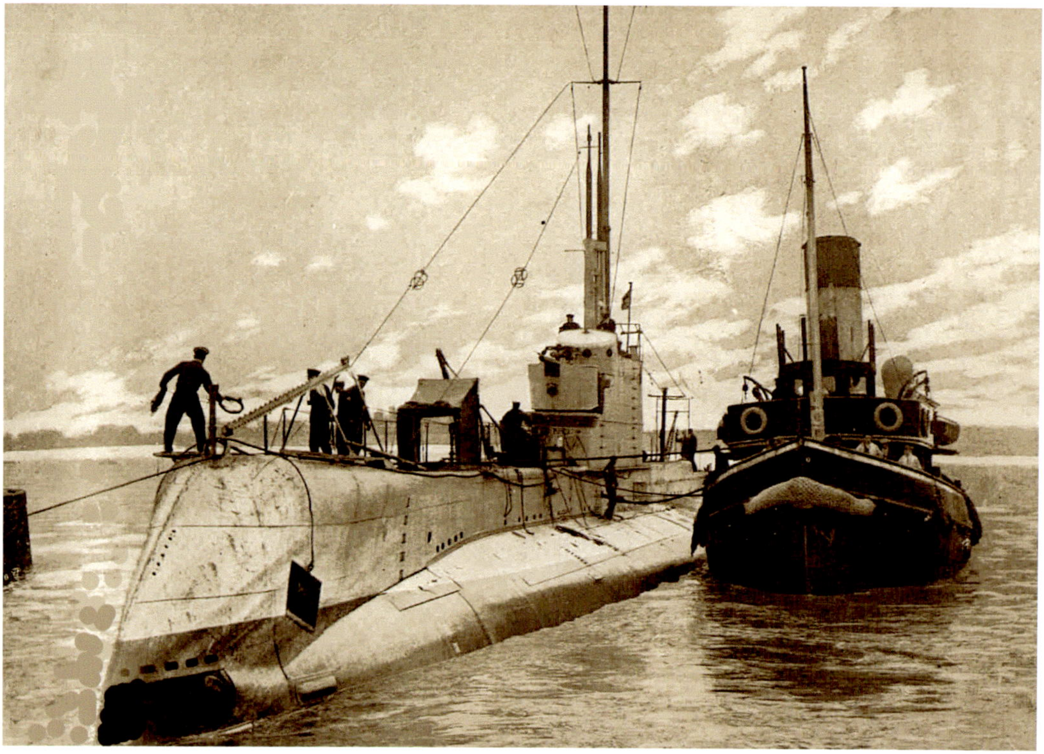

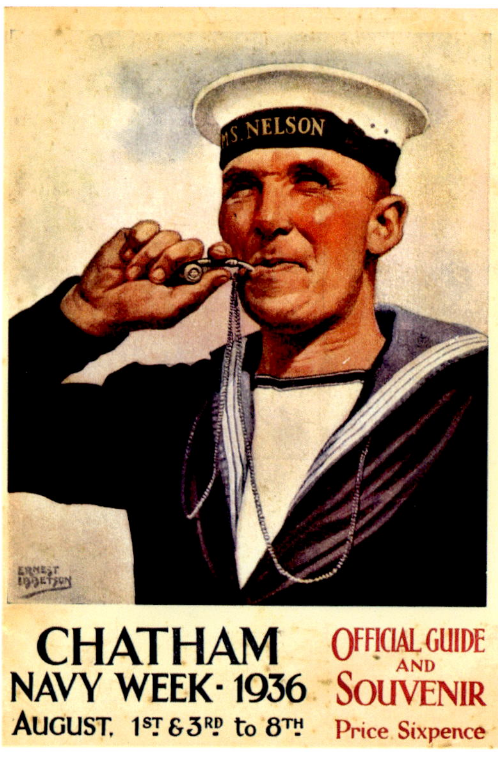

Above: His Majesty's Australian Submarine *Otway*, one of two 'Odin' class submarines built by Vickers-Armstrong at Barrow, lying off Chatham in June 1927. Commissioned at Chatham, she would serve briefly with the Royal Navy's 5th Submarine Flotilla before departing for Australia.

Left: Drawing huge crowds throughout the 1930s was Chatham's Navy Week, an annual event designed to allow the public to meet the navy. Held during the first week of August, this is the cover for the souvenir programme that could be purchased for six pennies. Following the Second World War, this event was transformed into Navy Days.

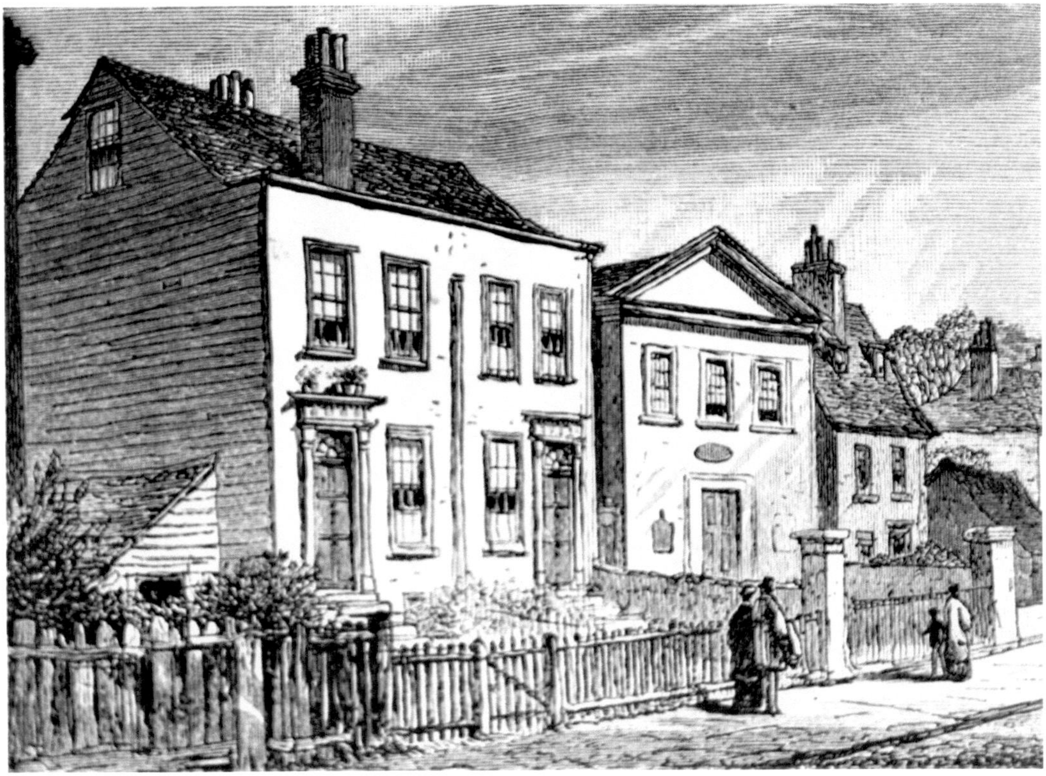

Above: An unfortunate rather than a memorable event was the demolition in 1941 of this, the home in St Mary's Place, The Brook, of Charles Dickens when a youngster. His father, employed in the pay office of the dockyard, having fallen into debt, had been forced to leave the more substantial residence previously occupied in Ordnance Terrace. The family moved to The Brook in 1821, the young Dickens remaining here until the following year.

Right: During the summer of 1985 the Tall Ships, sail training ships crewed primarily by youngsters, came to Chatham with a Parade of Sail that attracted large crowds to watch the ships as they passed along the river between the town and the dockyard. Using one of the basins of the dockyard as an assembly point, the race in which they were also participating was then known as the 'The Cutty Sark Tall Ships Races'.

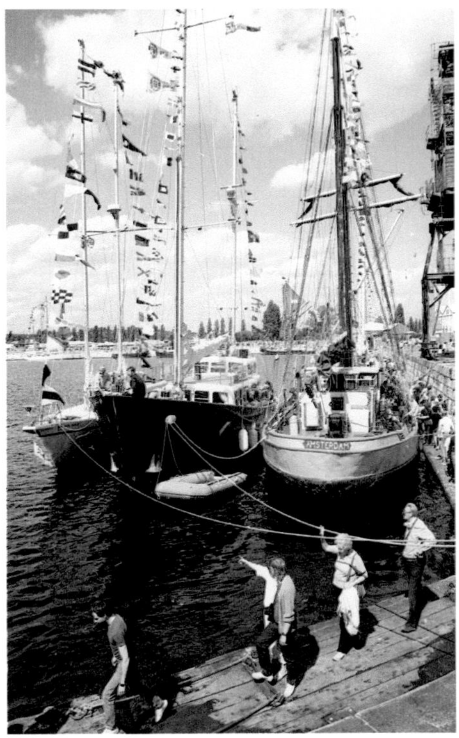

About the Author

Philip MacDougall has been researching and writing about the history of Chatham and the Medway Towns for a number of years. His first book, *The Story of the Hoo Peninsula*, was published in 1980. In all, he has written nearly twenty books on the area, including *The Book of Medway* (published in 1989), *Chatham Dockyard: The Rise and Fall of a Military Industrial Complex* (2012), *Medway Towns at Work* (2017) and *Secret Chatham* (2016). As well as writing about the Medway area, Philip has a recognised expertise in naval history, writing in depth on the supporting infrastructure of various navies across the world, concentrating especially on the eighteenth century. Philip has also contributed biographical material on selected naval officers for the widely acclaimed *Dictionary of National Biography*. In addition, he has family connections with the navy of the eighteenth century, an ancestor having served as Nelson's personal secretary during the naval wars fought against France, having first joined that future great Admiral at the Nore anchorage off the Isle of Grain in 1793.

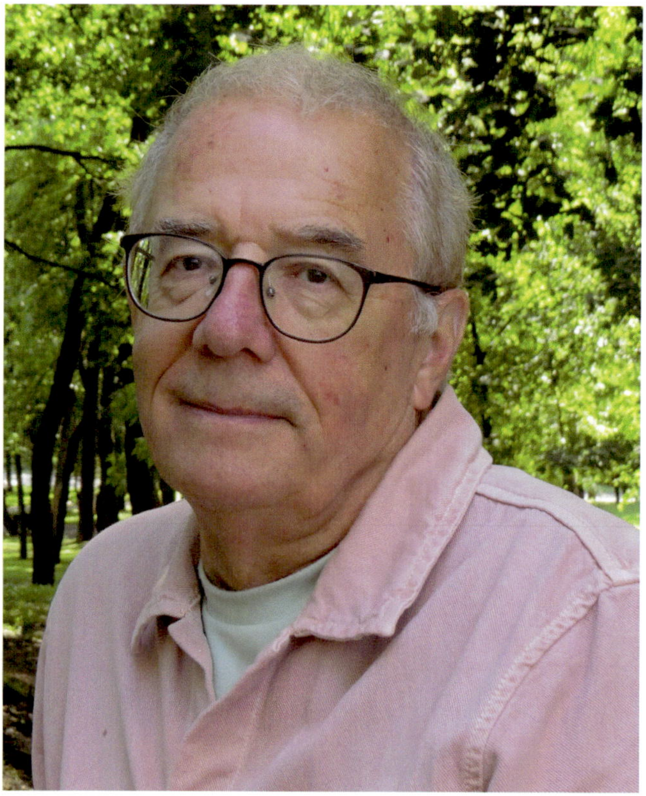